D0081134

RESTAURANT PLANNING, DESIGN, AND CONSTRUCTION

RESTAURANT PLANNING, DESIGN, AND CONSTRUCTION

❖

A Survival Manual for Owners, Operators, and Developers

Jeff B. Katz

John Wiley & Sons, Inc.

New York ♦ Chichester ♦ Brisbane ♦ Toronto ♦ Singapore ♦ Weinheim

This text is printed on acid-free paper.

Copyright © 1997 by John Wiley & Sons, Inc.

All rights reserved. Published simultaneusly in Canada.

Reproduction or translation of any part of this work beyond
that permitted by Section 107 or 108 of the United
States Copyright Act without the permission of the copyright
owner is unlawful. Requests for permission or further
information should be addressed to the Permissions Department,
John Wiley & Sons, Inc., 605 Third Avenue, New York, NY
10158-0012.

This publication is designed to provide accurate and
authoritative information in regard to the subject
matter covered. It is sold with the understanding that
the publisher is not engaged in rendering legal, accounting,
or other professional services. If legal advice or other
expert assistance is required, the services of a competent
professional person should be sought.

Library of Congress Cataloging in Publication Data:
Katz, Jeff B.
　　Restaurant planning, design, and construction : a survival manual
for owners, operators, and developers / Jeff B. Katz.
　　　　p.　　cm.
　　Includes bibliographical references.
　　ISBN 0-471-13698-0 (cloth : alk. paper)
　　1. Restaurants—Design and construction.　2. Restaurants-
-Planning.　I. Title.
TX945.K316　1996　　　　　　　　　　　　　96-18349
647.95′0068′2—dc20

Printed in the United States of America

10　9　8　7　6

Dedication

The idea to write this book has been on my mind for many years. Since I first got involved in the restaurant business, I have kept files of notes and sketches from projects I worked on. Too often, I have seen intelligent people stumble through the restaurant development process and shared these stories of problems, delays, and missed opportunities with my wife, Mary. I dedicate this book to her for enduring these tales and convincing me to start writing.

I also dedicate this book to the memory of my parents, Roy and Miriam Katz, who always encouraged and motivated me to pursue my dreams.

Preface

In the summer of 1962, I decided that I no longer wanted to go away to summer camp. Instead, I wanted to stay home and find a job. A few weeks into the summer, my Uncle Nat invited me to spend the weekend with him. We would drive to upstate New York, to a small resort lodge in Lake Placid. My parents had spent their summers there and told wonderful stories of The Placid Manor, so I was excited to visit.

This European-style resort offered a relaxed elegance and high level of service that many restaurateurs and hoteliers today refer to as "the great service and attention to detail that you don't find any more." My vacation immediately turned to work, as I was offered an opportunity to stay for the entire summer as an employee. Under the direction of Mae and Ted Frankel, the owners and day-to-day operators and the "big brother" guidance of their nephew, Stan Bromley, I worked in the kitchen, bakery, dining room, and wherever else I was needed.

At 14, my introduction to the hospitality industry was total immersion. Since we lived on the grounds, we were always available and were readily summoned to assist the guests or help out in the kitchen. The long hours and hard work were rewarding experiences and more fun than I could ever imagine having at summer camp. I spent three summers at The Placid Manor. The Frankels taught me well and instilled in me a passion for the hotel and restaurant business. I was fascinated with the hospitality industry and knew then that I would pursue a career in this field.

Passion for the restaurant business is not the only ingredient for success. Many restaurateurs will say, "you have to do your homework." The problem that many people have when getting involved in or expanding their interest in the restaurant industry is that they don't know the assignment! It is impossible to "do your homework" if you don't have the right text, know what page you should be on, or even understand the questions.

Doing your homework may be evaluting the need for a second server station in the main dining room or weighing the cost versus the added features of heavy-duty appliances over standard ones. Do you invest in a water filter for your beverages, or is the municipal water system good enough? Do you reduce the number of floor drains in the kitchen to save construction dollars, or do the benefits in maintenance outweigh the initial cost? This is "doing your homework."

The future economic and social success of a restaurant is often determined before the doors are opened to the public. How a restaurateur, developer, or operator plans, designs, and constructs a restaurant will greatly impact the outcome. That is the focus of this book. It is a tool to help the reader with his or her homework. By using it, restaurateurs and developers can plan, design, and construct a restaurant that works according to their concept and operating style.

JEFF B. KATZ

Contents

7 THE CONSTRUCTION PHASE: BUILDING YOUR RESTAURANT 211

❖

RESTAURANT PLANNING, DESIGN, AND CONSTRUCTION

Here's my plan, Steven . . . Marge will do the design, you will manage the construction, Susan will write the menus and recipes and I will handle the paperwork. Well, I think that covers it. What do you think?

One

Restaurant Development

People who do their job well make it look easy. This is a problem. When you try to communicate to others that what they are witnessing is really the product of hard work, serious effort, and extensive knowledge and experience, they are not easily convinced. They cannot see the long hours of study, training, and practice, nor the years of honing a skill to establish a groove or storehouse of knowledge. The errors in judgment or omissions that most professionals, in any business, experience are not visible. Often, the failures are not visible, as well.

Good ideas do not often work well on the first try. Smart developers and operators measure results. They observe what works and what does not, and they refine, modify, and polish ideas until they produce the desired results. If the results do not materialize, they regroup, abandon those ideas, and come up with new ones. Even familiarity with one aspect of the restaurant industry—food preparation and cooking, guest relations, marketing, or finance—does not necessarily mean that the many other necessary talents will be picked up easily. Casual observers and even those involved in some part of the restaurant industry see only scattered pieces of a business. Their experience or knowledge is very limited. Yet for some reason, they believe that they have sufficient background and skill to develop their own restaurant successfully. Even successful restaurant operators do not necessarily know or possess the skills required to develop a restaurant. Those who enter the restaurant industry from success in other fields often believe that their business acumen will fill the voids in their hands-on experience. What they don't understand is that there is, indeed, more involved than what they see or think they see.

Of course, planning and developing a restaurant is not rocket science. Many restaurateurs have succeeded in this industry without formal education or training. They haven't worked their way up through the business. They haven't worked in an allied field. They did, however, understand how to define their objectives and plan, execute, and delegate effectively. A critical part of that process was to fully understand the complexity of the undertaking; to prepare a plan of action; and to learn, acquire or hire the skills, knowledge, and resources necessary to implement their plan successfully.

The glamorous image of the restaurant industry draws players from diverse backgrounds. Hearts and egos are often the driving force. Reason and common sense are frequently abandoned. Personal opinions and theories, unsubstantiated or lacking convincing evidence, are often the basis for expensive, irreversible decisions. Casual comments become absolute requirements. The decision-making process that most savvy businesspeople would employ to purchase a power lawn mower is ignored. More time is spent discussing salad dressing or paint colors than in discussing budgets.

"You are clearly speaking of someone else," you say. Fine. But the real life stories of both budding and experienced restaurateurs indicate that there are a lot of "someone elses" out there. A woman decides to move her established restaurant to an old mansion in a neighboring town. Did she check applicable building and zoning codes? Parking? Did she develop a budget based on knowledgeable sources? These are basics, right? They weren't to her! There are always the stories of "no more space in the electrical panel for the toaster you decided to add," or "the tables don't fit in the dining room according to the plans," or "who was supposed to order that?" How about a seasoned restaurant company that goes $200,000 over budget because no one was monitoring the funds or questioning expenditures? "Impossible," you say. Well, it really happened; and it happens all the time.

The restaurant development process should be a rewarding, enjoyable, and successful experience. It is important to keep in mind that the development process is not an end in itself, but a beginning. The classic phrase, "The operation was a success but the patient died" certainly applies to restaurant development. The true measure of successful development is the financial success of the restaurant. Restaurant openings are deceiving. The beautiful space, or the confident owners and management smiling at the door, are not how most developers or owners measure success. Many restaurants appear to be successful. They are busy, the owner or manager is confident and cordial and the trappings of success are apparent: the right car, the stylish clothing, the flamboyant manner. All too often, perception is not reality. The image presented belies the true financial crisis that exists. The truth becomes clear only when the operation suddenly closes or changes hands and everyone wonders what really happened.

Armchair critics often say, "good concept, poorly executed" when discussing restaurants. They then begin to list the operational flaws they observed. Their focus is often on operational failures, which with corrective management, can frequently be restored. Unfortunately, this analysis addresses a small spectrum of the components that contribute to a restaurant's success. A useful analogy here is to the causes of airline crashes, which a friend shared with me. "An airline crash," he said, "is usually not the result of a single event or error. Rather, it occurs as a result of a series of events that, individually, are not catastrophic but cumulatively create an irreversible and unavoidable disaster."

The events that contribute to the success or failure of a restaurant begin with an idea or concept and end with effective implementation and performance. Along the way, hundreds of events occur. How each event is handled will contribute to the eventual success or failure of the restaurant. The focus here is on the development process, from the original idea, through the planning, design, and construction activities, and ending when the administrative loose ends are tied up and the restaurant is turned over to the management team.

The reality of restaurant development is that it is an evolving process. Changes and refinements along the way are expected and must be incorporated. In achieving their objective, space flights are off course 90 percent of the time. It is the constant evaluation of where they are and where they are going, and knowledge of how to make the necessary midcourse corrections, that enable them to reach their destination. Restaurant development requires the same constant monitoring and refinement. Toward that end, in this book we discuss in detail what is involved in the development process and provide tools and tricks as to how to effectively perform, delegate, and monitor the great variety of tasks.

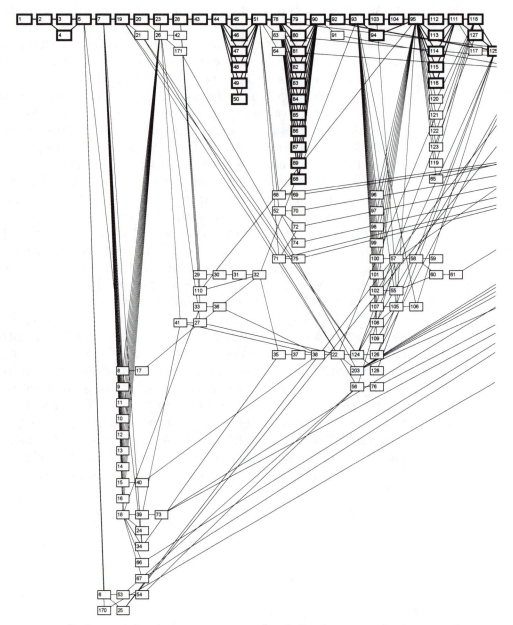

Restaurant development process. See following pages for key to reference

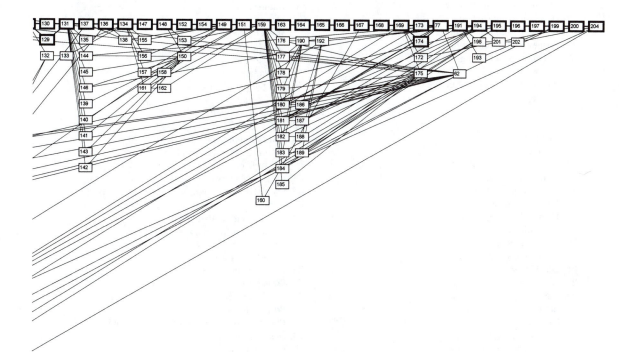

FIGURE 1.1   (*Continued*)

Key to Reference Numbers:

1. Idea to develop restaurant
2. Decision to take action
3. Prepare/refine general notes
4. Review with initial partners/advisors
5. Schedule exploratory meeting
6. Brainstorm concept
7. Prepare business plan outline
8. Concept
9. Menu
10. Market
11. Competition
12. Location
13. Design considerations
14. Management plan
15. Capital expenditures budget
16. Financial projections
17. Prepare supporting schedules
18. Determine business structure
19. Assess in-house talent
20. Assign responsibilities
21. Outside talent needs/search
22. Assemble development team
23. Business plan draft
24. Identify/resolve legal issues
25. Research
26. Planning budget
27. Funding of planning budget
28. Business plan draft review
29. List of unresolved issues
30. Assign responsibility for issues
31. Edit business plan draft
32. Finalize business plan
33. Financing plan
34. Legal issues
35. Investment documents
36. Funding sources
37. Presentation package
38. Funding
39. Establish banking relationship
40. Equipment lease package
41. Money management plan
42. Termination plan
43. Operation plan outline
44. Assign responsibilities
45. Staffing
46. Customer flow
47. Service flow
48. Kitchen procedures
49. Support facilities
50. Special tools/equipment
51. Operation plan draft
52. Operational plan finalized

53. Name selected
54. Legal use/protection
55. Sign code review
56. Logo/graphics
57. Signage design
58. Select fabricator
59. Budget review/update
60. Signage shop drawings
61. Signage installation
62. Preopening plan
63. Management team
64. Administrative procedures
65. Liquor license
66. Business license
67. Special licenses/permits
68. Staffing
69. Training and related activities
70. Marketing/advertising
71. Menu/recipe testing
72. Vendor/supplier contacts
73. Credit applications
74. Contract services
75. Opening inventories
76. Printed material
77. Coordination of owner provided equipment
78. Design program outline
79. Required spaces
80. Support areas
81. Space sizes/capacities
82. Access/adjacency/visibility
83. Design criteria
84. Special features
85. Utility requirements
86. Finishes/colors/materials
87. Special systems
88. Equipment requirements
89. Furnishing requirements
90. Design program draft
91. Design program finalized
92. Site criteria checklist
93. Site/location search
94. Site/location evaluation
95. Site/location selection
96. Adaptability to design program
97. Legal use
98. Licensing
99. Insurance
100. Zoning
101. Compatibility with neighborhood
102. Covenants/restrictions
103. Preliminary code review
104. Upgrade requirements

FIGURE 1.1 (*Continued*)

6

105. Site inspection
106. Existing document review
107. Utilities
108. Structural issues
109. Critical dimensions
110. Budget review
111. Lease/purchase contract
112. Price/terms
113. Timing
114. Contingencies
115. Inclusions/exclusions
116. Identify/resolve legal issues
117. Lease/purchase closing
118. Building inspection/code review
119. Identify applicable codes
120. Local requirements
121. Lease requirements
122. Covenants/restrictions
123. Field verification of dimensions
124. Assemble design team
125. Conceptual/schematic design
126. Establish procedures
127. Establish schedule
128. Assign responsibilities
129. Review with design team
130. Budget review/update
131. Review with owner for approval
132. Design build option
133. Value engineering
134. Design development
135. Preliminary review with code officials
136. Update design program
137. Update operational plan
138. Refine design
139. Architectural specifications
140. Structural specifications
141. Mechanical
142. Plumbing specifications
143. Electrical specifications
144. Equipment specifications
145. Furnishings/fixtures specifications
146. Special systems specifications
147. Review with design team
148. Review with owner
149. Construction documents: drawings
150. Construction documents: specifications
151. Construction documents complete
152. Review updated design program
153. Budget review/update
154. Schedule review/update
155. Coordinate details

156. Assign responsibilities for "by owner," "by others," "N.I.C."
157. Comprehensive review of documents
158. Revisions/owner approval
159. Bid process
160. Negotiated pricing/purchasing
161. Establish bidding/budget procedures
162. Qualify/select bidders
163. Monitor bid/pricing process
164. Review bids/pricing
165. Select contractors
166. Review contracts
167. Award contracts
168. Establish construction schedule
169. Construction process
170. Project management
171. Budget management
172. Field inspections
173. Coordinate changes: design program
174. Coordinate changes: field conditions
175. Shop drawing review
176. Architectural products shop drawings
177. Plumbing fixtures shop drawings
178. Electrical fixtures shop drawings
179. Mechanical systems shop drawings
180. Millwork shop drawings
181. Equipment shop drawings
182. Stainless steel fabrication shop drawings
183. Furnishings shop drawings
184. Specialty products/systems shop drawings
185. Owner/supplier provided items shop drawings
186. Millwork installation
187. Equipment installation
188. Stainless fabrication installation
189. Furnishings/fixtures installation
190. Custom/specialty item installation
191. Owner provided items installation
192. Final connection by general contractor
193. Coordinate owner provided items with preopening activities
194. Final inspections
195. Licenses/certificates
196. Certificate of occupancy
197. Sign-offs by landlord/franchise headquarters
198. Warranties/manuals/service agency directory
199. Preopening activities complete
200. Open to public
201. Walk-through by project manager and others
202. Punch list
203. Completion of all contractual/administrative activities
204. Restaurant development complete

FIGURE 1.1 *(Continued)*

❖   CHARTING THE RESTAURANT DEVELOPMENT PROCESS

The idea to open a restaurant originates from a variety of sources:

♦ You see a void and want to create a concept to serve this untapped market.

♦ A potential site sits vacant and you want to capitalize on this location.

♦ You have been thinking about and developing a concept and are ready to start your own restaurant.

♦ You enjoy a particular city or part of the country and want to live and develop a restaurant there.

♦ You own, manage, or are developing a building and want a restaurant tenant.

Whatever your reason, this germ of an idea begins to unfold and you begin to expand on it. To develop your restaurant effectively, you must be able to see the big picture—the individual activities that comprise the development process.

Figure 1.1 presents the activities that usually occur in the development process from "idea to develop restaurant" through "restaurant development complete," including all the intermediate activities. The purpose of this diagram is to illustrate how interrelated the activities are and to impress upon you the importance of coordination, communication, and overall management of the development process.

❖   DEVELOPING A RESTAURANT

Figure 1.1 is a graphic representation of the restaurant development process. Every restaurant development will use a different approach, vary the organization and priority of activities, and add, modify, or delete activities as necessary. The basics and the details of developing a restaurant, however, will be essentially the same.

Decision to Open a Restaurant

The decision to open a restaurant is a relatively simple first step that may have been your dream for years, or the opportunity may have just presented itself and you want to seize the moment. For whatever reason, you want to develop a restaurant. But the "idea" may remain dormant or may not be a high priority for you. It may take years for you to take the next step.

Your decision to take action initiates several other activities. You review and expand your notes on concepts, markets, menus, design, operating style, and restaurant details in general. At this time, you begin to share your ideas with trusted friends and potential partners. The energy and excitement grow. You plan a meeting to establish a plan of action.

Exploratory Meeting

The exploratory meeting focuses on how you are going to pursue the venture. You discuss concepts, operating style, menus, design, and other aspects of the proposed restaurant. Brainstorming is rampant. The enthusiasm and the collection of ideas and activities generated at this meeting must be organized and controlled. The development must be managed. The *business plan*—the first of three critical documents in the planning process—is discussed and outlined. Talents necessary to prepare the sections of the business plan are discussed. The abilities and talents of your core group are evaluated. In-house experience and capabilities are reviewed.

Research

Researching ideas and how other operators perform becomes a high priority. Perhaps you schedule trips to investigate successful or similar restaurants. Unfortunately, the idea of doing research is regarded as a luxury to many restaurateurs. They develop a budget for it, and when funds become tight, they delete it. Yet researching ideas and techniques, and seeing how successful operators perform similar tasks, should remain high priorities for several reasons. The most obvious reason is that you may learn something! Design and service ideas, equipment selections, and preparation techniques can be observed firsthand in working establishments. You may also see how not to do something. Concepts or ideas that you thought were workable are less satisfying or less feasible when seen in place or in action. A research trip may enlighten you as to seating options you hadn't thought of— booths accessible from both sides or interchangeable tabletops to accommodate large parties.

Following your exploratory meeting, numerous activities begin to unfold. When you realize that you do not have all the skills needed to perform all of these activities, you seek outside help. This requires research to find and evaluate potential candidates. It also requires a preliminary budget to pay for the services, so you develop a plan to fund and manage them. But, what happens when you collect the funds, sign contracts, begin work, and for some unfortunate reason, the restaurant development is abandoned? A *termination plan* sets the ground rules for how the planning budget is repaid or the remainder is distributed.

Financing Plan

The financing plan has several related activities that must be completed before your financing is, in fact, complete. Although it is possible to begin your search for funds and to make initial inquiries and contacts, this activity cannot be completed until these other activities are complete. Financing your restaurant development does not usually occur until you have:

♦ A solid draft of your business plan

♦ A termination plan

♦ Necessary legal documents for investors/partners

♦ A legal business structure/entity

♦ Procedures for managing these funds

♦ Supporting budgets/documents for equipment leases

It is evident why the development process becomes complex. If funding cannot be completed before other activities are finished, and still other activities cannot begin until financing is in place, your development time schedule begins to expand and individual responsibilities increase.

Operational Plan

This second critical document of your planning process is also comprised of several components. But you cannot start on this plan until you have completed at least a first draft of your business plan. Keep in mind that as you refine the business plan, changes may occur that will dramatically affect your operational plan.

As you can see, there are many related and unrelated activities taking place at the same time. As your development progresses, you and your partners will assume more responsibility and your development will grow as you add more professional talent. It may be necessary to delegate some tasks to others and possibly to people outside your organization. Assigning responsibility for these tasks and recruiting talent to assist, if necessary, adds to the series of events that make up this activity.

Many activities begin when you have a draft version of your operational plan. But you must remember that decisions are being made based on the information contained in the operational plan. Therefore, as this plan is refined and changed, the members of your development team must be updated. As long as your project manager continues to pass on to the team all changes in these documents, you do not need to wait for the final version to begin other tasks. The draft of the operational plan initiates five key activities:

1. The job descriptions of key management people

2. Staffing needs

3. Preopening plan

4. Design program

5. Menu development

Design Program

The design program is the third critical document in your planning process. The operational requirements established in the operational plan will dictate the physical components of the restaurant. Without a clear understanding of how you plan to operate and function and what spaces and amenities you require, the design team cannot design an effective space in which you can operate.

Site Selection

Site selection is shown as occurring after you have established your operational strategy and developed a draft design program. However, the search and selection of your site/location may occur prior to preparation of the operational plan and design program. Often, the location has been secured and a concept to fit the space is under development. It is no less important to prepare these documents and use them in evaluating your space. Although you may not be able to reject the location and find a more suitable one, you may be forced to modify your concept or space requirements.

Prior to embarking on site selection, you must have a draft design program and site criteria checklist for the use of the person responsible for identifying suitable locations. Once potential sites are found, a series of review and evaluation activities occur. Several activities requiring completion, resolution, investigation, and inspection must be performed before you can commit to a particular space and ensure that your selection is consistent with your design program. For example, both municipal zoning and building-related covenants and restrictions will affect the size, location, composition, and design of your signage. To make signage decisions before resolving these issues may be a costly error.

Design Process

The design process includes all the activities from the design program through the comprehensive review and approval of the completed contract documents. More than 75 activities are involved in this process and include:

◆ Overall project management

◆ Compliance with applicable codes and with your design program

◆ The coordination of the various design disciplines—architecture, engineering, interior design, food facilities design, graphic design, and many others—together with drawings and specifications

◆ Establishing and updating budgets and schedules

◆ Assigning responsibility for items that are "provided by owner," "provided by others," and "not in contract"

Construction Process

The construction process includes the activities from the bid/budget process through the completion of all contractual/administrative activities. Toward the end of construction, many earlier, unrelated activities start to interact. Owner-provided items such as phone systems, artwork, signage, furniture, and specialty finishes must be installed and coordinated with the general contractor. Scheduled inspections by building officials take precedence over all preopening operational activities. Coordination is critical.

Preopening Plan

The preopening plan, essentially a management activity, is considered a part of the development process because most of the activities begin very early in the development of your restaurant. As the restaurant construction draws to completion, several of these activities move into the facility and greatly affect the final weeks and days prior to final inspections and the certificate of occupancy.

Opening of the Restaurant

The opening of the restaurant to the public is not the completion of the development process. Without competent project management, the loose ends that remain untied can cause operational headaches weeks and months after opening. Delivery of equipment operating manuals, service directories, and the completion of unfinished construction details are an integral part of the development process and should not be overlooked.

There is a great deal of pressure and tension on a job site during the final days of construction and during the transition to opening to the public. This can be minimized significantly through effective planning, coordination and project management. To do this effectively, you must know and understand all the components that make up this complex process.

At every step in the development process, several activities repeat themselves.

♦ Periodic review of the development project with all involved

- ♦ Consideration and resolution of legal issues
- ♦ Updating the operational plan and design program
- ♦ Updating budgets and schedules
- ♦ Coordination of changes and refinements

The changes and refinements that inevitably occur in a restaurant development project require constant monitoring and coordination among the entire development team. These repetitive activities, if not performed, may result in serious errors, omissions, and oversights and sabotage your restaurant's development. Decisions, driven by emotions, egos, and outside pressures, also tend to derail the development process. Adhering to a structured approach will not diminish your enjoyment of the development process. On the contrary, it will enable you to focus on the issues that matter to you and let you enjoy the pursuit of your restaurant development.

T w o

Choosing and Managing Your Development Team

The development process involves all the activities that you, your partners, your hired professionals, contractors, vendors, and suppliers perform from your initial idea to develop your restaurant through the completion of construction and related administrative activities. At that point, the development process is complete. Once the building is complete and officially turned over to management, operational issues and decisions prevail. This distinction is significant: The skills and strengths necessary to *develop* a restaurant are not the same as those required to *manage* or operate a restaurant successfully. This will become more apparent as the details of the development process are explained.

There is a logical order to the development process, but it is not linear. You do not move neatly from one activity to another, from one decision to another. All of your decisions and actions will affect many other aspects of your planning. While the connection between relocating or changing the specifications of a piece of equipment and its related utilities requirements may seem obvious, this decision may also alter wall dimensions, the layout and design of adjacent equipment, fire protection requirements, hood exhaust capacities, or the need for wall blocking or special wall finishes. A change in the selection of a chair may change your seating capacity, storage space requirements (do they still nest?), or dining room flexibility. Changes in your seating layout will probably affect your lighting, HVAC zones, or placement of thermostats or interior partitions.

As your concept evolves and your service procedures change, tasks handled by a server in the dining room may shift to the kitchen. Duties assigned to the busser may be reallocated to a server. Decisions on how bread, salad, or condiments are stored and served will affect many aspects of your design. These changes and refinements will be reflected in your operational plan. This will, in turn, create a ripple throughout your development that affects many aspects of your planning, design, and construction.

You decide that the music system should be controlled at the host stand rather than from behind the bar. This affects wiring, millwork, and placement of zone controls. It also affects the design of the bar. Where conflicts occur, some compromises may have to be made. Moving the sound system to the host stand may free up valuable storage space behind the bar. But it may require that the host station be enlarged to accommodate the equipment. The change may make the host stand too large or may affect other functions. You will regroup and think about how important these changes really are to the integrity of your concept. If you must have them, you compromise somewhere else or you make it work by approaching it from a different angle.

Complex undertakings are often separated into more manageable parts. By understanding the components of the development process, you will realize that many aspects of the process are not foreign to you. In fact, you may be familiar with most of them. What may be unclear is how these pieces fit together to create a winning restaurant. This book delineates five phases of the development process. These phases have been established merely to break the process down into manageable parts. Each phase involves a series of activities that require certain skills, talent, or expertise. These phases are:

♦ Preparing a marketable business plan

♦ Refining your concept and writing the operational plan

♦ Preparing the design program

♦ Planning and design

♦ The construction phase: building your restaurant

To develop your restaurant effectively, you must address each of these areas. It is impossible to prepare a design program without having a clear understanding of your concept and operational procedures, which are detailed in your operational plan. How you decide whether you will serve your full menu in the bar will affect table sizes, placement of and accessories used at your wait stations, and traffic flow between the bar and kitchen. If you permit the conceptual design of your restaurant to begin without the benefit of a clearly defined design program, your design team may make assumptions that are incorrect. A decision that the coatroom will be staffed rather than self-service may alter its size and placement. If the bar is to cater to a slightly different market than the customer for the dining area, a small waiting area for diners may be necessary. Although you may respond to each phase in varying degrees of detail, totally omitting any one will create a domino effect of errors and omissions.

To develop your restaurant effectively, you must assemble the right team of talent to fill the voids in your knowledge, experience, or management skills. These people will assist you in planning, organizing, designing, and making key decisions about the operation and ultimate success of your restaurant. The members of the development team play a major role in defining and implementing the many details of your restaurant. As the conceptual ideas, notes, and mental images you have of this restaurant take shape, the decisions you make will affect aspects of your restaurant that you have yet to think about in any detail. Once you do think about them, you will make changes that will force you to rethink earlier decisions.

Teamwork is more easily talked about than accomplished. Simple human nature drives some team members to revert to form and refuse to share authority or responsibility. Other members may bicker about who gets credit for what work. By creating a collective ego, you will be able to accomplish far more than merely assembling a group of people who will work side by side.

1. *Choose your team wisely.* Each member will have his or her own agenda—defined or not—and none of them will have the vision, commitment, or stake in your restaurant that you have. This is not a criticism, but a fact. You, your partners, and investors have a financial and possibly personal risk in this venture. The members of your development team will probably have neither.

2. *Focus on your objectives.* Your ultimate goal is to develop and operate a successful restaurant. The restaurant's concept, market, and operating style should remain consistent with your vision as expressed in your business plan and refined throughout the development process. You also want to develop your restaurant on time, within your budget, and have a lot of fun doing it. You want to minimize your mistakes, omit or forget as little as possible, avoid compromises on your basic concept or operating philosophy, and be proud of your effort and your res-

taurant. Do not get sidetracked by issues and details that are not related to your development. The guest list for your opening party is not relevant now, nor is the ink color of your menus. Concentrate on what is important *now*.

3. *Play a very active role* in all phases of the development process. Many restaurateurs feel comfortable and confident dealing with their clientele and their staff and operating their restaurants, but they are unsure of the development process. As a result, they find excuses to delay or avoid making decisions, they fail to delegate key responsibilities to others who are more capable, or they gloss over details that will have a dramatic impact on their future success. Dealing competently with your development team will help ensure your restaurant's success.

Restaurant development is a dynamic process. Expect changes to evolve in your restaurant concept. Your concept will be refined and will change as you work out the details of space, flow, service procedures, the realities of food storage and preparation, and the constraints of your site or building. Expect these changes. Work with your development team to take advantage of these conditions and improve on your initial concept.

RECOGNIZING THE NEED FOR SPECIAL TALENT

The success of your restaurant will be determined, in part, by the attention you pay to the details. These details may become apparent to you only when someone asks the right questions or after you are open and you don't have the space or utilities you need. The people who know enough to ask these questions are your employees who work these areas, professionals or specialists involved with you in this project, or you and your partners who have seen these problems in other restaurants and have learned from your mistakes.

Having learned the importance of asking the right questions, many professionals understand the impact that your answers have on the other, seemingly unrelated, parts of your restaurant. This depth of experience or knowledge can be a very valuable asset. If you take advantage of it, you may greatly improve or enhance your restaurant development. Unfortunately, there are people who become involved in restaurant development who do not have the sufficient historical background or operational references necessary to see these relationships. It is, therefore, incumbent on you to monitor your development project or have someone on your team who can.

As a developer, restaurateur, or operator, your focus is on the overall impact that your concept and facility will have on your market and your profitability. Although you may have a general understanding of the component parts needed to develop your restaurant successfully, you probably have not had to examine and comprehend the development process down to its core. Your concern is that the facility, when turned over to you, works. How it evolves from a few notes scrawled on a napkin to a functioning restaurant is probably a little unclear. But you do know that you want to avoid adapting your operating style or service procedures to fit a poorly planned or executed facility. Too many restaurateurs have suffered the nightmare of setting up their new restaurant facility only to realize that "no one" considered where the waste container would go, where the coffee cups would be stacked, or where to plug in the toaster. This is not uncommon.

My friend George, a seasoned restaurateur, was reviewing the almost completed drawings his architect was preparing for his new steakhouse. His coffee supplier was looking over his shoulder and asked, innocently, "Where's the espresso machine going, George?" Well, George looked at the plans and then at his architect. The question was never asked until now! The idea to add an espresso machine came up during the design process, but the questions, "Who uses this equipment? Where does it go? What utilities are required? What related space or equipment is needed?" were probably never asked, confirmed, reviewed, or not clearly answered. Now, fortunately for George, there was time to correct the drawing rather than compromise his service procedures.

Office space is frequently tucked into a corner or not regarded as a significant space. In today's highly competitive and technologically intense restaurant industry, the office is a highly sophisticated control center. It may not need to be large, but it needs to be right. The conceptual plan for Claudes Bistro did not show any space for an office. When asked about this, Claude said, "We'll find a space for it. I think the landlord said he would give us some office space on the second floor." This is not smart planning and it exposes a deeper problem that can compromise his entire restaurant development. Whoever was doing the conceptual planning did not ask the right questions.

Time is measured differently in restaurant development than in day-to-day restaurant operations. Restaurateurs must react quickly—in minutes, maybe hours. A customer needs assistance *now*! An employee fails to show and you need to fill the void immediately—maybe you have an hour to find a substitute. You are accustomed to being in charge and in control, asking questions and getting quick responses.

In restaurant development, an engineer will get back to you with an answer in a few days. The building department needs four weeks or more to review your drawings. A supplier will get you specs or prices by the end of the week. You may not be used to waiting this long for answers and it is unsettling. The result is that you don't deal effectively or appropriately with the people on whom you must rely for information or decisions. You must either adapt to this different pace, which is not easy, or delegate the task to someone more skilled in dealing with this time frame.

Some activities are best left to those who have the appropriate temperament to deal with them. Attending a meeting with a building department official or sitting through a review or variance hearing may not be the best use of your time or the most efficient means to get the job done. When the city of Denver denied a local restaurateur's request for a revocable easement so that he could have a sidewalk patio and railing, the restaurateur called the zoning office and requested a meeting with the inspector at the building site. The official, happy to oblige, showed up. After a brief discussion of the request, the official reiterated his ruling. To support his decision, the official gestured widely and, walking the route pedestrians would be forced to take, explained to Michael, the restaurateur, that the patio and railing would require pedestrians to walk around his railing—a serpentine rather than a straight line—past the restaurant. He concluded that it was awkward and inconvenient. As it was his responsibility to protect the public welfare, he had to deny the request.

A negotiator familiar with the city zoning process would have regrouped and prepared his argument: specifically, that the serpentine route was more aesthetically pleasing to pedestrians, did not violate any sidewalk design standards, and would, in fact, promote the city's agenda of fostering outside patio dining. Additionally, he would line up his allies—neighborhood groups and residents supportive of the plan—and present his case in a manner that saved the patio for the restaurant and face for the official. That was not Michael's style. He became loud and threatening, and he cited the three other patios and railings on the same street, requiring a similar, curving path. He further told the official that he was going to do it anyway! Fortunately, Michael later agreed to turn the problem over to someone who understood how to approach the problem and solve it.

Very few people can develop a restaurant competently by themselves. Partnerships are formed among people with different strengths and complementary talents to plan and operate a restaurant. A strong foods person teams up with a front-of-the-house guy; a numbers cruncher joins forces with a people-person. Many small restaurant companies are successful because they combine a mix of talents that can at least oversee, if not perform, many of the required tasks. Large companies may have in-house staff to perform many of these functions. But even these people may not always have the depth of knowledge or experience to develop a restaurant. When they acknowledge the limits of their ability and are smart enough to select, oversee, and monitor the work of more competent outside professionals, their company wins.

When it is evident that neither the partners nor the management can perform a task, it should be delegated to someone who can. By recognizing when and where you need competent assistance, you will speed the development process and avoid costly blunders.

❖ # ASSESSING YOUR STRENGTHS

Effective restaurant development requires that you understand the varied talents required to complete the project successfully. You must determine objectively what tasks you and your partners can perform based on your talent, temperament, and the available time and resources at your disposal. Delegating a task does not preclude you from reviewing it, critiquing it, suggesting or making changes, or establishing the criteria for its execution. There are several trade-offs that you must consider before deciding to take on a task yourself or delegate it to a partner or an outsider.

Knowledge

Let's get this clear right now. You don't know everything. It makes no sense to risk the success of your restaurant by your taking on a task that you're not good at or don't really understand. You will simply make a fool of yourself if you insist on doing it. If you can't match your socks or can't comprehend spatial relationships, let someone else do the interior design. Take advantage of the professional talent that is available to make your restaurant a better place.

Being able to read drawings may not mean that you understand all the symbols and references. It may not mean that you can interpret them and determine if a detail is correct or if a conflict exists. The corporate office of an upstart restaurant company assigned the task of reviewing the construction documents for their franchise stores to a vice-president whose primary job was site selection and evaluation. He was given the added responsibility because he had construction experience. While he felt comfortable evaluating the drawings for the general flow of the restaurant and to confirm that all the required spaces were included, he could not check the elevations or details to ensure that recent operational changes were, in fact, incorporated. This was a critical task, one that had serious ramifications and had to be performed thoroughly and properly. The person assigned this responsibility was not sufficiently skilled to do this job. As a result, important changes slipped through the cracks and operational improvements were not implemented as quickly as hoped.

Your Time Versus Your Money

This is often a tough call. You cannot do it all by yourself, and usually, you cannot delegate and pay for all the work to be done by someone else. But you must decide what tasks can and should be done by you and your partners and which must be farmed out and be paid for to be done right. It is not uncommon to solicit help to provide "industry standard" formats or formulas for budgets and then do the math or produce the schedules yourself. It may be more economical to have an outsider review your work than to have them produce it.

Priorities

You have a schedule and you have a lot to accomplish. Recognizing that you can't do it all, you must decide what responsibilities are best handled by you or your partners personally. The timing of activities may affect your priorities. You may have more available time early in the development process and can devote more of your efforts to the activities that occur during this period—the business plan or financing. Your schedule may prevent you from getting too active in the design phase, but may loosen up in time to contribute during the construction phase.

Interest

Many developers will take on a job simply because it's fun. You'll work closely with your chef to develop recipes because you want to, even though it's not essential that you are intimately involved in this activity. You may elect to have nothing to do with the selection of furnishing since, in your opinion, as long as the chairs are comfortable and the tables spaced properly, the restaurant will work. If you are not interested in or passionate about a particular activity, you will probably not perform well.

Politics

Sometimes it is best to let someone else do your talking. As the central figure in your restaurant venture, you may not be the best one to deal with building inspectors or community groups who oppose your liquor license. Or you may find that by playing the role of the aspiring owner of a small business employer of local youth, and taxpayer, government officials will be more understanding when you deal with them directly rather than through a high-priced attorney or other professional.

A friend, Chris, wanted to get personally involved in the review of his drawings by the health department. He was proud of his concept and design and was looking forward to sharing his enthusiasm with the inspector. So he collected the information from his architect—drawings and equipment specifications. He even brought his sample menu and a sample of his china! The inspector was very nice and they both sat down in the conference room. This was a 125-seat restaurant of about 3000 square feet. It was all on one level, all new construction, a fairly straightforward design. The inspector looked at the equipment plan and then at the specifications, back to the plan and back to the specs and then just stared at the plan for 30 minutes. He didn't ask any questions and didn't say anything.

This enthusiastic restaurateur was fuming. "What in the world could he have been looking at for 30 minutes? He didn't say or ask anything! I could have redrawn that damn plan in that time!" Well, bureau-crats have their procedures and their pace. The plan was fine, and aside from the standard list of requirements that accompanied his approval, the inspector had nothing to say. Chris was furious that he had wasted his time meeting with a guy who really had no interest in his particular restaurant, didn't need to see his samples. To him, it was just another set of plans to review.

Roger, however, was successful because of his "humble, small businessman" approach. Many officials welcome the chance to give their opinion and tell you how they would do something. Too often, they are pressured, harassed, and belittled by designers, consultants, attor-neys, and other hired professionals who are trying to get their client's project approved and under construction. By appreciating the experi-ence that these people have with the building review process and ask-ing for their help or direction, you will be gaining important allies.

Roger met face to face with the plumbing review official to discuss his grease trap. The problem was simple. The code required a very large tank, larger and more expensive than Roger thought he should have. It was clear from his menu that he would not be doing much frying or using much grease. He asked the plumbing inspector to help him solve his problem, which was how to reduce the required size of his grease trap. There was Rog, harried, informally dressed, seeking help and advice from a guy who usually gets little respect or recognition from the people he serves. Together they came up with a plan to reduce the size of the grease trap.

WORKING WITH CONSULTANTS AND OTHER HIRED TALENT

To work with consultants and hired talent, you must understand how consultants and other advisors view you and your restaurant venture. There was an interview in the *Wall Street Journal* a few years ago (July 31, 1989, p. C-1) with a partner in a money management firm. When asked to define his job, he said, "the business of money management is not managing other peoples' money; it's the business of getting other peoples' money to manage." This was a very telling observation.

There are those who sell or market professional services and those who perform. You will be courted aggressively by those whose job it is to "get restaurants to design" or "construction projects to build." Their responsibility is to bring work into their company. Once you are landed, you are handed off to someone else and they are off to the next potential client. Sales and marketing professionals—this is a profession unto itself—will give you brochures, show you pictures of their work, and provide lists of other clients they have served. They will assure you that they can provide the skill and talent required to produce your restaurant.

To most consultants you are a "project," a source of revenue. They will prepare a contract that outlines their scope of services, propose a fee structure based on these services, and tell you how long it will take to complete their work. They will mention how excited they are to have this opportunity to work with you and how they will help you achieve the success that you are planning. They will be eager for you to sign their contract so they can begin work. Although many consultants do provide valuable and necessary services, their success is not tied to you or your venture. Their commitment, however sincere, is not as strong as yours. Your priorities are not necessarily theirs. They will not stay up late pondering the placement of telephones or wondering if you have enough deuces in the main dining room. You will!

There was a newspaper article that made this point very clear. A county commissioner was hired as a consultant by one of two resort area management companies. To some, this presented a conflict of interest since the commissioner would be voting on issues that could, potentially, affect his client adversely. When asked to address this conflict, he said, "I am a consultant, not an employee of [the company] and will be paid regardless of the success or failure of the ideas or recommendations I propose. . . ." How would you like to be paying big bucks to this consultant! The wonderful thing about his candor is that he laid his and many consultants' cards clearly on the table. What he really said was, "Hey, if my ideas don't work as well as I think they will, I will not suffer financially. I will have learned something at my client's expense, though, and will know better for my next client. . . ." He is sorry and you are out both time and money. In addition, you may have designed-in something that adversely affects your profitability and success.

By understanding how consultants view you and your restaurant, you can develop a healthy and satisfying working relationship with the ones you choose. You will know what to expect and will not set yourself up for disappointment. The nature of consulting work is that consultants have many clients. They need many clients and must be courting new clients actively all the time in order to pay their rent and maintain their business. After all, with their help you develop a successful restaurant, are very pleased with their work, thank them, pay them and you're gone! You're busy doing what you do best—operating your restaurant. However successful you are, you won't be needing their services again for at least a few years and probably more—maybe never.

You have a responsibility to yourself and to your investors and partners to select every member of your development team. Interviewing, evaluating, and selecting these players is a time-consuming and rigorous process. But due diligence requires that it be done thoroughly. There are nine general requirements that all your consultants must meet.

1. *Industry knowledge.* This is basic. Don't be the training ground for new talent. No other industry is "just like" the restaurant business. If you are expecting more from your development team members than simply providing a drafting service or word processing, knowledge of the restaurant industry is essential. General practitioners may provide guidance and direction in the early stages of your development, but why not align yourself from the very beginning with people who understand the language and nuances of your business?

2. *Experience with your type of restaurant.* You want people who have working experience with your specific type of operation. A fast-food restaurant is not the same as a specialty seafood house. The design and development requirements for an industrial feeding facility are not comparable to a family restaurant in a shopping complex or office building.

3. *Hands on experience in the work your require.* Meet the person who will be doing the actual work and get a commitment that this is the person who will be your contact. Avoid dealing with layers of bureaucracy, public relations types, or the "principals." The person who is making decisions or proposing options to you is the one you want to meet and feel confident with.

4. *Ability to be part of a team.* You have probably heard people talk of the extraordinary ability of a particular specialist and then add, "she's very temperamental" or "she really knows what works and is very opinionated. . . ." Nonsense! If a professional cannot be a contributing member of the development team who is able to listen to criticism and accept the owner's changes and decisions, you don't want her. This

type of consultant will destroy your development team, modify your concept to her criteria, and be more concerned with her own ego than your success. This is not her development; it is yours. Consultants must be team players and be able to subordinate their own agendas and egos for the sake of your development—that is nonnegotiable.

5. *A personality you can deal with.* Some people just don't hit it off. If you don't click with a consultant, recognize it early, accept it, and find another player. You will be dealing with enough contrary personalities beyond your control without inviting a mismatch into your team.

6. ***Resources to get the work done.*** Your team members must be able to get the job done. A great architect who has to use his friend's drafting table in the evenings will probably not be able to perform. A designer without access to showrooms or files of resources will not be able to show you the range of options available to you. Consultants without access to resources or the latest technology, or who lack knowledge of the materials available, are a shortcut to mediocrity. There are too many qualified professionals to choose from to compromise your team with a shortage of basic information.

7. ***Time to devote to your restaurant.*** Many consultants hate to say "no." They don't like to turn down work and may overbook their time. This is a disservice to you and can create unnecessary delays, poor performance, and cost you money. Sometimes it is difficult to tell beforehand if your restaurant project will be put on the back burner once you commit to working with a particular consultant. However, it will become apparent very quickly when you realize that they don't send their primary person to your development meetings or fail to meet a few deadlines. Let them know immediately, preferably during the interview process, that you will terminate their contract for poor performance. And define poor performance!

8. *A sincere interest in your restaurant.* Marketing representatives measure their success by the sales they generate. A steakhouse, employee cafeteria, fast-food place—it doesn't really matter. They get the lead, pursue it, and make the sale. You want more than that. You want to know that the firm you hire and the people who work with you have an interest in your success and really care about your restaurant.

9. *Belief in your concept, market, location, and your ability to perform.* Even those who care or take an interest in your venture may not be totally convinced that your timing, concept, location, or approach is

on target. The people you retain to assist you must be fully versed in your concept and be convinced that your plan is smart. You can't give them a pop quiz, but you should be able to tell from their attitude how committed they are to your project.

DETERMINING A CONSULTANT'S SCOPE OF SERVICES

When given an opportunity, an expert will offer advice on subjects outside his area of expertise. And he will do it with all the authority of his profession! Lawyers will provide counsel on operating procedures, food-service consultants will discuss lighting, and architects will try their hand at seating plans or color schemes. They do this for several reasons. The primary reason is that you let them! Almost everyone considers herself or himself an authority on the restaurant business. They eat out, understand service, and may even consider themselves accomplished cooks. By listening to their opinions, you are encouraging them to become involved in areas in which they are neither expert nor knowledgeable.

Normally, this is not a big issue and may even provide you with an interesting opinion or two. However, the reason it is important to recognize this tendency is that your encouragement gives them the false impression that their opinion in these areas has *value*. They will begin to devote their time and your money to thinking about and offering counsel on subjects that may interest them but on which they have no background or significant knowledge.

A marketing consultant was working on a preopening strategy for a family restaurant. He arrived on site as the furnishing and fixtures were being installed. Looking around, he began commenting on and criticizing the colors and fabric selections. The owner listened and started having second thoughts about her decisions. She became distracted from her efforts to get the restaurant open. The marketing wizard may or may not have been correct in his assessment. After all, colors and interior design are certainly subjective. But he was clearly not a professional interior designer or trained in interior design. His comments and involvement in this area were distracting and detrimental to the preopening effort.

Similarly, a restaurant critic and TV personality visited a popular restaurant that was in the final stages of a remodel. She, too, began criticizing the color selections and recommending color schemes that she felt would be more appealing. The owners, eager to please the local critic and reviewer, directed the painters to make the changes proposed. This change delayed the opening by three days!

Keep the services proffered by your consultants within their scope of expertise. It may seem expedient to delegate responsibility and authority for selecting specialty consultants or suppliers to your architect or contractor, but you may be compromising the quality of services you receive.

Many professionals will offer a "complete" range of services in the interest of project coordination. Architects, in particular, like to assume the role of project coordinator. They have established relationships with consulting engineers, interior designers, and specialty consultants, and they like to maintain these convenient relationships. The problem is that the experience, talent, and personalities of these professionals may not serve your best interests.

Contractors often like to include the purchase and installation of the foodservice equipment and some of the interior finishes—carpet, specialty flooring, lighting—in their general construction contract. Their primary motivation may be financial since their fee, whether fixed or a percentage of the cost, will reflect this additional service. Although they may stress the advantages to project coordination and timing, the downside of limited sources of supply or installation expertise may far outweigh the gains.

Foodservice consultants and interior designers prepare bid packages and often select the vendors and suppliers who are invited to bid. This is part of their "coordination and management" of their work and assures you, they will commonly claim, that only qualified companies bid on your project. Unfortunately, many small, highly reputable suppliers are excluded from this process. These smaller businesses may offer better service and competitive pricing.

Many of the specialized consultants you consider will promote the "package" approach. It is good marketing and from their perspective it is good business. You, however, must evaluate carefully which of the skills and services that they are proposing are truly their specialty and which are merely convenient. You accomplish this by establishing and following simple interview and review procedures. Initially, you will be approached by or will meet with marketing people. They will get your name or hear of your restaurant plans from a variety of sources: real estate or business brokers, newspaper articles, utility companies, or other resources that you have contacted.

While they are marketing to you, you must begin interviewing them. This is often awkward or difficult because they are courting you and feeding your ego. You may enjoy the process and forget to ask the tough questions. However you address these points, cover them completely.

1. *Check references.* Ask them for a list of restaurants whose development they have been involved in and the names and titles of the people with whom they worked directly. Visit the restaurants. Look at their work and talk to the people they worked with. Did they adhere to the concept? Were they easy to work with? How well did they communicate? Did they get their work done on time? What problems came up during the project, and how did they handle them?

2. *Learn their specific responsibilities.* Consultants sometimes take credit for work that they directed or coordinated but did not actually perform. Many marketing people use terms that make it unclear as to what their specific responsibilities were on a project. How many times have you heard someone say, "I did that restaurant. . . ." Well, what exactly do they mean by "did"? Equipment dealers and suppliers often say they "did" a restaurant when they mean they sold them the equipment or supplied the china, glass, and flatware. They may have made suggestions and, in fact, steered the owner toward a decision that really made a positive difference. But that does not mean you should entrust them with design decisions or the selection of china or equipment specifications. Architects and designers also claim broad-scope authorship of restaurant projects. Even as the project coordinator, they may not have been involved in many of the critical design decisions that affect operations.

3. *Clarify the specific services that are performed in-house.* Know which services are subcontracted out or provided by "associated firms." Many firms form alliances to submit a proposal for a development. These alliances or teams present their credentials as a package. They take this approach because, as a group, they can provide you with the full range of services necessary to complete your restaurant project and they believe that this "total services" approach will appeal to you. This shortcut clearly benefits them but may not benefit you. Evaluate each member of their "team" as an independent consultant.

4. *See the office.* See their company in action. Make an appointment or just stop by to take a tour of their facilities and chat with some of their staff. Look around. Get a sense of the types of projects that are in progress. They may say they are involved with many restaurants but you may not see any other restaurant projects "on the boards." Look at the equipment they have, and how well they are organized and managed. This will give you an excellent indication of their ability to perform.

5. *Meet the staff.* When you go into a restaurant or a retail shop, you can quickly pick up on the "feel" or "vibes" or "attitude" of the staff and management. This is what you are trying to sense when you visit potential consultants. The people who are working in the office—the secretary, administrative staff, drafting staff, executives—will project an attitude and work ethic that cannot be glossed over by a marketing person. Would you enjoy working with these people? Do they get along among themselves? Do they share ideas and appear to work well together? How well does management relate to them? Although you obviously cannot get an in-depth picture of the firm by a guided tour, you should be able to get a sense of how it works. Talk with them. Ask them questions about what they are working on. Get an idea of how knowledgeable they are and how much they care about the work they are doing.

6. *Look at their work.* Ask to see the work they did for other restaurateurs. What you are looking for is presentation, completeness, organization, and pride. You also want to like their designs. Are they proud of their work? Are they glad to show it to you, and do they point out things that made the restaurant work well or save time? Look at how they solved problems and addressed design issues. Have them walk you through the documents and explain the flow and organization of the documents. Without becoming an expert in the review of contract documents, you should see the order in their work.

7. *Make an assessment.* What do you think: Can these people do the job? Are you comfortable with their style and approach? Do you like the people? Do they want to work with you? Remember, you will be entrusting a portion of your success to their ability to perform. Your assessment of how the company truly reflects the marketing "spin" is an important judgment. Compare their strengths and weaknesses against those of the other companies you have interviewed. These people will be working for you and working with the other consultants you hire. It is critical that you have a high comfort level with their abilities and their people.

❖   CONTRACTING WITH CONSULTANTS

You will want to have a contract with your consultants. This agreement will clearly spell out what they will do, what they do not do, when they will complete their work, how and when they get paid, who reviews and approves their progress, and what they are and are not responsible for.

Contracts can be simple letter-style agreements or multipage legal nightmares. While everyone tries to protect against misunderstandings, you, as the buyer, should have a very clear understanding of the terms, conditions, and details of the agreement. If a consultant insists on using a lengthy, wordy, legal-sounding document ("my legal counsel requires us to use this contract"), you should understand it thoroughly and have your attorney read it. Many negotiators make one point very clear. Everything is negotiable! If a consultant is unwilling to delete an objectionable paragraph from a standard contract, you have three choices:

1. Accept it if you feel you can.

2. Demand an addendum with wording that is acceptable to you.

3. Find another consultant who will accept your terms.

The fact is that regardless of the contract, if you are not satisfied with the consultant's work, or if you do not perform as agreed, you will either have to negotiate a settlement or have it out in court. Many business-people say that if you have to go back and look at the contract after you have executed it, you've got a problem.

There are several items that you will want itemized in your agreement.

1. *Detailed scope of services.*   Their services must be itemized. It is not enough to write "prepare financial projections." You must know if this step includes supporting schedules, the number of scenarios covered, who determines the expense categories, how many times you can change the operating statistics, and so on. Similarly, "prepare contract documents (drawings and specifications)" is also too vague. You need the specifics. Most professional associations provide their members with standard contract forms: leases, architectural and interior design contracts, construction contracts. Even though these are standard

forms, read them carefully and question any areas that you do not understand. Some agreements require actions or information from you that you cannot provide. Architectural contracts frequently indicate that the owner provides the design requirements. You may prefer that the architect assist you in this endeavor. If so, you may have to alter the agreement to reflect this added service.

2. *Time required to perform.* When will they start, and how long will it take them to complete each phase of their work? Are there review stages so that you can make changes or corrections? What constitutes completion? All parties involved in your planning process will rely on information provided by other members of your development team. Meeting deadlines often depends on several different entities working together and providing information to each other on time. One delay will inevitably cause a chain reaction that delays the entire process.

3. *Information required from you or others.* Since all the work on your restaurant is interrelated, what information are they going to research and provide, and what do they need from you or your other consultants? Will they get this information directly, or is it your responsibility to collect it and pass it along? Consultants are often maligned for taking your information, putting it in a nice format, and then taking credit for it. Well, sometimes another viewpoint can shed needed light on a subject: filling in blanks, asking relevant questions to get needed additional detail, or providing insight into operational requirements.

4. *Resources that consultant will use.* How will they accomplish their work? Compatible computer software, access to showrooms and trade sources, and knowledge of specialty manufacturers and custom designers of specialty products can be determining factors in the selection of a design professional. The availability of crews and the clout that a contractor has with their subcontractors and suppliers may affect schedules and therefore your selection of one general contractor over another.

5. *Total fee.* What will their services, as detailed, cost, and which costs are fixed and which variable? Many consultants base their fee on a percentage of your total project cost or a percentage of the cost of the work performed under their contract. So if the cost changes, so does their fee.

6. *Additional costs.* There are usually "additional" fees or costs involved. Direct expenses such as phone, courier services, printing, postage, travel, parking, and so on, are generally additional. These should

be listed and any markup over actual cost indicated. The additional costs for services not included in the base proposal must be clearly defined. These would include changes made to designs after approval or other services—studies, surveys, expanded scope of design—that are not part of the original contract.

7. *Availability for meetings.* You will want your consultants to be available to you when you need them. Realizing that this is impractical, consultants often restrict their attendance to specific benchmarks or review points. Attendance at additional meetings will cost you either an hourly fee or a fixed fee per meeting. Be sure that the number of meetings included in the base fee is reasonable and will cover the entire process in which they are involved (planning and design or construction, or both). They should include telephone conferences and fielding questions over the phone as part of the base fee. If not, be sure that you understand the limitations.

8. *To whom consultant reports.* Establish a very clear chain of communication. Each of your consultants must report directly to your project manager. While consultants will and must communicate directly among themselves, you want your project manager to be aware of *all* correspondence and communication. Your project manager should not create any bottlenecks or limit the flow of information. He must, however, make sure that the most current information is in the hands of the right people and that decisions are not being made without your knowledge.

9. *Identity of consultant's contact person.* When you have a question or comment, you need to know that there is someone at the office who knows you and your restaurant project and can get answers for you. The person assigned to you should be actively involved in your project. Steer clear of the principals unless they are actually involved. The more corporate layers you have to sift through, the longer it will take to get an answer. And like the old game of "telephone," your question probably will have lost its original meaning before you have an answer.

❖   # TIMING

All members of your development team will tell you that they should be involved in the project from the very beginning. They will tell you that even though their particular talent does not come into play until later in the development, their input in the early stages will benefit you and your restaurant. Involve them when their talents are needed, not before. In the very early planning stages, the operational details of your concept are evolving. You need to surround yourself only with people who understand and can contribute to this specific effort.

Committee decision making is a slow, tedious and often an unproductive process. Many restaurateurs are owners of small businesses who don't have the luxury of time or the patience to sit around and discuss issues to death. They get information and make decisions. They don't "talk;" they "do." By bringing in team members too early, you may become bogged down in discussions and conferences with people who cannot truly contribute professionally.

❖ MANAGING THE DEVELOPMENT TEAM

One person must be given the responsibility and the authority to coordinate and manage the development team. Ideally, this person should be a partner in the development—someone who has a vested interest in its success. If no partner or investor qualifies for the job, select a person whose judgment you trust and whose allegiance is totally directed to your concept and ideas.

As with any position, you need a clear job description and a job specification. This person is your project manager or owner's representative. He or she is the quarterback, the person who directs and coordinates the interaction of all the other team members. The job description explains the tasks and duties for which this person will be responsible. The job specification defines the characteristics that this person must possess to be effective in the job.

Job Description

The project manager or owner's rep will be responsible for:

1. *Preparing a directory* of all team members (including company name, areas of responsibility, contact, address, phone, fax, and other

pertinent information about the person and company) and distributing it to all members.

2. *Attending all meetings*, taking detailed notes (decisions made, decisions to be made, due dates, persons responsible) and sending copies of these notes to all members whether or not they attended the meeting.

3. *Acting as the liaison* between consultants, and between consultants and owners.

4. *Receiving, reviewing, and where necessary, acting* on meeting notes or memos from meetings with consultants, suppliers, government agencies, or others.

5. *Acting as agent* for owner to approve or authorize invoices, decisions, material selections, and so on.

6. *Expediting* the restaurant development project—monitoring deadlines and due dates, demanding performance, mediating disputes.

Job Specification

The person you select must be:

1. *Well organized.* All the information relating to the restaurant development must be readily accessible. This person will be setting up and maintaining these files.

2. *Good communicator.* Whether written or spoken, information and communication must be direct and clear. For the right decisions to be made, this person must feel as comfortable presenting options as in offering clarification on complex issues or getting the right people (consultants) to state their case.

3. *Demanding and able to handle confrontations easily.* Team members will have strong opinions and views. Your owner's representative will have to mediate these conflicting opinions and solve problems as they arise.

4. *Able to deal effectively with bureaucracy.* This is not easy. Using the system to your benefit rather than fighting it takes a certain temperament. The project manager must understand this and choose the appropriate tack. He or she must be able to work within the system.

5. *Decisive.* The owner's representative must be able to evaluate the information and make a decision. Giving partial answers or "maybe's" doesn't cut it. This is not to suggest that the manager should rush into a decision before he or she is ready, but once all the information needed to make an informed decision is available, a decision must be made.

❖ # MAKING DECISIONS

If your restaurant is ever going to be developed, you will have to make decisions. Many people postpone making decisions until they have checked every angle and gotten input from everyone they know. Some believe that "no decision" is the best decision. Others make quick decisions just to avoid confrontation or to get on with their project. Well, whatever your style, there are nine keys to the decision-making process.

1. *Understand the question.* What is it exactly that you are being asked to decide? If a consultant asks, "what style of chair do you have in mind?" What does he want to know—color, arm or armless, padded seat, size? You may have to ask the consultant questions to get to the meat of these questions. When an architect asks, "how comfortable do you want the bathrooms to be?", is she asking about the quality of the fixtures, the number of toilets you want above those required by code, or the quality of the finishes? By understanding the reason for the question and what the consultant is going to do with the answer, you can then respond properly.

2. *Know the impact of your decision on the other aspects of the development.* No decision is an island. Every time you decide something, it will have an influence on some other area of your restaurant: budget, space, service, table layout, lighting, and so on. Many consultants view their contribution as most important. You've got to have an effective air distribution system, but the ductwork layout does not necessarily take precedence over the lighting plan. The chair that your designer selects meets all your requirements for comfort, style, and price, but doesn't stack or nest. How does this affect your storage? Your staff needs easy access to the wait station, but the location costs you a four-top. Tough decisions. But by knowing how each individual decision affects other parts of your restaurant, you can begin to evaluate your options.

3. *Define your options clearly—all of them.* There are always choices. There is more than one right way to do something. Although your consultants may give you a choice of A or B, don't accept those as the only options. Think about what you are trying to accomplish and how else you can solve the problem. There is an old puzzle that may help open your mind: connecting a series of nine dots arranged in a square using only four continuous straight lines:

The secret is to draw two of the lines beyond the boundaries of the square of dots:

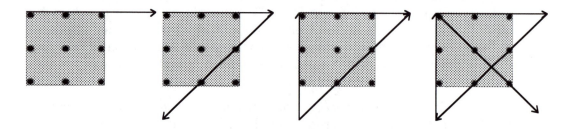

The lesson here is to "think outside the dots." Don't get into a rut and consider only options that are tried and true. Why not consider turning the wait station 90 degrees or flipping it? Why not move the bar 2 feet or to the other side of the lounge? Why does the door have to go there?

4. *Be sure that you have all the information to make an informed decision.* You can get the information you need to make your decision from many places. By bringing the question up at your development

meetings, you will get comments from all your consultants. That is one resource. If you need more background or other perspectives, you may have to see how various solutions work for other operators. Go to restaurants that have done what you are considering and talk with the people who must live with the decision: servers, management, kitchen staff, and others. Talk with customers or friends who have experienced the consumer side of the decision.

It is perfectly acceptable to solicit opinions from people outside your development team: professionals and interested amateurs. You are not bound to rely only on those professionals who you have retained to assist you. Be careful to distinguish professional advice and opinions from unsubstantiated beliefs. This can be tricky, since many professionals offer comments that cannot be supported by example or experience.

5. *Check your ego.* It is difficult for many entrepreneurial business-people to admit to having a bad idea or, worse, that someone else has a better solution to a problem. You may not like it, but for the sake of your restaurant and your future success, try to manage your ego and recognize good advice when you hear it.

6. *Avoid "yes-men."* Along this line, if you surround yourself with people who always agree with you, why not just buy a mirror and save money? Some developers handicap themselves and their project by falling into this trap. Be vigilant not to surround yourself with people who always agree with you and will not challenge your ideas or opinions. You might make a casual comment about the placement of a wait station or style of chair, and soon find that it has been implemented into the plan. Decisions can be made without a lot of discussion, resulting in flaws that could have been avoided easily with a more challenging team.

7. *Don't be pressured into making a decision before you are ready.* Each member of your development team has a schedule that she or he is trying to maintain. They may want to complete your project before the holidays or by the end of the month. They may be starting another assignment soon and need to shift their staff. Whatever their agenda, they may push you to make decisions so that they can complete their phase of the work. Do not fall prey to this pressure. Make your decision after you are comfortable with the facts, the choices you have, and the impact that your decision makes on the other aspects of your restaurant.

8. *You can change your mind.* Making changes often costs time and money. You will be discouraged every step of the way from making revisions or re-thinking an earlier decision. Stand your ground! You are building a restaurant, your restaurant, perhaps the only restaurant you will ever own and certainly your livelihood for many years.

A two-week delay or a few hundred or a thousand dollars may not be a high price to pay to get something right. Consider the consequences of not making a change or correction and the years of inconvenience or operational compromise you will live with. Obviously, you should avoid making changes, but accept the fact that you will make mistakes and forget things until after a decision has been made and you will be forced to take corrective action.

Do not be bullied by your consultants or give in to the threats of delays, cost overruns, or other ploys to keep you on some arbitrary schedule. You must remember that you will operate with the decisions you make today for many, many years. Weigh the long-term gain against the short-term savings.

9. *Give your decision clearly, explicitly, and in writing.* Once you have made a decision, make sure that everyone understands it and adheres to it. You will not always make popular decisions or get total agreement from your development team. Some members may attempt to override your decision, ignore it, or claim to have misunderstood what you meant. This is why your project manager coordinates communication among the team members and puts everything in writing.

❖   ASSEMBLING YOUR TEAM

To build a team that can accomplish your objectives, you must first determine what positions must be filled. To do this, you will take each area of the development process, list the activities and decisions associated with these areas, and identify the talents needed to perform these tasks.

Preparing a Marketable Business Plan

Your business plan presents your overall idea for your business. It discusses the specifics of your concept, operating style, location, and financing requirements and projected revenues to your potential investors, lenders, and partners. While there are consultants who can assist you with this phase, you and your partners must provide the core information. Many operators know what they want but cannot write or present it in a comprehensive, well-organized document. Similarly, knowing the check average you plan to achieve or the cost of some of the development components is not sufficient to prepare detailed budgets or financial statements. There are several skills that are required to write a marketable business plan. One person does not necessarily have to be given the task of preparing the entire document. Each component can be assigned to one or more people.

Drafting a Plan. Since this is your concept, you are the one who must put your initial thoughts on paper. Do not concern yourself with format, grammar, or style. The essential point here is that you get your ideas, operating philosophy, and key components of your plan in writing. You may choose to assign the research or fact finding for the various components of the business plan to other people; listing competitive operations or doing market analysis, for example. If you assign the drafting of these sections to others, you should review the information and any conclusions they draw to confirm their findings.

Writing and Editing. You can't sell what you can't explain. The writing must be clear and well reasoned. The text should use language that investors and lenders can understand. Be careful with industry buzzwords. Although they indicate an intimacy with the industry, they may be foreign to potential lenders and investors and your point may be lost. Terms such as *check average*, *covers*, or *deuce* should be explained.

Independent writers, if they are not involved with your development, may misinterpret some of your notes or ideas. Therefore, it is necessary that you read and edit their work for content and correct presentation of your ideas. The writer must use a word processor since you will be editing this document many times before you are satisfied with the final product. You will want to print your document on a laser printer so that the copy quality is very clear and easy to read.

Work from an outline; follow a format used by other, successful business plans; use a guide written specifically for your industry; or hire a professional writer who is familiar with the restaurant business. Regardless of your writing ability, you must be the one to provide the basic information. After all, it is your concept and restaurant that is being explained, and the business plan will be the basis for developing the details of your restaurant.

Presenting a Menu. The discussion and presentation of your proposed menu must go into sufficient detail to whet the appetite of your readers. Restaurants have a romantic appeal to many investors. By presenting the menu with all the glamor and showmanship that you will apply to the restaurant itself, you can lure your reader into the concept and make him a part of the restaurant. Use the style of writing that you intend to use on your actual menu. Produce a mock-up, if possible. The person who writes this section could be your chef or the partner who is focusing on this part of the operation. Even if this person is not comfortable writing finished copy, he can get the essentials down in draft form and your writer can polish it.

Developing a Budget. Your budget must be very detailed and complete and must have some basis in fact. There are guides and books that will give you detailed budget breakdowns. A budget that is too general indicates that you do not really understand the complexity of your undertaking. The person who puts the budget together does not need to be an accountant or bookkeeper but should be detail oriented and know where to get estimates and realistic budget figures. You may even break the budget into sections and assign different people different sections. For example, if you are working with a specific general contractor or know a contractor familiar with restaurant construction, you may meet with him to get budget estimates for the construction section. Your prospective foodservice supply and equipment dealer will help you determine your equipment budget. Calling specialty suppliers for estimates or unit costs will give you realistic prices for these items. Your chef can work on budgets for his area while your dining room manager can develop the budget for hers.

Preparing Financial Statements and Supporting Schedules. There are standard formats for restaurant financials that must be followed. Although you may delegate the task of preparing these statements to an accountant or bookkeeper, you must participate in establishing the criteria for sales revenues and provide or agree with the backup for the supporting schedules, related costs, and line item expenses. Since these projections are based entirely on your concept, market, operating style, and location, you must ensure that the revenue, expenses, and accompanying schedules are consistent.

Setting Up a Business Entity. There are considerations regarding taxes, personal liability, reporting procedures, and many other factors that will determine the type of business entity under which you operate. Knowledgeable legal counsel is essential. Attorneys are specialists. A good corporate attorney may not be adequately familiar with liquor license law. An attorney who concentrates on business entities may not be the best one to review your lease. Many accountants specialize in setting up business entities and may work with an attorney to provide a package that addresses both the legal and financial management issues.

Packaging. Visually, your business plan must project the style and image of the restaurant you are developing. A plan for a family restaurant will be presented differently from that representing a flamboyant café. Graphics, your logo, and the type of cover will all make an initial impression on your reader. Your local quick print shop can offer many suggestions. A brief meeting with a graphic artist can steer you in the right direction.

Financing

Getting funding for your restaurant development is a multistep process. Many different talents may be needed to complete the process. Now that you have your completed business plan, you can't just set up a stand on the corner or hand them out at the bus stop. Who gets one; who do you call; who presents the plan to potential investors?

Sources of Funding. There are professionals who broker investments such as yours. Before committing to anyone, find out the kinds and sizes of deals they sell (if you are trying to raise $60,000, someone who deals in millions isn't the right person to approach). You need to know their commission structure and what their fee includes and excludes. Be sure to check references. You or your partners may contact friends, relatives, or business associates. Soliciting money for a venture requires a certain temperament. In some cases, your personal appeal may be required. In others, an outsider may be able to present your information more convincingly.

Representation. Someone has to communicate with potential investors and partners. He must answer questions, get more details, and so on. This is a critical time in your development, since without funds, your restaurant will not become a reality. This position must be considered a very high priority. You are busy moving ahead with your planning. Others may be waiting for the green light to begin their work. No one has adequate funding to get basic supplies. It is a frustrating time in your development, but this frustration can not be allowed to show through to your potential investors. A less sensitive third party may be better able to communicate.

Legal Documents. Legal documentation for investments requires the services of another legal specialist. Although one attorney may wear many hats, do not assume that your attorney and golfing partner can fulfill all your legal needs.

Money Management. What do you do with the invested funds during the development process? Who is responsible for disbursements, lien waivers, and similar documents? Someone must be assigned the responsibility for managing and accounting for the money. Your bookkeeper or accountant could accomplish this. Do not minimize the importance of this job. Many lawsuits emanate from poor fiscal management.

Refining Your Concept and Writing the Operational Plan

While you are soliciting your financing, you can be refining your concept. Taking the operational details of your business plan, you now flesh out these details, getting into the specifics of how you plan to execute the concept and operating style you described. Your business plan presented your concept in broad strokes, with many ideas stated and described but not necessarily thought through completely. Now is the time to refine and delve into these ideas, procedures, and approaches to customer service. The information and details you prepare here will become an integral part of your design program.

Customer and Service Procedures. It is fine to say that you will use tray service to deliver food to the table and that bussers will remove dishes by hand to a service area, where they will temporarily hold them in bus boxes. This level of detail in a business plan is perfectly acceptable. Now, however, you must figure out how this will really work. What size and shape of trays will you use? Where will the trays be stored while in service? How about the bus boxes? How many will be kept at the side stand? Will the bussing station be separate or a part of the wait station? What other items—water, ice, and so on—will be stored there? These are the types of questions and the level of detail that you must address, since the answers to these questions will be the basis for your design.

When you put this information down on paper, format is not important. It is the raw data—the details—that are essential. This procedure is usually a collaborative effort. You and your partners, along with your manager (if selected), servers from your other operations, or your food-service consultant, will literally map out the procedures of your operation from the time the guests walk in the door to the time they leave. Who greets them? Where? What tools, materials, or space does the host need? Who gives them menus? Where are they stored? The questions go on until you've covered every aspect of your service procedures. Just get it down on paper, organize it, and review and refine it. Have it typed or neatly printed so that you can incorporate it with the package you will provide your designers.

Kitchen Procedures. In your business plan, you presented your menu and discussed the preparation of some key items. Now you will go through the menu, item by item, and document the raw ingredients: how they are purchased (fresh, frozen, dry storage), their storage requirements (refrigeration, freezer, dry storage, secured or open shelving), the stages of preparation and the tools, space, and equipment required, how they are held after cooking, where they are set for pickup, who picks them up, and so on. This will enable you to determine what storage, prep space, tools, equipment, and serving space you need. Your chef or kitchen manager will participate in this activity. As you develop these requirements, you will probably revise your service procedures, adding, deleting, and transferring responsibilities among your service staff.

Administrative Needs. Every operator has his or her own style of management and administration. What functions are performed in your office? Is your bookkeeping done on or off premises? Do you need to hold management meetings in your office? How many desks or workstations will you need? What about daily cash handling and reporting? These are the kinds of questions that the operator/manager or partner in charge of these activities must answer since he or she is the person who will be performing or directing these functions.

Staffing. In your business plan, you calculated your payroll based on staffing charts or used a similar method. Now, with the refinements you have made to your operating procedures, you need to rethink your staffing and be more specific about positions, workstations, job descriptions, employment requirements, and so on. You need to know how many people you will actually be hiring to staff your operation. Then you need to determine where these people will clock-in and store their personal belongings, change into their uniforms, and what tools, space, and accessories they will need to perform their jobs. This task may be assumed by one of your managers or partners. Here, too, the details of your operation, developed and described in this section, will be of great assistance.

Space Requirements. Don't be put off by the heading "space requirements"—you are not required to do math or draw. What you need to determine are the various pieces of your restaurant. Just list them in no particular order. Once again, the important thing is to get it down on paper. Begin at the front door and walk through your restaurant listing all the spaces that come to mind: entry, host, coatrooms, retail area, phone booth, waiting area, bar, lounge seating, and so on, all the way through to the back door. Don't concern yourself at this point with sizes or the relationship of one space to another. You and your partners can write this list or get your managers to do it. The purpose of this list of spaces is to form a basis for your design program, which will be discussed shortly.

Seating Requirements. It is amazing how many restaurateurs let their design team determine the seating requirements for their restaurant. This is not the seating *layout* but your requirements: How many bar stools and lounge seats do you want? What is the mix of seating units for the dining room (2's, 4's, 6's)? What kind of seating do you prefer: booths, tables, banquettes? You discussed some of this in your business plan, but you may not have been as well versed in the details of your concept as you are now. Table sizes and shapes as well as chair sizes and styles are addressed here.

These are operational decisions, not necessarily design or aesthetic decisions. The operator, owner, or creator of the concept must make these decisions.

The Design Program

The design program outlines the criteria that the design team will use in designing your restaurant. The required spaces and their specific features and characteristics will be detailed in this document. Your architect may coordinate the preparation of the design program. While she will use your business plan, budgets, and operational plan as the basis for this document, the design program is concerned primarily with the physical requirements—space, utilities, circulation, materials and finishes, furnishings/fixtures, and equipment—that are necessary for your restaurant to function according to your operational requirements. The design program is the general "recipe" for the design of the restaurant. Leave out a necessary ingredient and the finished product will not meet your expectations.

An architect working on the conceptual plans for a restaurant/grill wanted to show the owner a variety of building designs. In an attempt to get some fresh ideas, she handed the project to an associate. The associate, a very talented designer, came back with an unusual and attractive design scheme that caught everyone's attention. The only problem was that it did not include all the required elements or ingredients. There was no "balcony dining area" or "alcove off the bar for private parties." The plan was quickly dismissed without further discussion. Thus any good ideas that may have been included in the design were overlooked. The problem was quite simple. The associate did not read the design program. He saw an opportunity to create an exciting restaurant and used his own ideas about what should be included. Without a written design program, you run the risk of omitting key operational ingredients of your restaurant.

The design program can be coordinated and prepared by you, your project manager, or by your architect/designer. Whoever prepares it must work closely with those who developed the restaurant concept or are responsible for operating the restaurant. This may include your general manager, chef, dining room manager, or other key personnel.

Site/Building Selection

You have indicated in your business plan who your market is and where, in general, you want to locate. Now you will be seeking out specific locations. If you have developed your plan based on a pre-selected site or location, this is the time to make sure that the space still meets your needs and requirements. Like most other professionals, real estate brokers and leasing companies specialize. An excellent residential home broker probably will not have a good grasp of the commercial restaurant market. Brokers who concentrate on general retail or office space may not have a keen sense of what's available in the restaurant market either.

Prepare a checklist of the features and characteristics that you require. Indicate which are essential, which are desirable, which would add to the value of the space, and which are mere wishes. There is no sense pursuing a space that has a fatal flaw. This checklist will spell out your criteria very explicitly. This checklist should include:

- ◆ Lease or purchase
- ◆ Raw land or existing building
- ◆ General terms: length of lease, budget
- ◆ Legal use: licensing requirements, such as liquor, cabaret, dancing
- ◆ Location requirements: access, egress, visibility, neighborhood or section of city, specific streets or intersections
- ◆ Size: area required, number of levels, parking
- ◆ Utilities: specifically, issues that may be problems, such as natural gas, electrical load, grease trap, exhaust ducting

♦ Architectural features: patios, views, ceiling heights, windows, street-level access

Interview and select a company and broker/agent who knows the area that you are considering, specializes in restaurants, and is active in the location-finding business. It is not enough to find the right company that deals in your particular market and is familiar with your location and industry. You must also find the right person within that organization to work with you. Your broker, like every other member of your development team, should read your business plan and review your design program. This will familiarize him with your concept, space requirements, and other important factors relating to your restaurant site. He will review your checklist and offer suggestions and refinements.

Spread the word to many professionals. Let more than one broker know of your needs. Meet with several and present your concept, location requirements, and timetable. Review your requirements with these agents and add to the list based on their comments and suggestions. They will ask critical questions that may help you refine your requirements. As a potential tenant, you are not limited to dealing exclusively with one agent. By involving several from different companies or areas of specialty—freestanding buildings, office parks and complexes, retail centers—you will get good coverage throughout your planned market area.

Brokers like exclusive agreements and claim to be more aggressive on your behalf if they know you are working solely with them. In many cases, this may be true. However, a commitment on your part requires an equal commitment on their's. If you agree with an exclusive arrangement, demand intensive action and set standards that you expect your broker to achieve, such as scheduled site visits or update meetings. Give yourself an out if your broker does not perform. Offering exclusivity for a limited time period such as 30 days gives you an opportunity to evaluate her performance at short intervals.

Professional real estate brokers are one of several sources for locating your site, building or space. You or one of your associates can drive around your prospective area and scout out buildings. Once you have found some of interest, call the owner or landlord or have your broker do the legwork. Keep in mind, though, that researching a potential site takes time and a knowledge of what to look for. This is one reason to use the services of a professional broker. Broker fees are usually paid by the landlord but calculated into the rent. Keep in mind, too, that unless the broker finds the right location and you sign a lease, she does not get paid. So her motivation is to root out all potential locations and ensure that they meet your requirements.

Your broker will determine many things about a potential site before she takes you there to inspect it.

1. *Satisfies your basic space requirements.* There is no reason to go any further if the space is too small or too large or doesn't meet any of your other basic requirements of orientation, level, location, visibility, or accessibility.

2. *Legality of business.* Do the applicable municipal codes and building covenants permit your specific use? Can you operate during the hours you require? Many multitenant buildings restrict or specify your hours of operation. Can the premises be licensed for liquor service? You would be surprised how many restaurateurs commit to a space assuming that they can be licensed, only to realize that the surrounding neighborhood will oppose and win the battle to prevent the licensing.

3. *Available utilities.* Are the utilities adequate for your needs? Your broker, using your design program, will have a good idea of the utilities you require. She can get a clear answer from the landlord or owner as to what utilities are available, their capacity, and any restriction or limitation on the use of sewers, grease traps, gas, water, heating, air conditioning, ventilation, and electrical service.

4. *Architectural/interior features.* Your design program describes the architectural features and elements that are necessary for your concept. These may include high ceilings, large windows, corner entrance, basement storage, and alley access for service. The features found in a particular building, following your inspection, may not meet your needs. But at least you have narrowed your search significantly and reduced the time you spend inspecting potential sites.

5. *Terms of lease/purchase.* Lease terms vary greatly and are usually negotiable. Your broker will present to you the terms and conditions listed or as defined by the landlord. By comparing these proposed terms and conditions with your pro-forma financials and your capital expenditures schedule, you'll have a reasonable indication of whether or not you can afford the space.

6. *Adverse conditions.* Are there covenants, restrictions, or other provisions that may affect your restaurant operation? Leases, building rules, and other nongovernmental restrictions imposed by condominium associations or management companies may inhibit your

ability to build your market share. How do adjacent tenants, planned developments, or construction plans affect your proposed business? Competitive restaurants planned for adjacent lots or buildings may dissuade you from this location. Highway expansions and rerouting of roadways can divert your intended market, block access to your restaurant, or delay your opening.

7. *Lease terms.* The cost of your space includes many individual items. It may include a base rent plus a percentage of your gross revenue, common-area charges, utilities (metered or a percentage of the total), general building maintenance, association fees, common advertising fees, and other fixed and variable charges. You also may be required to post deposits. Or your lease term may begin long before you open for business, requiring additional capital expenditures beyond your budget.

Leases can be 2 or 200 pages in length. Regardless of length or complexity, you will want an attorney to review the terms and conditions of your lease. Select an attorney who knows your concept and budgets, understands restaurants and restaurant leases, and who is working for you. Your broker, while finding a space for you, is really working for the landlord, since the landlord is the one who will pay her commission. There are brokers who act for you as the lessee, and you pay their commission. Although this may appeal to you, they are not lawyers and you should still use an attorney or other qualified professional to review the lease.

You and your partners should read and understand the lease. Do not rely solely on your attorney to read and interpret the lease details for you. As an operator, you will pick out terms and conditions that you may not want to have included. These may seem innocuous to your attorney but may be critical to you. Some leases require the restaurant tenant to be responsible for cleaning and maintaining the public restrooms since, according to the landlord, the restaurant and the restaurant patrons are the primary users. To your attorney this may not be a big issue. But to you as the operator this involves staffing, supplies, and the maintenance of an area totally outside of your control. Read the lease.

The Design Process

This is the area where your ideas and your concept are transformed into a restaurant facility—on paper. The "on paper" part is critical because you will have the opportunity to see how it works and make changes before you commit to concrete, wood, and nails. All the pieces that make up your restaurant facility—dining room, kitchen, bar, storage, heating and air-conditioning systems, electrical, plumbing, furniture/fixtures, and equipment—will be decided during this phase.

Designing a restaurant can involve a dozen or more different design talents. The management and coordination of these professionals is the responsibility of the project manager. When dealing with design professionals, you are often working with big egos, sensitive personalities, and highly opinionated people. Just remember whose restaurant it is and that it is the design program and the concept as created and modified that drive the design process.

Every design decision made by any member of your design group will affect some other aspect of the design. No design decision is isolated. Therefore, whenever a decision or change in the design is made, look for its effects throughout the design.

Restaurants are very complicated buildings. Dimensions are critical. An error of inches can reduce your seating capacity or prevent a piece of equipment from fitting properly. Utility requirements and their placement are complex. Where cleaning is essential, adding surface-mounted utilities causes health hazards and maintenance headaches. The degree of detail and the coordination of many trades is highly demanding. You want all those involved in the design process to be very familiar with restaurant design. Regardless of how talented they may be, if they have not designed restaurants similar to the type you are developing, they will not have the depth of knowledge necessary to do the job right.

Unless you or your project manager specifically designate the team member who will perform these services, they will be provided by the professional who:

♦ Takes the initiative to claim it

♦ Traditionally performs it

♦ Wants to add it to his services to increase his involvement in the project

♦ Has it assigned to him by the project architect

or, it won't get assigned and won't get done!

The talents that make up your design team may include:

1. *Project manager.* The project manager acts as the owners representative to oversee and manage the development process. Too often, a distinction is made between the needs of the front-of-the-house (public

areas) and the back-of-the-house (service and support spaces). This results in a pushing and shoving contest among your consultants—very unproductive, time consuming, and stupid! It is the responsibility of your project manager to make it clear to every member of your development team that you are developing one restaurant. How it functions is a result of how well the entire facility is designed.

2. *Project architect.* Architects, traditionally, coordinate the design process. They develop the conceptual floor plans and prepare or coordinate all of the contract documents—drawings and specifications—that become the working drawings for the construction of your restaurant. Many states require that your drawing be prepared or reviewed and signed by a licensed architect. But architects do not have all the answers or all the talent to accomplish this. The many consultants and specialists involved in the process are often retained and managed by the architect. The primary objection to this approach is that their priorities and criteria for the selection of these professionals may not be the same as yours. If an architect has an interior designer on staff, she may not solicit proposals from outside designers even though their talents may be more suitable for your restaurant.

Many architects have established relationships with consulting mechanical, electrical, and structural engineers. While these professionals may be familiar with the requirements of restaurants, they may not be the best choice for your facility. There may be other firms that have a better understanding of your particular concept and have a depth of experience not found in your architect's regular stable of consulting firms.

Your architect may argue that a good working relationship among the consultants on the design team is critical to the effective coordination and smooth development of the contract documents. She is absolutely correct. But these relationships can be established quickly and should not limit your choice of talent. Besides, she can learn to work with a new consulting engineer if the new one has more experience and better skills to help design your restaurant. This is one of the major reasons for having a team manager whose loyalty is to the owner and not affected by convenient relationships among consulting professionals.

3. *Code review specialists.* This service is often provided by your project architect. But it is worth your time to learn how effective they are in performing this task. All industries have specialists who work in obscure phases of a business. This is one of them.

Building and related codes are complex and often contradictory. The plumbing code may require four toilets in the ladies room, whereas the health department may require five. The building code may permit something that is prohibited in the fire code. Consultants who study these codes and know the people in the various departments who enforce these codes can interpret them properly and get clarification on conflicting rules. You can not assume that your architect has designed your space to comply. Even if she follows the code as written, departmental and individual interpretation can cause you to suffer loss of time and go through a redesign of your space.

Code consultants are often employed on large projects. If your restaurant development is within this type of project, the primary architect for the developer may retain this professional and can provide the guidelines that your architect needs for your specific space. While a code review consultant cannot guarantee that his work and research will avoid unfavorable interpretations, his knowledge and experience will certainly minimize the chances.

4. *Specification writer.* Specifications are the written text that accompany the drawings. These specifications spell out in exacting detail the quality and type of materials to be used, construction methods to be employed, and what is included and excluded in the work to be performed by each trade. It is, however, important to ask how they prepare their specs. Most specifications consist of standard verbiage gleaned from specialized software programs. Unless they are carefully reviewed and edited, some of the text may not apply or may not cover key issues that affect your restaurant.

What you see on your drawings is not always what you get. Phrases like "by others" or "N.I.C." (not in contract) can cost you dearly. An item such as a towel dispenser or rack for remote compressors may be shown on the drawings. But if it is not clearly detailed or assigned to a particular trade it may not be provided or may be regarded as an extra, at additional cost. Specification writers are sticklers for detail. They coordinate the drawings with the specifications so that they are consistent and cover all aspects of the construction documents. They will review the specifications of other consultants to ensure that they are consistent with the overall set of construction documents as well. How well these specialists perform and how well their work is coordinated and integrated into the contract documents will have a great impact on your budget, customer and employee comfort, your ability to rearrange or add equipment, seating flexibility, maintenance, and the cost of doing business.

5. *Consulting engineers.* Your restaurant development, regardless of how small or large, may require the services of consulting structural, mechanical, and electrical engineers and possibly others, such as acoustical, lighting, or environmental engineers. Consulting engineers are licensed by the state. Their license is the result of schooling and passing a state or professional licensing exam. Their professional stamp may be required for a building permit. There are choices and options in the design of the structure, mechanical, plumbing, and electrical systems. The placement of columns or depth of ceiling joists is not limited to only one way. Ductwork, plumbing lines, electrical circuitry, the location of electrical and access panels, and mechanical gear are not determined solely by the engineer. There are operational considerations that may take priority. This is why your consulting engineers must understand restaurants. They must know that changes may need be made to accommodate equipment placement, seating, circulation, or other operational needs.

♦ *Structural engineers:* design the building structure—the components that hold up the walls, floors, ceilings and roof, raised floor areas, decks, balconies, and stairways. They need to know restaurants because they need to know that a crowd of people dancing to rock music on a balcony does not always adhere to the posted occupancy limits or people-per-square-foot charts in building codes. Railings need to handle people leaning on or against them or bouncing into them. Restaurant equipment is heavy and is often rolled over the floor.

  Floors need to be able to handle these loads without any flexibility that will crack tile or epoxy flooring. You may have specialty features—waterfalls, overhangs, ceiling-mounted stuff—that must be properly engineered and secured. This is the role of the structural engineer.

♦ *Mechanical engineers:* design the heating, ventilation, and air-conditioning systems and plumbing system. They locate your hot and cold water connections, floor sinks and drains, gas and steam lines, and their connections. Here, too, the placement of grease traps, water heaters, and control panels for exhaust hood systems may need to be altered to accommodate the operational needs of the restaurant.

♦ *Electrical engineers:* determine the overall electrical power requirements, circuitry, placement of outlets, panels, and switches, and in some cases, the lighting design. The initial placement of electrical panels, switches, and controls often conflicts with equipment and storage shelving. Engineers who are sensitive to the requirements of restaurant design understand this and work to resolve these conflicts.

6. *Specialty consultants.* These professionals are brought into a project because the specific needs of your restaurant demand it. These specialists, if used properly, can save you time and money because they have access to unique products and ideas, they know the latest technology and how it can apply to your restaurant, and they have the experience to know how their recommendations will work in your restaurant.

♦ *Acoustical consultants:* often retained to control noise from outside sources (adjacent tenants, airports, traffic), create zones within a restaurant (isolate a dance area, reduce kitchen or equipment noise, compensate for hard surfaces throughout a restaurant space), or direct sound where live entertainment is a major factor. Materials and techniques that they employ may be less conspicuous or more effective than traditional methods commonly used by architects.

♦ *Lighting consultants:* provide specialty lighting fixtures, automatic dimming systems, artistic lighting designs, and specialty lighting for artwork, mood lighting, or lighting that is coordinated with a sound system. These consultants have access to or manufacture custom light fixtures that consulting electrical engineers may not be aware of or have access to.

♦ *Sound system consultants:* design complete sound systems, selecting and specifying equipment, locating speakers, zones, and volume controls, and providing complete installation. These systems may include intercoms, paging, or entertainment packages.

Interior Architecture and Design. The design of the interior space, which includes the size and shape of the bar, changes in floor elevations, location, and shape of walls and railings, ceiling treatments, selection of furniture, fixtures, accessories, colors, and materials— anything that affects the look, feel, image, or mood of your restaurant falls under the domain of interior architecture and design. This is not to say that the interior designer will be responsible for all these areas. The allocation of responsibilities within this area is often unclear. That is because there is no clear line between interior design and the overall architecture of the restaurant. What is important, though, is this. You want your design team to understand that the location of walls and raised areas within the restaurant is not just an aesthetic decision or structural decision but an operational and functional decision as well. Seating, service flow, and sight lines to the kitchen are affected by these decisions. Often, the architect will assume the responsibility for the location and shape of the interior walls and then turn the space over to the interior designer.

As with all members of the design team, they must work together to address and solve these issues.

Food Facilities Design. Many restaurateurs realize that they need assistance selecting and specifying their kitchen and bar equipment and the equipment they will need at the service areas throughout the restaurant. Often, their local supplies and equipment dealer will contact them—salespeople always find out about new restaurants—and offer to assist them. Many dealers have in-house designers and they offer free or low-cost design services to get the purchase contract. There are also professional foodservice consultants who specialize in the design and specification of your foodservice equipment. Their approach is that they are not influenced by specific manufacturers because they do not benefit from rebates or other dealer incentives. They specify only what you need because their fee is not based on the amount of the sale.

The scope of services allocated to the food facilities designer or kitchen designer is too often limited to filling a space with equipment. Your concept may require certain storage, preparation, and cooking equipment and sufficient space for these functions to be performed properly. Foodservice consultants are trained to design these work environments. They understand how the work is performed and may best be suited to plan these spaces. These consultants will often suggest modifications to the plan to better accommodate equipment or flow within the kitchen and service areas. Their recommendations can greatly improve the function of your restaurant without compromising design.

Graphic Design. The design of your logo and signage represents your image and reflects your concept and overall style. Your logo and name appear in your marketing and advertising material. The design of your graphics and the way you present your name and logo are very important and should be done professionally.

Purchasing Services. Your interior designer will specify the furnishings, finishes, and accessories that go into your restaurant, but that does not necessarily mean that they should purchase these items for you. There are many companies whose professional expertise is in purchasing, freight management, and installation of these items. These companies purchase the specified furnishings or can find comparable products at considerable savings. Their expertise is in having resources. They work with furniture manufacturers, alternative suppliers, and have direct access to manufacturers because they deal in large volume and specialize in this niche. Purchasing services coordinate freight shipments, inspection for damage, verification of quantities and specifications, staging, and delivery to the site as well as uncrating and installation. They often work on a percentage markup over their cost or a fixed fee for the total job. These purchasing services may also provide the foodservice equipment for your restaurant and can provide the same scope of services as they do for the furniture and furnishings.

Construction and Construction Management

The building process turns your plans into reality. But regardless of the care that went into the planning and design of your restaurant, field conditions will require changes, modifications, and in some cases, compromise. There will always be unknowns in construction. Specified products or equipment will not be available. Factory specifications will be modified. Code compliance will demand changes in your plans. Demolition of existing conditions will reveal surprises that could not have been foreseen.

Approaches to the Project. There are four general approaches to building a restaurant:

1. Competitive bid
2. Negotiated bid
3. Design/build

4.   Acting as your own general contractor

Competitive Bid.   This is the most traditional approach to construction. Your design team produces a complete set of construction documents. Several general contractors are interviewed, selected, and are given the drawings and specifications to bid. They, along with their subcontractors, provide you with a fixed dollar amount to construct your restaurant according to the contract documents. You, as the owner, choose the contractor based on his bid and other selection criteria detailed in the specifications.

The advantages of this approach are:

1.   The prices quoted are usually very competitive.

2.   You can compare prices and, where permitted, acceptable alternatives.

3.   Your contract documents are very complete, with all areas clearly defined and specified.

4.   Because of the completeness of the documents, the owners' involvement can be minimal during the construction phase.

5.   Field decisions are minimized.

The disadvantages are:

1.   Quality may be compromised since you are essentially comparing contractors' prices rather than the abilities of their crews and subcontractors.

2.   Contractors may include "allowances" that do not reflect the true cost.

3.   You do not have a choice of subcontractors or suppliers.

4.   There is a built-in adversarial relationship between the architect and the contractor.

5.   Architectural and other design fees may be higher since detailed contract documents are required.

Negotiated Bid.   Once you have completed drawings and specifications, you interview and select one contractor to work with. This contractor reviews the contract documents and assembles his costs based on these documents. He will often make suggestions to save money or modify materials for ease of construction, better delivery or availability, or other considerations. Negotiated bids often include a fixed or negotiated percentage fee.

The advantages of this approach are:

1. This approach is less adversarial than competitive bidding.

2. There is a greater team effort to manage costs and improve design.

3. Design costs are lower because more decisions are made directly with contractor.

4. An experienced contractor can be highly effective in contributing to the design process.

5. The comfort level with the contractor is already established.

The disadvantages are:

1. The architect's control over the project is diminished.

2. The system of checks and balances between architect and contractor is compromised.

3. Decisions and changes may not be well coordinated.

4. Owner involvement is greatly increased.

5. The choice of subcontractors may be limited.

Design/Build. This approach involves your contractor early in the design process. It requires that you select and commit to your general contractor and use his knowledge of restaurant construction, sources of available supply, realistic pricing, and his construction-related resources (subcontractors, etc.) to help you and your design team plan and design the most cost-effective restaurant.

The advantages of this approach are:

1. Your design team can discuss options on structural and other building systems with someone who has priced and built them.

2. Your contractor can provide accurate budget pricing and a realistic timetable for construction.

3. You can discuss various approaches to designing systems with the people who actually provide, install, and service them.

4. Your contractor and his subcontractors (mechanical, plumbing, and electrical) can provide the necessary engineering drawings.

5. You save time by being able to apply for permits and begin construction as soon as the contract documents are ready.

The disadvantages are:

1. You are committed to this contractor and have no comparative costs.

2. The engineers working for the subcontractors may not be familiar with the latest technology available, but recommend what they are familiar and comfortable with.

3. Your contractor may rely heavily on tried-and-true methods and materials and not want to try different and possibly better approaches to the design.

4. The contractor may not have the necessary resources of supply available to him at the most competitive prices.

5. The contractor and architect may not agree on basic issues of construction.

6. Drawings are often incomplete, relying heavily on field decisions.

Acting as Your Own General Contractor. This can work for remodeling or small construction projects. When you "general" your own project, you hire, direct, and coordinate all the trades on the job. To be effective, you must understand the construction process and how trades interact and coexist. It has been done very successfully. It has also produced costly and time-consuming nightmares.

The advantages are:

1. The owner is often on the job site anyway.

2. The owner can track and manage the schedule.

3. You save fees associated with job supervision.

4. It is very rewarding to see the restaurant take shape.

The disadvantages are:

1. Your ego—you know less than you think you do.

2. You must have experience dealing with construction.

3. Scheduling construction is extremely complex.

4. You may not have the pool of resources that contractors acquire over years of work in the field.

5. This is a full-time job that detracts from other, possibly more important activities that only you can perform.

Carrying Out the Project. Whichever method you select, the people who actually perform the work will play a significant role in making your restaurant a reality. Do not think that once the drawings and specifications are complete, your restaurant will simply take shape. Many events can occur that will alter your plans and force you to make changes. Because of these unknowns, the selection of those companies that will do the work or supply the materials is very important.

Just as your architect will coordinate and make decisions concerning the design process unless you specifically delegate that responsibility, so will your general contractor make the decisions regarding the subcontractors who will work for him. Although some of his choices may be quite acceptable, his criteria and motivation for selecting them may not be in your best interest.

The involvement of you or your project manager in the selection and review of these trades and suppliers has many benefits. Apply the same selection criteria to them that you applied to your consultants. Although many contractors and suppliers are involved, do not avoid getting involved yourself. No one understands your restaurant concept as well as you do. The field decisions that will be made must be made based on operational considerations as well as cost, time, and availability factors.

General Contractor. This is a pivotal position. The general contractor's job is to coordinate the construction of your restaurant. He determines the schedule, the timing of the various subcontractors' involvement, purchase, delivery, staging, and installation of materials, and essentially, puts it all together. All questions, comments, and communication on the job site go through the general contractor. Depending on the size of the general contractor's company and their approach to your specific project, they will either use their own staff to do some or all of the work or contract the work to others. Some very successful contractors are essentially project managers/brokers. Their strength is managing and coordinating the construction process—finding the best people for specific tasks. Others have on their own payroll the people they feel are the best at what they do.

Framing Contractor. The layout of your walls and partitions, platforms, soffits, and dropped ceilings is done by the framing crew. The demands of restaurants are different from those of residential homes or office space. Blocking for wall-hung or ceiling-hung equipment and the exactness of dimensions are reasons why even the framing crew must know how restaurants are put together.

Drywall and Finishes Contractor. Drywall and some finishes are installed by a separate contractor. Where there is excessive moisture, special types of drywall or adhesives for finishes may be required. Contractors familiar with restaurants are aware of this and can flag these concerns if they are not clearly spelled out on the construction documents.

Electrical, Plumbing, and Mechanical Contractors. These three trades install the primary systems in your restaurant. Sure, they are following detailed drawings and specifications, but as mentioned earlier, field conditions change. Conflicts that did not appear (or were not noticed) on the construction documents are painfully obvious here. It is left to these contractors, the general contractor, and your owner's representative to resolve these problems in the best interest of the restaurant. Contractors unfamiliar with restaurants may not recognize the implications of the conflict and simply relocate their utility connection. Such actions can cause major problems when you go to connect your equipment.

Refrigeration Contractor. Walk-in coolers and freezers generally arrive unassembled. The contractor who puts them together may or may not be responsible for connecting the refrigeration system. Locating the compressor for easy maintenance and placing the coil inside the box for maximum circulation and to avoid obliterating shelf space take planning and restaurant knowledge. Many restaurants use remote refrigeration packages. The compressors for the walk-ins, reach-ins, and even the ice machine are located away from the heat and grease of the kitchen. This is often done to make servicing the equipment easier and to keep the equipment cleaner. It is the refrigeration contractor who runs these remote refrigeration lines and installs the compressor unit. He will also be responsible for calibrating and adjusting these systems.

Finish Carpentry. The installation of finishes such as wall paneling, baseboards, door trim, built-in shelving, and millwork is rarely detailed on drawings. This job, although it seems very straightforward, can affect operational details of the restaurant. How trim is installed affects cleaning and maintenance and, in some cases, how appliances fit.

Millwork and Cabinetry. These items are frequently detailed by your architect or interior designer. The millwork fabricator, in return, does a "shop drawing" that shows in greater detail exactly how he will build these items, where equipment or appliances provided by others will go and all dimensions. Coordination of the items that fit in and on this cabinetry and the way they are installed and fastened requires an understanding of the nature of their use and abuse.

Specialty Suppliers and Vendors. The suppliers and installers of the telephone system, sound system, fire/burglar/security system, computer system, and so on, are often unfamiliar with the other trades on the job. Their sole responsibility is to get their systems installed. But where they put boxes, outlets, sensors, or speakers has a big impact on the other trades and on your operation. Many of these specialty systems may not have been detailed on the construction drawings, so coordination of their work is the responsibility of the general contractor and the project manager.

Carpet, tile, specialty wall finishes, and equipment installers all focus on getting their jobs done. You can not assume that these people know the abuse that restaurant traffic and general wear and tear have on their work. The effects of heat, moisture, and heavy use may determine the type of adhesives used, trim details, or how a material is installed and secured. Knowing how equipment is used will affect exactly where it is installed. Decisions like these require an understanding of restaurant construction.

Project Administration. Keeping track of all the activities that are going on during the development process: contracts, budgets, invoices and billing, change orders, managing money and keeping records of disbursements, lien waivers, and the like are important. If this task is not handled competently, it can cause the downfall of the restaurant before you open.

Inspections. Who determines when a task is completed and if it is done properly? Who represents you when something needs to be fixed, changed, or done over? Decisions like these must be made by someone who has the best interests of the restaurant foremost in mind. Expediency, convenience, or accommodating a subcontractor cannot be a motivating factor. Inspections take place throughout the construction process. They are not tied to the inspection schedule of the building department or the convenience of the general contractor or the subs. Your representative will be on the site often, seeing that the work is progressing according to schedule, answering questions, noting how the pieces are fitting together, and determining if there are potential or real problems or conflicts. Your inspector will prepare reports of his visits and keep you informed of noteworthy developments, problems, and decisions that must be made.

❖   # FOLLOWING THROUGH

The successful development of your restaurant, from its conception through construction, involves dozens of people who are interdependent. Choosing the right people to assist you and managing them is a big responsibility. You cannot build your team, assign someone the job of representing you and your partners, and then sit back and watch. The dynamics of this group and the outside influences that will force you to make changes and compromises require you to be a very active participant. The checklist shown in Figure 2.1 can be used to assign responsibilities and track deadlines.

DEVELOPMENT TEAM CHECKLIST

Activity	Name/Company	Due Date

Business Plan

◊ Draft plan

◊ Writing and editing

◊ Menu presentation

◊ Budget development

◊ Financial statements

◊ Supporting schedules

◊ Business entity

◊ Packaging

Financing

◊ Sources of funding

◊ Representation

◊ Legal documents

◊ Money management

Operational Plan

◊ Customer and
   service procedures

◊ Kitchen procedures

◊ Administrative needs

◊ Staffing

◊ Space requirements

◊ Seating requirements

Design Program

◊ Draft design program

◊ Update

FIGURE 2.1   Development team checklist.

Activity	Name/Company	Due Date

Site Selection

◊ Checklist _____

◊ Select broker/agent/
representative _____

◊ Find potential sites _____

◊ Evaluate sites _____

◊ Review lease/purchase
agreements _____

◊ Negotiate lease/purchase _____

Planning and Design

◊ Interview/selection _____

◊ Project manager _____

◊ Architect _____

◊ Code review consultant _____

◊ Specification writer _____

◊ Structural engineer _____

◊ Mechanical engineer _____

◊ Electrical engineer _____

◊ Specialty consultants _____

◊ _____

◊ _____

◊ _____

◊ _____

◊ Interior architecture
and design _____

◊ Food facilities design _____

◊ Graphic design _____

◊ Purchasing services _____

FIGURE 2.1 (*Continued*)

Activity	Name/Company	Due Date

Construction

◊ Interview and selection   _____

◊ General contractor   _____

◊ Subcontractors   _____

◊   _____

◊   _____

◊   _____

◊   _____

◊ Specialty suppliers/
vendors   _____

◊   _____

◊   _____

◊   _____

◊ Project administrator   _____

◊ Field inspector   _____

FIGURE 2.1   *(Continued)*

T h r e e

Preparing a Marketable Business Plan

You prepare a business plan to sell your idea for a restaurant to potential lenders, investors, and partners. To do this you must present an organized, well-documented, and complete picture of what you want to do and how you plan to do it. Your business plan is also your opportunity to put all your ideas and thoughts into a comprehensive and cohesive document. It is your opportunity to refine and polish the details of your concept. It is your chance to set your plan on paper and view it objectively, to be sure that it says what you intended, and that the restaurant sounds like the one you had in your mind's eye.

There are certain skills and knowledge needed to prepare some of this information. Where you lack these skills, you may have to seek assistance from others. Bankers, small business seminars, professional associations, schools, and government publications can provide background and direction for little or no fee. Try to avoid significant cash expenditures before you have established your budget and determined how you are going to fund it.

As in sports, everyone has an opinion about restaurants and the restaurant business. They get emotional about it; they enjoy expressing their views and being critics. Your business plan, therefore, should tap into the positive aspects of these emotions and draw your reader—your potential partner, lender, or investor—into the drama, the imagery, and the ego gratification the restaurant will create.

Creating excitement and interest in your restaurant, although essential to securing funding, is still secondary to the content of your business plan. What you say, how you say it, and how you support your ideas with facts, figures, assumptions, and examples will either build on the interest you create with your prose or cause your readers to abandon your project merely as a wild dream and an excuse to take their money.

Give your proposed restaurant a name, even if you are not certain that this will be the actual name you end up with. A name personalizes your business plan. It gives a life to your plan. You and your readers can begin to identify with the restaurant and to feel a kinship with it—refer to it by name whenever you can. You will often hear consultants refer to projects as the "proposed restaurant." This is very businesslike, dry, unexciting, and boring. It results in your restaurant, your dream, your "baby" being regarded as just another deal to consider. You do not want that! You want your reader to identify with your plan and to develop a strong, positive mental image of your restaurant. You want him to think about it and discuss it as if it were a real place. Giving it a name will help accomplish this.

Each component of your business plan is a building block that contributes to the whole. They are all interrelated. Your ideas, theme, style, and operating philosophy must apply consistently in all areas. You will write, edit, rewrite, and refine this plan many times: three, five, ten, . . . however many times it takes to make you comfortable with your presentation. You will probably refine an idea in one section that affects one or more earlier sections. This is expected. Don't rush and don't compromise the content to "get it done" or meet an arbitrary deadline. Your business plan is the basic component of your entire development plan. If you are not thorough here, you may endanger the success of your restaurant.

❖ THE COMPONENTS

Formats and names vary, but the essential ingredients of a business plan for a restaurant remain the same. There are 11 components to your business plan:

1. Concept statement

2. Menu

3. Market

4. Competitive operations

5. Location

6. Design considerations

7. Management plan

8. Capital expenditures schedule

9. Financial projections

10. Proposed business structure

11. Appendix

Potential restaurateurs enter the business from different starting points. Some have a location—a town or a building—and want to develop a concept to put in it. Others have a particular concept in mind—a neighborhood grill, a French bistro, or a breakfast/lunch operation—and want to find the right location. Still others know that they want to develop a restaurant but are flexible as to concept or location. They are looking for an opportunity and will adapt to what they find. Wherever you start, your business plan will still contain the same components, but the order will vary.

Start with what you know. If you have a firm grasp of your concept, begin with that and build your case. Your plan, if presented in one paragraph with all the details omitted, may read like this.

> This is my concept and my proposed menu. It is geared toward this market. The competition for my concept is [. . .]. I believe that locating here [part of town, specific building, etc.] will draw our intended market. We need this much space and must design the restaurant to accommodate these critical elements. The key design features of our restaurant will be [. . .]. Here is a brief description of our management team, style, and approach. We expect the entire project to cost [$ . . .]. The restaurant will generate gross revenues of [$ . . .] and expenses will be [$ . . .]. Let's set the business up like this, unless you have an alternative idea, which, of course, I will listen to. By the way, here is a sketch of what we want to do and how we think the space will lay out. I have also included some background on my management team. Thank you.

If you have a great location crying out for a restaurant, you might approach it like this:

> You know the old Bleeker Building downtown. Well, the first floor is available. It sits right in the heart of downtown, adjacent to the conference center and across from the train station. It's ideal for a restaurant. Most of the people who work in the area are [. . .] and the crowds that come downtown at night enjoy [. . .]. These markets are strong Monday through Friday both day and night and very strong on Saturdays after 4:00. Our concept and menu will satisfy these markets. The space can handle [. . .] seats. Designwise, we need to consider [. . .]. I've got a strong management team and organization. We could remodel and open it for [. . .].

The capital expenditure Budget, financial projections, business structure, and appendix information remain the same. Simple on the surface—complex and detailed when you get into it.

Concept Statement

Opening Line. The concept statement must tell the reader what you intend to do. It answers the question: "OK, I'm listening, what's your idea?" This is the opener that will either entice your readers to continue to read through your plan or cause them to throw it away. It must be clear, direct, and present your core idea in one or two sentences. It must also instill confidence in readers that you know what you are doing. This opening statement carries a big burden. For example:

> I have spent the last 27 years cooking, studying, eating, and enjoying Northern Italian food. The passion for fresh pastas, homemade sauces, roasted meats and vegetables, and rich sweet cheese desserts has been passed down through generations of my family. It is now time for me to create my own restaurant that brings these wonderful, delicious foods to our city.

or

> Willie's & Archie's will be a comfortable neighborhood tavern serving traditional sandwiches, soups, salads, blue-plate spe-

cials, and full dinners. This "locals" restaurant will be the perfect place for informal gathering and relaxing with friends over a cocktail or meal.

or

Sports bars and grills are gaining in popularity and becoming profitable meeting, drinking and eating places for male and female fans of all ages and lifestyles. My experience managing restaurants coupled with my love of sports will make The Ballpark an authentic, fun, and profitable enterprise.

Then you expand on this idea. You are creating a picture of your restaurant for your readers. As they read this, they are trying to get a sense of how the restaurant is going to feel to them. Is it inviting or reserved, loud or intimate, laid back or pretentious, fast-paced or relaxed? Your discussion should cover the following topics.

Theme. What is the theme, image, or dominant design style of your restaurant, and how are you going to present this to your customers? Sports bars clearly have a "sports/athletics/professional team" theme. Photographs, pennants, sporting apparel and equipment, graphics, style of seating, and uniforms can all be used to make this theme come alive. More subtle themes, such as "informal dinnerhouse," must be described in terms of period in time, an era, or a locale.

Sneakers is a sports bar and restaurant that remembers the grand old days of sports. Authentic memorabilia featuring sports legends and paraphernalia from popular, obscure, and international sports will fill the rooms. These will set the tone for Sneakers. Dioramas of locker rooms, the old team bus, and other snapshots of early life on the sports road will add to the imagery. But our technology will be strictly twenty-first century. Eighteen channels and 43 TV sets will provide wide-screen sporting events, live and on video from around the globe.

or

Ryan's Roadhouse will play on the early 1940s—a relaxed, fun-loving environment slightly outside the boundaries of the city and of the law.

or

> Mabel's will be a contemporary, elegant restaurant catering to residents and businesses in the North Lake district. This will be an unhurried establishment with fine china and tableware, spacious seating, American antiques and replica furnishings, and an extensive menu of American fare.

Atmosphere. This refers to the overall feel within the restaurant. It includes the decoration, furnishings, type of materials used, colors, and lighting. You are creating the mood.

> The Bayside Grill will be a lively, fast-paced seafood restaurant. Hardwood floors, checkered tablecloths, and servers in knee-length white bib aprons embroidered with our logo will serve our large entrée platters of fresh fish.

or

> Old ships' lanterns and big brass chandeliers styled after boating accessories will provide general lighting. Nautical-style candle table lamps will give light and character to the table. The tables themselves will have inlaid maps and antique artifacts.

Style of Service. This refers to how you plan to present and serve your food and beverages. How are your guests treated when they arrive? How are the food and beverages served? Is there a salad, dessert, or appetizer bar? Are there captains and waiters, team servers? What about bussers? How are dishes moved in and out of the dining areas: by trays, hand held, or by cart service? What about bussing: Will you use trays, bus boxes, or carts? Discuss different dining areas, if you plan to have them, such as an informal lounge with a limited menu, main dining area, or banquet facilities.

> Customers will be greeted at the door and invited into the lounge for cocktails while their table is being set. A full-service antique bar with 14 stools will be the dominant design feature and focal point in the room. Guests can also enjoy the more intimate solid wood tables, sitting in overstuffed chairs and

being served by a cocktail waitress. The host will escort them to their dining table, present the menus, and refresh their drinks, if necessary. The wait staff will be responsible for presenting the specials, taking their order, and serving their food. Servers will use the traditional large oval trays and tray stands. The busser will be responsible for clearing the table, serving and refilling water glasses, and refilling coffee if the server is not available. Bussing will be done using trays and tray stands for full tables or by hand for smaller items. Bussing and service stations will be placed discreetly in the dining areas.

Seating. Seats and tables are your stock in trade. Your total seating and how these seats are allocated—number of tables and table mix—will be used in calculating your gross revenue and will affect your capital expenditures budget. Give seating a lot of thought. Table sizes, flexibility, style of seating—booths, banquettes, chairs—and the mix of sizes—deuces, four-tops, six-tops, community tables—have an impact on your total seating capacity and number of seating units. Mention kids' seating, accommodations for large parties, or special functions.

The owner of Geranium's, a small natural foods restaurant with very limited seating, was very sensitive about the effectiveness of his seating layout. He and his designer came up with five different seating schemes that offered maximum flexibility. His plans ranged from 12 tables/42 seats to 15 tables/38 seats. He chose the most tables since he believed that by seating more "parties," he could increase his customer counts. He also realized that all his tables would not always be at capacity; that, at times, a deuce or threesome would sit at a four-top. The extra tables would offset this shortfall. Some restaurants have "celebrity" or "feature" tables that are highlighted in some manner. These tables may be large round tops that seat 8 or 10 and have a chandelier over the center. Or the feature may be a booth in a very visible location off the entry. These are the seating characteristics that need to be explained in this section.

Sophie's will have a total seating capacity of 193 in the dining areas and 36 in the lounge. The dining area will have a small room adjacent to the main dining room that can accommodate 20 to 40 people (depending on seating layout) for private functions. When set for regular dining, this room will seat 30 people comfortably. The main dining room will feature booth seating and freestanding tables for two, four, and six people. The lounge will have a corner bar with 12 bar stools. These stools will be upholstered, with padded backs. Guests will be encouraged to eat at the bar and at the small cocktail tables, especially if they are having cocktails and appetizers or coffee and dessert. The lounge tables will be 24-inch rounds and 30-inch rounds, as listed below.

Seating Chart. The use of a chart to show the seating mix is a simple way to show the number of tables, table sizes, and total seating by area. This information, even though preliminary, gives the impression that you have thought this through and understand your concept very well. Many operators believe that the number of "parties" you can seat is a more accurate measure of capacity than the total number of seats. If two restaurants each have 150 seats but one has 43 tables and the other has 48 tables, the one with 48 tables may be able to serve a greater number of people.

SEATING CHART: DINING ROOM

Table Size	Quantity	Seats/Table	Total Seats
30-in. round	5	2	10
30-in. by 30-in.	5	2	10
36-in. by 36-in.	30	4	120
54-in. round	4	6	24
Booths	5	4	20
	49		184

SEATING CHART: BAR/LOUNGE

Table Size	Quantity	Seats/Table	Total Seats
18-in. round	4	2	8
30-in. round	8	4	32
Booth	7	4	28
Bar	1	16	16
	23		84

Days and Hours of Operation. This is a simple statement that has a tremendous impact on your overall business. What you say here will be used in preparing your financial projections and operating expenses. In determining your operating hours and days, you must consider the demands of your market and the type of restaurant you are developing. What are the eating habits of your clientele? What day or days of the week do you close, if at all? If you serve lunch Monday through Friday, is there a market for lunch or brunch on the weekend? Many downtown restaurants serve lunch and dinner Monday through Friday and dinner only on Saturday, closing on Sunday. Do you serve a Sunday brunch but otherwise open for lunch and dinner only? What are your hours? Do you open for lunch at 11:00 or 11:30? Do you serve continuously throughout the day, or do you stop serving lunch at 3:00 and reopen for dinner at 5:30?

Many restaurants keep the bar open throughout the day even when the dining room is closed. Or they serve a limited menu, often to comply with liquor laws. These decisions will directly affect your staffing and gross revenue.

The Drifter will serve lunch and dinner Monday through Friday and dinner only on Saturday. Since our market is primarily the weekday business community and the Saturday downtown shopper, the restaurant will be closed on Sundays. Lunch will be served from 11:00 A.M. through 3:30 P.M. A limited menu will be offered in the bar between 3:30 and 5:30. To attract the after-work crowd, we will offer drink and food specials from 4:30 through 7:00. Dinner will be served from 5:30 through 10:30. The restaurant may remain open later as business warrants. On Saturday, we will serve the full menu through 11:00 P.M. The bar will be open until 2:00 A.M. every night.

Some restaurants are seasonal and close for weeks or months at a time between seasons. If this applies to you, discuss it here.

Since Vivaldi's caters primarily to the local tourist market, we will be closed during the last two weeks of April and the month of September, when the tourist traffic cannot support our business. We will use this time to take care of necessary repairs, plan for our next season, shop for new items for the gift shop, and give our staff vacation time. Our business volume during our active season will generate the revenue to sustain us during this downtime.

Special Features. Entertainment, dancing, displaying art by local artists, retail sales, and major banquet or party facilities require special mention. These are potential revenue sources that are outside the regular food and beverage sales of the restaurant. What they are and how you plan to feature them are discussed here.

Max's Supper Club will have live entertainment Fridays and Saturdays from 9:00 P.M. through midnight. The club will feature local dance bands and occasionally bring in a nationally known act for special functions. During the week, a D.J. will operate out of a booth adjacent to the dance floor. Prior to the live music or D.J. program, our CD sound system will provide music in the restaurant. We plan to gain a reputation for the quality of our entertainment and attract a dinner crowd that will stay through the evening.

or

Retail sales of our popular hot fudge sauce as well as our logo-embroidered clothing and accessories will provide an additional source of revenue. Our distinctive logo will be featured on sweatshirts, T-shirts, hats, and coffee mugs. These items will be prominently displayed at our host area and available for sale by the wait staff or the host. The popularity of these types of items and the promotions we are planning will generate considerable sales of these products.

or

Banquets and special functions will be a major market source for Bruno's. Our facility will be ideally suited to accommodate parties of 20 to 120. It is our intent to pursue the corporate business meeting and dinner party markets as well as local community and private social functions. Our style of service and design are naturally suited to these sophisticated markets.

Your Operating Philosophy. Here is your opportunity to discuss your personal style, abilities, and experience. This is a chance to build on the comfort level you have been establishing through the methodical and organized presentation of your concept. This closing statement to your concept explains why you feel strongly about this business and this idea. It is not a long-winded, self-promoting piece. It is a brief, almost incidental comment. What your trying to say is, " I know how to do this, trust me!"

> Service to our customers and our attention to detail will make this restaurant a success. Our technical skills, knowledge of food and beverage, familiarity with the market and the community and our ability to react to the demands of the marketplace will give us the competitive edge. Dawson's will generate a reputation for offering our customers personal service, quality products, fair prices, and a great place to eat and relax.

Menu

Many articles, books, and food-service consultants will tell you that your menu is the backbone of your restaurant. Well, it is and it isn't. *It is*, because it will determine your equipment requirements, affect your floor plan, influence your staffing and service procedures, and obviously, determine who will patronize your restaurant and the prices you can charge. *It isn't*, because your equipment will be highly versatile and can be used to prepare many different items. Your floor plan, except for special features such as display rotisseries, salad bars or retail areas, can be adapted to accommodate a variety of menus and concepts. Changing or refining service procedures is often done even if your menu does not change. Your market will expect you to update and modify the menu. Finally, your pricing structure or range of selling prices is more a function of your concept than of the specific items you have on your menu.

You do need to have a clear grasp of the types of menu items that you will serve, any ethnic or regional orientation that you are planning, and your price range, but you do not need to know the details of sauces, methods of preparation, accompaniments, or garnishes. In the mind of your readers, however, the discussion of your menu is an extremely sensitive and vital part of your business plan. Here is where every lender, investor, and potential partner has an opinion. "What?", they will think as they read your plan, "He's not serving gnocchi with that?" or "How can he not have swordfish on the menu?" But the ideal response you are looking for is, "Oh, wow, what a great place this is going to be. Hey, Charlie, listen to this menu *we're* gonna have."

So although you are not committed to the details of the menu you present in your business plan, you will want your menu to appear detailed and well thought out, even to the point of having a sample menu in a format similar to what you envision, pricing and all. Remember, you are building an image.

Specialty bar drinks and your wine list are discussed here also. If you use fresh juices or have house drinks, discuss them and their presentation. Don't regard the bar and lounge as something everyone has or as "just your typical bar and lounge." Give it character! Begin your menu discussion in general terms and then get specific. Be descriptive.

> The Armory will be moderately priced and feature steaks, chops, seafood, and chicken entrées. The salad bar will be offered with all dinners and will have over 27 items, ranging from the traditional lettuce, spinach leaves, tomatoes, and cut vegetables to artichoke hearts, pepperoncini, raisins, and pickled watermelon rind.

or

> The display meat counter will exhibit the cuts of beef and fresh fish that we will serve. Customers will be invited to select their cuts and watch our chef prepare their entrées.

or

> The specialty of the house will be our homemade soups. The corn chowder and vegetable soup will be featured daily and a third soup will change daily. This soup may be a cold potato soup or gazpacho in the summer months or a hearty steak and cheese or barley soup in the fall and winter.

or

> Desserts will be baked on premises. Fruit pies, rich cakes, and our locally made ice creams will be served.

The bar and lounge can have a character very different from the main dining area, even to the point of giving it a separate name.

> Hermit's Bar will have a world-class collection of single-malt scotch whiskey, prominently displayed. We will promote ½-ounce tastings in special glasses. Our beer and wine selection will be extensive, featuring microbrews and wines from small, boutique wineries.

or

> Our specialty drink list presents both alcoholic and non-alcoholic concoctions that will promote our image as a turn-of-the-century farmhouse. The specialty glasses will help to enhance this fun, informal, rural environment.

Be sure to describe the actual menu itself.

> Our menu format and type style will accent our Mexican decor. The in-house computer-generated menus will provide us with a quick and inexpensive format for updating our selections and adjusting prices to reflect changing market conditions. Following is a sample menu [or "A sample menu is attached"].

Here is where you insert a copy of your menu if it can be copied to fit on standard paper without losing its appeal. Don't attempt to bind an odd-sized menu into the business plan, since it will make the document difficult to handle and read. Include pricing on the menu, even though you have not calculated the true selling price. You want to make it look as complete as possible.

Market

Your markets are the different groups of people you expect to patronize your establishment. These markets, sometimes referred to as segments, will frequent your establishment on different days, at different meal periods, and possibly, in different seasons. Breakfast may draw the local business crowd, students from local schools, or tourists having breakfast before the museums or amusement park opens. Retail shoppers may stop in for late-morning snacks. Lunch may be primarily government employees from adjacent office buildings, executives from the downtown core, retirees enjoying the relaxing atmosphere and views from your deck, or the blue-collar crowd from the local plants and factories. Your evening trade may be totally different: theatergoers, sports fans, conventioneers, families from the surrounding neighborhood.

You must know your market intimately. This means that you may have to do some research. You must know when they will come, how often, how much they will spend, what kind of music they like, the foods they like to eat, and the kind of service and atmosphere they expect. You must know if they are primarily couples, singles, or large groups. Do they want privacy or exposure? You will have a good, general understanding of them already since you have developed your concept to appeal to them or know them well enough to develop a concept to serve them. But this is where you make your case that your concept and this market mesh well together. Here you explain, in some detail, who they are, where they work and live, when they will visit you, how often, and how much they will spend. You will also discuss how large these various market segments are, how stable they are, and if they are seasonal.

If you are a seasonal business, discuss the rhythm of your seasonal business and your expectations of business during the various phases of the year based on this rhythm. Ski resorts, for example, have more than just "ski season" and "not-ski season." A study done for a Colorado resort hotel divided the year into eight seasons, with each one representing a different level of business activity and catering to a different mix of market segments. What this means is that you must analyze your market and market segments and determine when, throughout the year, they are available to patronize your restaurant. Broad generalizations indicate a lack of knowledge or research. Statements such as "Our restaurant will serve the business community" do not go far enough. Is this your only market? Can it sustain lunch and dinner six or seven days a week? This section of your business plan defines the extent of your customer base. If it is too shallow or if you are dependent on too few market segments, you may be limiting your potential sales or exposing your restaurant to the economic state or whims of a small group.

Your markets, their size and projected frequency of patronage, and their stability are critical factors to your economic success. Make this point clear in your business plan.

The Blackstone Inn caters to several stable market segments. Our lunch clientele will be the local business crowd from neighboring office parks, which are populated with several multinational corporations and regional offices. These parks are very successful and expanding, as noted on the chart in the appendix. The management and middle-management executives as well as administrative personnel enjoy eating lunch out. Our garden patio and carry-out service will be a major attraction to this market. We will also attract many of the local social clubs and women's organizations that need space for meetings and gatherings of 20 to 35. Our private meeting facilities are ideally suited to this market.

or

The large population of blue-collar workers from the Excel Corporation as well as the many, smaller manufacturing facilities in and around the Fairway Industrial Park are a strong, diverse and healthy source of lunch business.

or

The cocktail crowd will come from the business segment as well. Our proximity to the affluent Regis area of town will attract those wishing to enjoy a cocktail without worrying about a long commute home. We will also draw from this crowd for predinner cocktails.

or

Harper's dinner business will be predominantly conventioneers. The success of our convention center complex has resulted in year-round activity that is expected to continue and grow. This market enjoys the type of atmosphere and menu that we offer and will account for 75 percent of our dinner traffic. The balance of our dinner customers will be local couples and others attending shows and events at surrounding theaters.

or

Sports fans are our market. There are thousands of them—men, women, and families—who will enjoy our inexpensive foods, high-energy staff, game room, memorabilia covering our walls and ceiling, gift shop, and, of course the 53 TV sets and 18 cable channels of nonstop sports. This growing market seeks out clean, well-managed, safe places to enjoy watching their favorite team.

Present your market segments as real people. Mention specific neighborhoods and the names of large companies or businesses. The restaurant business is about people and personalities. You must continue to reinforce this image.

Competitive Operations

Of course, no one can do what you do. The guy down the street has lousy burgers. You have no idea why anyone goes to Murphy's, since his steaks are small and the soup must be from a can. The truth is, these other operations, whatever their failings, are presently attracting and serving your potential customers. And they are your competition. Evaluate them objectively: Who goes there, and why? What do they serve? How will your restaurant differ from theirs, and why will you draw some of these customers some of the time? You will probably not put them out of business. Your presence may even bring more customers to the area and build business for all of you.

Critical mass is a term that marketers use to try to justify the positive side of more restaurants coming into an area that already has a few good ones. "More restaurants coming into your neighborhood will create a critical mass and draw more people. This can become a 'restaurant row' or 'restaurant district.' We can all join together and form the 'Uptown Region'." Well, maybe it will; and maybe you can. The fact is, you want to develop your restaurant to serve these markets because you believe that you can do it profitably. The owners who are already there think that they can, too. You are not developing your restaurant so that you can form an alliance with your competition. It will probably be the operator who feels most threatened by your presence who will suggest the formation of a group.

Do not belittle the competition or ignore them. Your objective is to know your competitors—their strengths and weaknesses—what they do right that attracts your potential customers, how effective they are, and how you are positioning your restaurant to attract your share or more of these patrons. Begin with a statement that acknowledges these restaurants. Then add a general comment about why the market is not saturated or why your restaurant will prosper amid this competition.

There are several restaurants in the downtown core that cater to our potential customers. It is our belief that while they also serve lunch and dinner, our menu offerings, price structure, and style of service will draw customers from these operations to our restaurant.

or

While Griswold's and The Pier both cater to the family dinner market, the growing residential population and neighboring office park developments are creating a larger, more diverse market that can easily support another, more moderately priced restaurant.

Discuss each competitive restaurant briefly. Mention their style, pricing, markets, and distinguishing features. If you are aware of other restaurants being planned or that are under construction, or if any existing restaurant has plans to expand or remodel, discuss this, too. This is an area that can be overlooked by inexperienced researchers. It may be easy to see and evaluate what is existing in your market. But you must investigate what is planned for buildings that are currently vacant, for lease or sale, land that is under development, or unannounced plans of current restaurateurs.

The Trader is a fine-dining restaurant that features continental fare. They cater primarily to the special occasion, expense account, and upper-end dinner guest. Their pricing is considerably higher than ours and their menu offerings are very limited.

or

Broadway Grill caters to our market. They are an established and successful operation. While their menu is similar, our rotisserie-cooked chickens and meats will enhance our menu and appeal to our market. Additionally, our meeting facilities will satisfy a growing demand that they do not have the space to serve.

Conclude by recognizing and clearly stating that there is room in the marketplace for you to thrive along with these other successful, competitive restaurants.

While there are many successful restaurants in the Chambers District, the demand for our style of service and menu is growing among the young families that are moving into this community.

or

Although The Corner Grill and Hasting's Market appeal to our clientele, there are three important reasons why we will prosper in this marketplace. First, unlike the existing restaurants, we are a family-oriented restaurant with comfortable seating, small dining rooms, and a children's menu. Second, we have a convenient, covered drop-off and ample parking. Third, the market is growing rapidly and these existing facilities cannot accommodate this increased demand. Our new, well-designed restaurant will cater to this growing market.

Location

Every decision you make regarding your restaurant is critical. But it's easier to change your menu than it is to change your location. Location has always been one of those "don't be wrong or you're dead" decisions. Consequently, everyone concentrates on this, often to the exclusion of or at the expense of other, equally important decisions. The good news about discussing your desired location in your business plan is that you are not committing to anything. You are not signing a lease and not locking yourself into a building that doesn't work for you.

Be as specific as you want to be in describing the features you want or need. At this point in your development, you are beginning to establish the criteria that you will use to develop your site-selection criteria. This will also give your readers a space to conjure up in their minds to go along with your concept. The discussion of your proposed location will include the part of town, the neighborhood, or in some cases, the names of buildings you would consider. General access and visibility and other features you consider critical to your success are discussed here. You are interested in establishing, in general terms, the type of location that is best suited for your concept.

The Kitchen Cafe will be located in the southeast part of the city, close to the interstate, and within a short driving distance or inexpensive cab ride from the major hotels and business corridor. Since our dinner business will draw heavily from the large surrounding residential population, it is essential that there be ample parking and easy access from the residential areas. The patio area, an important design element for this market, will face south and be shielded from the highway.

If you have developed a concept to fit a specific site, you must describe the features and advantages of the site.

The Craig Building, located downtown at 1735 Eighteenth Street, is in the heart of the downtown financial and business district. The street-level location, with its large windows and corner entrance, provide excellent visibility and access to our primary market. The adjacent parking garage and "after 6" free on-street parking provide easy access for our dinner clientele.

Maps can provide a good visual to indicate an area of a city or the relationship of the specific site to important market sources. The map should:

♦ Be clear and readable

♦ Orient the reader to the location and its relationship to nearby landmarks

♦ Be drawn to scale with the scale indicated

Ideally, you should use a commercial map and highlight key areas and features, mask information that is extraneous or confusing, and focus on the primary area. Hand-drawn maps work only if they are professionally done and meet the criteria for effectiveness.

Design Considerations

Along with location, there will be, no doubt, spatial features and infrastructure considerations regarding the space that will be essential to the success of your restaurant. Let's start with the basics. Although some of these items may seem obvious, many older buildings or buildings that are not presently restaurants do not have and may not be able to get these basic amenities at a reasonable cost:

◆ Natural gas

◆ Adequate water service

◆ Electric capacity

◆ Sewer or grease traps

◆ Location and availability of exhaust duct access

◆ Trash storage

◆ Delivery access

Moving on to more aesthetic concerns, you'll need to consider location within a building, patio space, ceiling height, windows, street access, parking, signage requirements and restrictions, and of course, zoning and licensing. Discussing these items now will show your reader that you understand the importance of these factors to your success. Additionally, these design considerations will become a part of your design criteria and will influence your site and location search.

Our street-level location and large windows will provide excellent visibility and show off our large, ornate bar. The high ceilings will allow us to construct a small mezzanine area overlooking the main room, for private functions.

or

Our menu demands an extensive exhaust system and the availability of natural gas. The Grier Center has ample capacity to accommodate our needs.

Management Plan

Now that you have presented the concept in great detail and with tremendous enthusiasm and conviction, how do you plan to pull it off?

Who is going to manage this restaurant, and what is your management plan? You cannot simply state that "I will manage this restaurant myself and hire competent assistants" and expect potential investors to be comfortable. There are exceptions, but don't set yourself up for failure. Besides, regardless of how competent you are, most restaurant ventures require more than one key person to manage and operate a successful restaurant. This is where you name your team, describe their responsibilities, and explain your overall management procedures.

Be brief and use an outline or simple paragraph form. The essential ingredient here is that you have a specific plan for managing and controlling the restaurant as a business. Start with a general comment on the management structure, the control procedures, accounting procedures, and security provisions. Then elaborate on the positions and, where possible, give names and credentials.

> The Rockville Grill will be managed by a team consisting of a general manager, bar manager, and floor supervisor. Using the Restco point-of-sale system, we will maintain tight control over all sales and receipts. This system, regarded as an industry standard, serves as a time clock, ordering system, and inventory control system. Reports generated by this system will be used by our in-house bookkeeper to prepare daily reports of sales, labor, sales mix, and server performance.

or

> The general partners have each been involved in the restaurant business for 14 years. They have been responsible for opening and managing several full-service restaurants and they understand the details of successful management. They have proven themselves in the business, as can be seen in their résumés, which are attached.

or

> Operating policy and strategic planning will be the responsibility of the two general partners. The day-to-day management of the restaurant will be the responsibility of the general manager, who will report directly to the general partners.

Capital Expenditures Schedule

This is a detailed, line-item listing of all expenditures that you will make prior to opening the restaurant. It covers every dollar you will spend, planning, developing, designing, building, furnishing, equipping, staffing, training, and supplying the restaurant up until the day you open. Some of these categories may not apply to your situation. The essential element here is that you have all your expenses covered. Many restaurants fail because they are underfunded. By preparing this schedule and providing supporting documents where necessary, you will have a better picture of the true cost of opening a restaurant. This schedule has been developed and refined over the past 18 years. You will add categories, change the titles, and claim that we omitted something. Good for you. Add to it or change it. The important thing is that you fill in all the blanks.

At this point in your budget process, you will be using estimated costs developed by you based on experience or in collaboration with potential contractors and suppliers. Many contractors will work with you in order to have an opportunity to bid on your restaurant when you are ready. Others may want to charge you a fee to help assemble your costs. Work with contractors and suppliers who are very familiar with restaurants. They know what is involved, and what restaurant components cost and will be able to provide reasonable estimates. Begin to build a file of these sources. Although you should not commit yourself to using them, they can provide valuable information. Use the worksheet shown in Figure 3.1 at the end of this chapter to develop your capital expenditures schedule. These reference notes will detail what is included under each category.

Planning. This category covers your initial planning activities. In the beginning stages of your development, you will incur costs. Although you may pay for these out of your own pocket, since you probably have not yet raised funds for this venture, they must still be accounted for.

Preparation of Business Plan. You may pay someone to help you write it or research it. This also includes the cost of typing, printing, and binding it.

Legal. There are legal expenses involved in setting up a corporation or business entity. Legal fees to review your business structure and prepare the appropriate legal documents must be budgeted.

Accounting. Cost for assistance in preparing projections or budgets is included here.

Research/Travel. You may visit cities or restaurants to study ideas or concepts. Research is a vital component of restaurant development and should be included in your budget. This includes travel, lodging, food and beverage expense, and film and processing.

Administrative. This item includes the cost of telephone, fax, courier services, copies, and other incidental out-of-pocket expenses, which always add up to more than you think.

Site/Building Acquisition. This includes costs associated with finding and securing your site or location.

Fees/Commissions. You may pay referral fees, finder's fees, or broker fees to people who find you a suitable location.

Appraisals. The cost of an independent appraiser to evaluate site or existing facilities, furniture, fixtures, or equipment is included here.

Inspections. This item lists the cost of an independent inspector to check site for construction defects, hidden problems, utilities, and other building-related items that will affect your use of the space. You may also have an architect or engineer do a "code review" to ensure that the building is in compliance with current codes or to determine, at least initially, what is required to meet code. This inspection focuses on handicapped access, adequate utilities, proper ventilation, access and egress, and parking. Issues of approved use or zoning are usually resolved by your agent before a site is pursued.

Legal. Legal fees to review lease or purchase documents and assist at closing are included here.

Surveys. Land surveys identify property lines, location of utilities, utility easements, and other features of the site or building. These are often required with new construction, additions, or major remodels.

Deposits. Prepayments of rent and security deposits for utilities service are included here.

Administration. Administrative and management costs related to developing your project are listed under this heading.

Licenses and Permits. This item includes legal fees and costs associated with securing a liquor license, including neighborhood surveys and petitions, mailings, and informational meetings for the community and neighbors. This line item also includes the cost of business licenses, sales tax licenses, and related expenses.

Temporary Office. Many restaurateurs set up offices outside their home or current office prior to opening. The cost of this space, including rent, deposits, and parking, are listed here.

Phone/Fax. The cost of the office phone is listed separately unless it is included in the office rent.

Supplies. This line item includes the supplies that are required to set up an office and establish the initial files and records for your restaurant development.

Expenses. The cost of meals, meetings, local travel, and entertainment related to the development process is included here.

Contract Services. You will be retaining professional services to assist you throughout the development process. These may be fixed-fee contracts, hourly agreements, or percentage of cost agreements. Be sure to list the cost or estimated cost of all agreements. As the development progresses, you will be updating this line-item budget and adjusting these fees accordingly.

Project Manager. You may elect to hire someone to act as your agent to oversee and manage the construction of your restaurant. These services may be performed hourly or on a fixed fee.

Architecture. Fees and expenses for architectural services are included here. Reimbursable expenses are usually additional. Put in an allowance for this amount that will be updated.

Code Review. Fee is hourly or fixed and is usually included in basic services provided by your architect. But on large or complex projects, this may be an additional service.

Specification Writer. This service, too, is often included in the basic scope of services provided by your architect. But where special systems or product installation is required, such as flooring or acoustical wall or ceiling systems, or where the coordination of multiple trades is required on large developments, a specification writer may be employed.

Engineering. Fees charged by consulting mechanical, electrical, structural, acoustical, and other specialty engineers that may be retained by you or your architect are included here. Here too, reimbursable expenses are additional and should be noted.

Interior Design. This may be a separate fee from your architectural fees, even though your architect may provide these services.

Food Facilities Design. This consultant is a specialist in the design of your kitchen, bar, and service areas and the selection and specification of your equipment. Some equipment dealers offer this service. If they do not charge a fee for this work, it will be reflected in the cost of the equipment they sell to you.

Graphic Design. This person is usually an independent designer working for you, although their work must be coordinated with that of the design team. Charges can be a fixed fee or hourly.

Purchasing Services. These firms typically charge a percentage of the cost of items and related services purchased on your behalf.

Construction. The cost of building a restaurant involves many components. It is recommended that you break these costs down so that you can manage them more easily and understand what is and what is not included in the various contracts you sign. When you establish your construction budget initially, you will be basing many of your costs on a "standard of finish" that you will attempt to convey to your contractor and his subcontractors. Basically, you are making it clear that you want a "Ford or a Cadillac." This standard that you establish will be reflected in the selection of hardware, lighting fixtures and switches, toilet fixtures, and general construction materials. This standard will also be used when the contractor and subcontractors provide "allowances": minibudgets for groups of items (hardware, light fixtures, floor coverings) based on square footage or similar factors.

General Construction. You will probably have a general contractor build the basic restaurant for you. However, many aspects of construction are performed by subcontractors and specialists whose costs may or may not be included in the general contractor's fee. This breakdown will help you determine where the costs are and what is covered.

Fee and Permits. Many contractors include an "allowance" for these costs. If the amount of the allowance is not sufficient to cover the actual cost, you will be required to make up the difference. Therefore, it is wise to get accurate assessments of the fees and permit costs.

Mechanical. This is the cost of your heating, air-conditioning, and ventilation system. Parts or all of your kitchen exhaust hood system may or may not be included in this budget. It should be included either here or in the kitchen equipment budget.

Plumbing. This includes all water piping, vents, and drains. Specialty fixtures such as exotic faucets in the rest rooms or janitor's sinks may not be included in this contract. Some kitchen fixtures, such as hand lavatories or janitors sinks, may be included in the plumbing contract rather than in the foodservice equipment budget. Final connection of foodservice equipment should be included in this budget.

Electrical. All electrical work is included here. However, some specialty lighting may be part of the interior design package. Specialty systems, such as telephones, sound systems, alarms, or lighting packages, may be provided by specialty contractors, and only the primary wiring is included in the electrical contractors budget. These items must be clarified. Final connection of foodservice equipment should be included in this budget.

Refrigeration. The refrigeration systems for your walk-in coolers and freezers and other refrigerated equipment may require field installation and calibration. Remote systems require refrigeration lines to be run from the units to the remote compressor location, usually inside walls and ceilings during construction. The cost of this specialty work should be listed here. This work may be included in the foodservice equipment contract and provided through the equipment supplier.

Special Finishes. There are some restaurant floor finishes (poured epoxy, staining of concrete, exotic marbles) and wall finishes (stainless steel flashing, fiber-reinforced plastic wallboard) that are provided and installed by specialty contractors and may not be figured into your general construction budget. These items should be added here.

Special Systems. Water filtration systems, air purifiers, and special lighting controls may be listed here.

Specialty Items. These items are often overlooked in the budget process since they are traditionally outside the scope of work provided by the general contractor or the subcontractors. However, there will be work related to these items that will be performed by the general contractor and subcontractors. The cost of electrical wiring and junction boxes, water connections, chases, and blocking must be included in these line-item budgets.

Signage. Exterior building signs, window signs, and similar directional signage are included here. Include the cost of the sign, shipping, and installation. Installation is usually done by a signage company, not the general contractor. As noted above, the power required for the signs and any construction details required for mounting the sign should be part of the general construction budget.

Landscaping. Exterior plants, trees, grass, and sprinkler systems are included in the line item. Fences, railings, fountains, outside or interior planters, and flower boxes would also be included.

Sound System. This item includes CD players, tape players, speakers, and wiring. Include the cost of CDs and tapes. Electrical power and outlets required for this system and related carpentry or construction should be included in the general construction budget.

POS System. Most restaurants use computerized point-of-sale (POS) systems. These systems are sold directly to the owner/operator, not purchased through a contractor. The budget for this item should include installation and startup. These systems often require specialized wiring and telephone lines that would be included in the electrical budget line item.

Computer System. This is the office computer system used for accounting, word processing, and similar tasks. This is usually separate from the POS system. Include the cost of software, installation, and startup. Here, too, these systems often require specialized wiring and telephone lines, which would be included in the electrical budget line item.

Carbonated Beverage System. This is usually provided directly to the operator by the beverage supplier. There may be costs associated with these systems. Chases for the syrup lines, power, water, racks to hold the product, and installation of the system may have associated costs.

Liquor System. This may be part of the equipment package or contracted for independently directly by the owner. Costs similar to those listed with carbonated beverages may apply.

Beer System. Draft beer systems, either remote or self-contained, may be arranged for outside the foodservice equipment contract. The same associated costs as above may apply.

Telephone System. This is usually a separate contract. Wiring may be included in the electrical contract, but not the equipment. These systems may require conduit and power, which will be part of the electrical budget.

Security System. Fire/burglar alarms may be required by code but not included in the budget. This is usually provided by an independent company but may need to be interwired with other building systems.

Safe. Most operators buy their own safe and have the contractor anchor it in the office. The line-item budget should include delivery and setting in place.

Furniture/Fixtures and Equipment. Traditionally, these items are not part of the general construction contract. Allowances are frequently made for these items until the specifications become more detailed.

Carpet. Include carpet, pad (if used), freight, taxes, and installation in this item.

Specialty Flooring. This may be subcontracted out to a specialty installer and includes tile, marble, wood planking, and special coatings and finishes.

Wallcovering. This is usually supplied and installed under a separate contract as specified by the interior designer. The line-item budget should include the fabrication, hardware, delivery and installation.

Window Treatments. Shutters, curtains, drapes, blinds, and so on, are included here. They are usually specified by the interior designer. The line-item budget should include the fabrication, hardware, delivery and installation.

Lighting. Most lighting will be specified and provided under the electrical contract. However, some chandeliers and other accent/decor lighting will be specified by the interior designer or specialty lighting consultant.

Specialty Millwork. The front and back bar, server stations, host stand, food bars, wine displays, and other specialty cabinetry and millwork may not be included in the general construction contract. These items may be part of the interior furnishings and fixtures package designed and specified by the interior designer. There may be costs associated with these products that may fall under the general construction budget.

Decor Items. These are decorations and accessories that accent your restaurant. Photos, artwork, display tables, and so on. Include the cost of delivery and installation with these items.

Kitchen and Bar Equipment. This equipment is usually provided by a restaurant supply company or purchasing service. Your foodservice consultant or kitchen equipment supplier will specify this equipment and then provide an itemized breakdown of the cost. These professionals can usually provide a reasonably accurate budget estimate.

Chairs, Tables, Table Bases, Booths, Bar Stools. Budget these items separately, as the quantities of each will change as your restaurant plans are refined. Be sure to include the cost of fabrics, which may come from a different source.

Freight and Taxes. This can be a large number and is not included in the cost of these products. They are usually added at the time of billing. Your supplier can provide a reasonable estimate of these costs, usually a percentage of the purchase amount.

Delivery and Installation. Your equipment and furnishings will need to be stored off site until you are ready for them. There are companies that specialize in this work. They will store, inspect, deliver, uncrate, assemble, clean, set in place, and adjust and calibrate your furniture and equipment. These services are often provided by the company from which you purchased the products, either directly or through a subcontractor. This should be kept as a separate line item, rather than lumping it into the total furnishings or equipment budget. As you refine your budgets and develop subschedules for these categories, you can better manage your overall budget and evaluate where to make adjustments.

Supply Items. These items are often purchased close to opening and are not always budgeted for. They can account for many thousands of dollars.

Office Supplies. This includes everything from pens to paper to bank drawers, bulletin boards, clip boards, and so on—all the items needed by the office or offices.

Kitchen Smallwares. These tools and accessories are not part of the equipment package. These include pots, pans, spoons, ladles, thermometers, inset pans, utensils, and similar items. Some small appliances, such as hand-held mixers, blenders, and can openers, are not included in the equipment package and must be accounted for here. Most equipment suppliers will provide you with a checklist or catalog to assist you in ordering these items. Most will also work with you to develop a realistic budget amount.

Cleaning and Janitorial Supplies. Mops, buckets, squeegees—these items, too, will be found in your supplier's catalog. Some companies have programs for cleaning chemicals. Here, too, they will provide realistic opening order budgets.

Bar Supplies. Mixing glasses, matting, bar glassware, bartenders' tools, and small appliances such as blenders and mixers are not included in the equipment package and must be included here.

Tabletop Accessories. These are the salt and peppers, sugar caddies, flower vases, candles, serving dishes, trays and tray jacks, and other dining room service supplies.

China, Glass, and Flatware. The initial order for these items will include a reserve or backup supply, often 1.5 to 2.5 times the number of seats in your establishment. Your supplier can give you a cost per seat to use as a budget figure based on the style and quality you are planning to use. This figure includes all plates, glassware, and utensils.

Matches. Many restaurants have custom matches printed with their name and logo. These often need to be ordered a few months prior to opening because of overseas printing. There are companies that specialize in printing matches and coasters in a variety of sizes and shapes.

Menus. Based on your menu style, a printer or your equipment supplier can give you budgets to use for menu covers. Although many restaurateurs now use their in-house computers to print their menus, the covers may still need to be included in your budget.

Guest Checks. Many of the new POS systems generate their own checks. But some operators still use preprinted guest checks or custom-printed check presenters.

Manuals. You will be preparing and copying employee training manuals. The cost involved in preparing, printing, and binding these documents should be noted here.

Miscellaneous Printed Forms. You will use many forms: employee applications, evaluation forms, tests, checklists, inventory forms. Even if you plan to prepare these on your in-house computer, the cost of printing should be budgeted here.

Preopening Operating Expenses. Prior to opening, you will incur expenses that must be paid prior to generating any income. Although some purveyors will give you terms to carry you through opening, don't count on it now. Prepare realistic budgets for these items. Toward the end of construction, unexpected expenses may squeeze your overall budget. Although these items occur toward the end of your development, they are critical to your success. Compromising them because of insufficient budgeting will be a costly error.

Payroll. This includes the cost of staff during training and for setting up the restaurant. This may include a general manager and chef or kitchen manager starting months before opening as well as employees coming in to help set up the restaurant prior to the start of official training. Payroll costs associated with training are included here.

Inventories. Opening inventories can amount to significant cash expenditures. Although some or all of these costs may be available on terms from your supplier, new restaurant operators are often required to pay for these initial orders if credit has not been established. Even with credit terms, payment may be required prior to opening the restaurant to the public. There are rules of thumb used by many operators to estimate these costs, based on projected volume: food, one-week supply; liquor, one month; beer, one week; wine, varies with wine list; paper, one month; chemical and janitorial, one month.

Recipe Testing. You will be purchasing food, beverages, and supplies to use when testing recipes. These costs are in addition to preopening inventories and usually occur before you place those orders.

Preopening Parties. These events, held for the press, influential locals, and friends are frequently used as training sessions for staff and a shakedown of the restaurant. Include the cost of staffing as well as the cost of food, beverages, invitations, postage, and advertising.

Hiring and Training. Recruiting staff involves numerous expenses. These include ads placed for employees, agency fees, the cost of outside trainers, rental of meeting rooms to hold training sessions, rental of audiovisual equipment, and incidental expenses.

House Banks. These banks are the startup cash needed at cashier stations, the bar, and for making change in the course of business. It also includes petty cash funds.

Advertising and Promotion. These programs may be funded, in part, by trade out with radio stations, magazines, or newspapers. But some portion may require prepayment. These outlays usually occur before opening.

Lease Payments. Equipment leases, including foodservice equipment, dish machines, ice machines, and POS systems usually require initial deposits or advance payments.

Telephone. The telephone service will be operational prior to the opening of your restaurant. Payments for this service will be made from this budget until the restaurant is open.

Rent. Your lease may require that rent begin on a particular date whether or not you are open for business. These monthly payments must be budgeted.

Auto Expense. You and your management team will do a lot of running around prior to opening. The expense of operating automobiles for the business may include insurance, maintenance, fuel or lease payments.

Dues/Subscriptions. Many restaurateurs join local or national trade associations, subscribe to trade magazines or newsletters, or join the local chamber of commerce. These membership dues and subscription payments are budgeted here.

Utilities. Utility service is switched from temporary to primary as soon as it is feasible. The cost of these utilities—gas, electric, water, and sewer—may be due prior to opening.

Working Capital. This is often the great black hole of restaurant development. Of course, everyone knows that you need money set aside to operate your restaurant until the cash flow is sufficient to carry it. But in reality, it is too often a bogus figure that is never funded. Undercapitalization—not enough money—is an all-too-frequent reason for restaurant failure. Good concepts, well executed, and with excellent potential for success can fail if the financial obligations associated with them cannot be met in the early months of business. The amount dedicated to working capital is often underestimated. Ideally, you want to have six months to a year of fixed expenses covered. Realistically, many operators budget one to three months. Because they have underestimated other preopening expenses, this fund is depleted in the early weeks or months.

Contingency Fund. Your plans will change, ideas will emerge that cost money, you will forget something, or the price of some items will go up. This line item is not a slush fund for extravagance but a realistic resource for unplanned events. If you don't have a contingency fund, you will use your working capital prior to opening and put your restaurant's future success in jeopardy. This fund can be as little as $15,000 to $50,000 or as much as 5 to 10 percent of your budget.

Financial Projections

Attempting to predict the future is always a risk. Your objective here is to present a realistic prediction of your projected revenue and expenses and to support your predictions with schedules and calculations that an investor, lender, or partner can understand. Many restaurateurs present revenue and expenses at three levels of business: low, medium, high; or pessimistic, realistic, optimistic. Some project their revenue over five or ten years in order to show investor returns. Operations that are seasonal may present their revenue based on seasonal dates rather than months.

When preparing financial projections, follow the format generally accepted by the hospitality industry. Use the "Uniform System of Accounts for Restaurants" published by the National Restaurant Association, or the industry reports published by some of the hospitality accounting firms. If you do not use an industry-accepted format, investors and lenders may question your understanding or familiarity with the industry, and you will be putting your credibility in jeopardy. The formats presented in Figures 3.2 to 3.4 at the end of this chapter are based on industry standards. Your restaurant may require additional expense categories, or some of those shown may not apply. The important thing is that you have presented this information in a realistic manner and have the supporting schedules to back up your numbers.

Revenue. The money generated from the sales of food and beverage, catering, retail product, or other activities is your revenue or sales. There are four basic approaches to determining these figures.

1. *"We can do" approach.* There are restaurateurs who, after talking to their friends in the business or reading about other restaurants' volume in the trade press, determine that "we can do at least 1.5 mil." Then, they allocate this number between food and beverage sales, and that is the gross revenue figure they use. The advantage of this method is that it is quick, easy, and doesn't require a lot of thought. The disadvantage is that it has absolutely no basis in fact or reasonable assumptions. Presenting a revenue projection that is not supported credibly will create immediate suspicion by your reader and taint all of your other figures.

2. *"Dollars per seat" method.* Some industry reports are based on data collected from restaurants throughout the country and sorted by type of restaurant and location (city, suburban, downtown, etc.). These reports calculate a "sales per seat" number computed from the information they receive. The accuracy of the raw data is usually not verified and the base upon which the calculations are made may not include any operations that are reasonably similar to yours. These are "industry averages," statistics that are interesting if you want a general overview. But they are not intended to be used for calculating your specific revenue. Although this resource may provide a benchmark to compare your projections to, using it to calculate your projected revenue does not take local conditions into account. The advantage of this method is that you are using revenue numbers compiled by industry authorities. The disadvantage is that they have no relevance to your particular restaurant.

3. *"Customer count times check average" method.* This method requires that you understand your market and know how you will be pricing your menu. It involves calculating your average food and beverage checks by meal period or daily and multiplying this amount times the number of customers you expect to serve by meal, daily or monthly. There are variations of this method that use daily, weekly, or monthly gross revenue calculations and then allocate these sales to food and beverages based on your intended mix. Retail sales and other revenue sources are calculated separately. The advantage of this method is that it is based on the particulars of your market, menu, and style of operation. The disadvantage is that it takes time and requires information that you must compile and evaluate.

4. *"Historical" or "comparable restaurant" method.* This method works well if you are duplicating or replicating an existing concept and have historical data that you can use. The caution here is that you consider variances in the market size as well as any operational changes you are considering that will affect your check averages or customer counts.

Unless you are duplicating a concept that you know intimately in a market comparable to the existing market (method 4), it is recommended that you take the time and make the effort to use method 3. If you use a spreadsheet program on your computer, you can study many variations until you are comfortable with the numbers. The following chart can be used manually or set up in a spreadsheet program to calculate your revenue (method 3).

FOOD AND BEVERAGE SALES FOR _____
(Day of Week, Typical Week, High-Season Day, etc.)

Meal Period	Customer Count	Food Check	Beverage Check	Total Food	Total Beverage
Breakfast	93	4.75	0.50	441.75	46.50
Lunch	172	8.95	1.25	153.94	215.00
Dinner	195	14.75	5.25	2876.25	1023.75
Cocktails/late	76	2.50	7.50	190.00	570.00
	536			3661.94	1855.25

Using this method, you can try a variety of scenarios. Your resulting gross revenue projections will have a schedule to support them, even if your assumptions may be loose.

Other Income. Many restaurants also have retail sales of home-made foods, T-shirts, hats, and other trinkets. Here too, you need to determine unit sell prices and quantities that you expect to sell.

Cost of Goods. Use the industry standard format. The cost of goods is calculated separately for food and for beverages. Many operations separate beverage into liquor, beer, and wine, since they each have different markups. As a restaurateur, you can determine, based on your menu and concept, the cost of goods you want to achieve. You can also "cost out" some of your entrée items to determine if you are using realistic numbers. Your "food cost" will vary from menu item to menu item. You may sell a New York steak that has a cost of $6.50 for $18.95. The cost of goods for this menu item is 34 percent. A chicken salad may sell for $8.75 with a cost of $2.25 and a food cost of 26 percent. Most operators aim for an overall or composite food-cost percentage that works for their concept in their market. This is the percentage that will be used in your projections.

Expenses. There are five ways to determine your expenses.

1. *Percentages of revenue.* This method assumes that your expense varies directly with fluctuations in your food, beverage, or total sales.

2. *Fixed amount.* This method assumes that the expense is fixed whether you are open or closed and does not fluctuate with sales volume.

3. *Seasonal.* This method assumes that the expense is affected by the time of year: snow removal as part of maintenance, for example.

4. *Combination.* Some expenses have a fixed base with a marginal increase with increased sales. Others, such as rent, may be calculated as a base amount against a percentage of gross revenue.

5. *Staffing charts.* With restaurant payroll and other line-item expenses that include hourly or contract services based on hourly rates (snow shoveling, valet, security), it is best to graph your projected needs and determine the costs based on the projected hours and hourly rate. Software spreadsheet programs, programs specifically designed for staffing and scheduling, or the following manual chart can be used.

STAFFING CHART: DINING ROOM, TYPICAL WEEKDAY

Position	Rate	*Hours*												*Hours*	*Total*
		7	8	9	10	11	12	1	2	3	4	5	6		
Server	4.25													7.0	29.75
Server	4.25													6.5	27.63
Busser	5.00													5.5	27.50
Host	5.00													7.0	35.00

Expense categories and terminology vary with types of restaurants and how detailed your cost control system will be. The key is to use categories that provide you with a means of tracking your expenses accurately and measuring the effectiveness of your control systems.

Net Profit from Operations. This number indicates your profit from the restaurant operation before taking into account taxes, debt service, or other nonoperational expenditures. The structure of your business will determine how these profits are allocated.

Reference Notes. It is often necessary to provide supporting schedules or explanations for your method of calculating expenses. Using a reference note keyed to the line item is a simple, straightforward approach that allows readers to check this information if they want to, but does not interrupt their train of thought.

Proposed Business Structure

One purpose of your business plan, as mentioned earlier, is to sell your ideas for a restaurant to your potential investors, lenders, and partners. To do this, you must present them with a proposal to which they can respond. Think about the response you want from your reader and address your business structure toward that goal. The business plan, as presented here, is *not* a legal document. You must have proper legal and financial counsel when you solicit funding for your restaurant. There are specific laws that govern how you can solicit investors and what you must provide them. You are not using this business plan to solicit funds. It is intended to provide information on some of the critical issues that may be raised by your potential lenders, investors, and partners. Ideally, you want them to express strong interest in your restaurant venture and to request the legal documents pertaining to investing in your restaurant for review. The business structure addresses these points:

1. *How much money you require to develop your restaurant successfully?* This is a straightforward statement. Your capital expenditures schedules details the line-item expenditures and the total amount.

> The Mountain Man Restaurant can be developed for $1,850,000. The funds will be used as shown in the capital expenditures schedule.

2. *When do you want it?* Make your timetable clear. Short schedules may prevent potential investors from participating. Long time frames may cause interest to wane. Be realistic. Improbable deadlines undermine credibility.

> The development of The Fishmonger is expected to take eight months, following successful funding of this venture. All funds will be held in escrow until we have 100 percent of our investment needs committed. We have been informally scouting locations and would like to begin development within three months. To meet this schedule, we must be fully funded by March 31.

3. *Who will control the funds and how they will be disbursed?* Investors want to know that their investment will be properly controlled and spent as presented in your business plan.

> All funds will be maintained in our separate Pier 12, Inc. development account maintained at the Shoreline Bank, Shore Road branch. Disbursements will be made as required by the general partners. Accounting for this project will be handled by Block, P.C., an independent accounting firm. Financial reports will be distributed monthly.

4. *What do I get for my money?* How is my principal repaid and/or my interest reimbursed? Show either in your financial statements or as a separate schedule how your investors will benefit from their investment. Also discuss any special benefits they receive as "owners" of the restaurant: signing privileges, house accounts, discounts, and so on. Investors in restaurants like to enjoy the owner role and flaunt their involvement.

5. *What input, if any, do I have in this business venture?* Define your investors' responsibilities and limitations fully and clearly. Their interest and enthusiasm in your (their) restaurant may cause them to overextend their authority and compromise your management.

> The day-to-day management of the restaurant will be the sole responsibility of the general partners. Investors and limited partners may direct their questions and comments to the general partners. Only management and the general partners may discuss policy, procedures, and restaurant concerns with employees or customers.

6. *Can I sell out my interest? If so, how and who determines the sell price?* Investors like to know that they can get out of their investment, if necessary, without a lot of hassle or cost. Explain in general terms how this will be accomplished, keeping in mind that the legal documents will explain this in detail.

7. *Show me the legal agreements.* This is the primary objective of your business plan. You want the legal documents to be prepared by an attorney who is competent in this field, knows the laws related to this type of investment and business structure, understands your objectives, and has a thorough understanding of your business plan. Be sure that you read, understand, and agree with the entire document before you present it to your potential investors.

Appendix

You may include an appendix in your business plan. The appendix contains supporting information that is not related directly to the text or is of a size that makes inserting it into the body of the plan awkward. This may contain:

1. *Conceptual floor plans.* Architectural drawings or sketches can be effective in showing potential investors the size, orientation, and overall scheme of your restaurant. Avoid complex drawings since most investors are interested in a general overview.

2. *Exterior and/or interior renderings.* For those who cannot readily understand floor plans, rendered (colored or shaded) perspective sketches of the interior or exterior will provide a picture of your idea to complement your text.

3. *Resumes of key persons.* This is an opportunity for you to elaborate on the skills and background of your management team. It adds credibility to your claims of experience and competence.

4. *Sample menus.* Many people invest in restaurants because of the showmanship associated with it. Your menu, more than anything else, exemplifies this image. A mock-up of your menu will bring this image to life.

5. *Photographs of specific artifacts or design elements.* Providing photos or samples of items that are critical to the success of your restaurant builds on your commitment and attention to details. Although not necessary, this may persuade some investors.

6. *Newspaper articles and awards.* Public relations is always welcomed and shows that you are recognized and respected among your peers, active in the community, and serious about your work.

❖   PRESENTATION GUIDELINES

The presentation of your business plan—the cover, type style, format, binding—will reflect on your professionalism. Word processors and high-quality photocopiers make assembling a high-quality document inexpensive. Here are some basics that should be followed to make a professional impression.

1. *Paper.* Plain bond paper or a high-quality white paper is expected. Fancy or expensive papers may suggest an extravagant style or disregard for budgets.

2. *Type style.* Make sure that the document is free of typographical and grammatical errors. Have it read by someone who can check grammar, tense, terminology, and spelling. Use a standard font such as Times Roman or Helvetica. Do not use a type that is cute or difficult to read. Use only one typestyle for the document.

3. *Format.* Break your text into small paragraphs. Use bold headings, bullets, and numbers to highlight key points. Delineate each section clearly. It is important to number pages so that parts of the document can be quickly referenced. Tabs and dividers are expensive and unnecessary.

4. *Cover.* If you have a logo or typestyle for the name of your restaurant, use it. If you have a sketch or rendering of your proposed restaurant, put it on the cover. The cover should be simple, contain the name of the restaurant, the title of the document ("Business Plan"), your name, address, phone, and fax, and the date. Some business plans are numbered so that the distribution can be controlled.

5. *Binding.* Use a simple binding that allows the reader to open the document easily and fully. Plastic spiral-type binding works well and is available at most retail printing shops. Staples are awkward and can fail.

6. *Special effects.* Colored photocopies of renderings or the use of color for the cover may add visual impact but are not necessary. Oversized menus, plans of the restaurant, or photos can accompany your business plan and can be highly effective if they are well prepared. Color boards of interior concepts work well in presentations and can be reduced for color copying. Do not use or include anything that is sloppy, unprofessional, or not directly related to the business plan. Rough sketches, poor-quality copies or photos, or excessive documents on the market or region that have no direct bearing on the potential success of your restaurant are frivolous and may detract from your overall presentation.

CAPITAL EXPENDITURES SCHEDULE

Category	Amount
Planning:	
Preparation of business plan	
Legal	
Accounting	
Research/travel	
Administrative	
Total	
Site/Building Acquisition:	
Fees/commissions	
Appraisals	
Inspection	
Legal	
Surveys	
Deposits	
Total	
Administration:	
Licenses and permits	
Temporary office	
Phone/fax	
Supplies	
Expenses	
Total	
Contract Services:	
Project Manager	
Architecture	
Code review	
Specification writer	
Engineering	
Interior design	
Food facilities design	
Graphic design	

FIGURE 3.1   Capital Expenditures Schedule.

Category	Amount
Contract Services (*Continued*):	
Purchasing services	
Total	
Construction:	
General construction	
Fees and permits	
Mechanical	
Plumbing	
Electrical	
Refrigeration	
Special finishes	
Special systems	
Total	
Specialty Items:	
Signage	
Landscaping	
Sound system	
POS system	
Computer system	
Carbonated beverage system	
Liquor system	
Beer system	
Telephone system	
Security system	
Safe	
Total	
Furniture/Fixtures/Equipment:	
Carpet	
Specialty flooring	
Window treatments	
Lighting	

FIGURE 3.1　(*Continued*)

Category	Amount
Furniture/Fixtures/Equipment (*Continued*):	
Specialty millwork	
Decor items	
Kitchen and bar equipment	
Chairs	
Tables	
Table bases	
Booths	
Bar stools	
Freight	
Taxes	
Delivery and installation	
Total	
Supply Items:	
Office supplies	
Kitchen smallwares	
Cleaning and janitorial supplies	
Bar supplies	
Tabletop accessories	
China, glass, flatware	
Matches	
Menus	
Guest checks	
Manuals	
Miscellaneous printed forms	
Total	
Preopening Operating Expenses:	
Payroll	
Payroll taxes and benefits	
Food inventory	
Liquor inventory	
Beer inventory	

FIGURE 3.1   (*Continued*)

Category	Amount
Preopening Operating Expenses (*Continued*):	
Wine inventory	
Linen inventory	
Paper inventory	
Chemical and janitorial inventory	
Recipe testing	
Preopening parties	
Hiring and training	
House banks	
Advertising and promotion	
Lease payments	
Telephone	
Rent	
Auto expense	
Dues/subscriptions	
Utilities	
Working capital	
Contingency fund	
Total	
Grand Total	

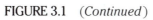

FIGURE 3.1   (*Continued*)

GRISWOLD'S GRILL
Pro Forma Financial Statement
Typical Year

	Amount	%	Reference Number
Revenue:			
Food sales			
Beverage sales			
Total food and beverage sales			
Retail sales			
Total revenue			
Cost of Goods Sold:			
Food			
Beverage			
Retail			
Total cost of goods sold			
Gross Profit:			
Food			
Beverage			
Retail			
Total gross profit			
Expenses:			
Payroll			
Management			
Kitchen			
Service			
Taxes and benefits			
Total payroll			
Management fee			
Linen and laundry			
Kitchen and bar supplies			
China, glass, flatware			
Janitorial supplies			
Office supplies			
Paper supplies			
Music/entertainment			
Utilities			
Repair/maintenance			
Telephone			
Administrative			
Insurance			
Legal and accounting			
Equipment leases			
Rent			
Total expenses			
Net profit from operations			

FIGURE 3.2   Financial statement format A.

THE SALISBURY INN
Pro Forma Financial Statement
Shown at Three Levels of Business Activity

	Low		Medium		High		Reference Number
	$	%	$	%	$	%	
Revenue:							
Food sales							
Beverage sales							
Total food and beverage sales							
Retail sales							
Total revenue							
Cost of Goods Sold:							
Food							
Beverage							
Retail							
Total cost of goods sold							
Gross Profit:							
Food							
Beverage							
Retail							
Total gross profit							
Expenses:							
Payroll							
Management							
Kitchen							
Service							
Taxes and benefits							
Total payroll							
Management fee							
Linen and laundry							
Kitchen and bar supplies							
China, glass, flatware							
Janitorial supplies							
Office supplies							
Paper supplies							
Music/entertainment							
Utilities							
Repair/maintenance							
Telephone							
Administrative							
Insurance							
Legal and accounting							
Equipment leases							
Rent							
Total expenses							
New profit from operations							

FIGURE 3.3 Financial statement format B.

THE OLD CABIN RESTAURANT
Pro Forma Financial Statement
Year 1 through 5

	Year 1		Year 2		Year 3		Year 4		Year 5		Reference Number
	$	%	$	%	$	%	$	%	$	%	
Revenue:											
Food sales											
Beverage sales											
Total food and beverage sales											
Retail sales											
Total revenue											
Cost of Goods Sold:											
Food											
Beverage											
Retail											
Total cost of goods sold											
Gross Profit:											
Food											
Beverage											
Retail											
Total gross profit											
Expenses:											
Payroll											
Management											
Kitchen											
Service											
Taxes and benefits											
Total payroll											
Management fee											
Linen and laundry											
Kitchen and bar supplies											
China, glass, flatware											
Janitorial supplies											
Office supplies											
Paper supplies											
Music/entertainment											
Utilities											
Repair/maintenance											
Telephone											
Administrative											
Insurance											
Legal and accounting											
Equipment leases											
Rent											
Total expenses											
Net profit from operations											

FIGURE 3.4

F o u r

Refining Your Concept and Writing the Operational Plan

Your business plan explains your concept and operating style in general terms. In it, you are painting a picture of your restaurant; presenting an image that will convey to your readers the general feel, style, ambiance, and niche of your proposed restaurant. It is an overview, a summary. Now you must fill in the details. You can no longer just talk about your restaurant operation in loose generalizations. You have to figure out the details to make it work.

When you mentioned in your business plan that "the meat counter will display the cuts of beef and fresh fish that we serve," you were creating an image for the reader. Your intent was to let him "see" the crowds standing at the counter, letting the feel of the meat market—the tools, butcher block tables, bib aprons, and wood floors—sink in. That was fine imagery and, hopefully, served its purpose. You will now expand on this idea. You will plan the size of the meat counter. How many customers do you need to service at one time? When you plan your refrigeration needs, you will list display refrigeration, backup walk-in cooler space, and any self-service that might be needed. Consider how you want shelving arranged and the type of shelving you need. How product is received and handled may affect these decisions. Therefore, you may have to do some research to determine your true needs. The size, shape, and materials for your work surfaces must be listed.

Equipment, tools, and displays of accessory products must also be considered. If you are dealing in retail, over-the-counter sales, packaging and cash handling will also be factors. It is not uncommon to draw sketches of how you envision tables or stations positioned. Staffing and workstations are described in the operational plan. The casual phrase "the wait staff will present our fresh baked breads to the customers" will be examined in detail. Where is the bread baked? Are they rolls, pieces, or slices? Where is it held, and is it served warm? Is the bread displayed or kept discreetly at a side stand? How is it presented? In what? There will be many more questions to answer about how the bread gets from the bakery or storage area to the guest. The objective is to think through every aspect of your restaurant operation from the moment your guest first approaches your restaurant (front door or parking lot/valet) to the time he or she leaves. You will study and document these activities from the guests' viewpoint, as an employee and as a supplier/vendor. Discuss and document how you plan to do things, what you need to operate properly, and what you want your guests to experience. You will think through what space, equipment, collateral space, and other operational needs must be considered to make the restaurant function effectively.

You are defining your restaurant in detail. You are making decisions about service and space that will be used to prepare the design program that your development team will use to plan and design your restaurant. The procedures you establish for your host will translate into how the host area is designed and built. If your servers use trays and tray stands, space must be planned for their use and storage. If you use tablecloths or cloth napkins, space at the wait station(s) must be allocated for storage of clean and soiled linen. These are operational issues that you must decide.

Brainstorming and numerous rewrites are common and encouraged. This is an exciting, evolutionary process. The details of your operation have not yet been decided. So this is not merely documenting how you plan to run the restaurant. Rather, you are creating the operational style and systems that will determine how your restaurant is planned and designed and, ultimately, how well it functions. You decide that bread will be served warm from roll drawers at the wait station by the busser. Later, you decide to feature your home-baked bread and have the server present it from strategically displayed baskets placed throughout the dining room. The important issue here is to think through what is required to accomplish this. How big are these baskets, and where can they be placed or displayed without getting knocked over or interfering with other functions at the wait stations?

You must understand the impact that each decision has on the overall development of your restaurant. Moving the responsibility for one element of service may alter the design of your wait stations and the pickup area at the kitchen. If, for example, you decide to use food runners instead of servers to place entrees at the table or decide that soup should be ladled up by the line instead of the wait staff, how does this affect the requirements for space and equipment at the server station and the line? Consider what happens when you decide that guests can eat at the bar as well as at bar tables. The bartender needs setups and a method of communicating with the kitchen. Procedures for transporting food from the kitchen to the bar must be decided. Soiled dish holding at the bar and from the bar to the kitchen must be considered. Server stations may need to be planned for or modified. The very design of the bar top may change to accommodate dining.

This is not the time to compromise. As you work out the details of service and expand on how your guest experiences your restaurant, do not concern yourself with how your ideas will fit in the actual space plan and design of the restaurant. Jon Bell was opening a small, neighborhood restaurant and considered takeout a major revenue center. But he was unsure about where this activity could be staged and the space required to accomplish it. He began to rethink the merits and logistics of takeout. At this point in his planning process, how the components of takeout were going to fit should not have been his concern. The important fact was that he considered takeout a primary element of his restaurant concept and wanted it to be a part of his operational plan. If during the design process, space or flow became an issue, that would be the time to think through the takeout operation and consider alternatives.

DEFINING THE
❖   # ESSENTIAL ELEMENTS

Restaurateurs often create files with pictures, clippings from trade magazines, and notes covering everything from tabletop accessories to uniforms to design details to food presentation ideas. Organizing, refining, and tailoring these ideas into a cohesive, comprehensive document that clearly explains how your restaurant is going to function is the essence of the operational plan.

The document that you create—the operational plan—will provide the background for your development team to prepare the design program. How detailed you are in writing the operational plan will determine the thoroughness of the design program, the effectiveness of your restaurant design, and ultimately, the success of your restaurant. The statement "I'm a customer; walk me through your restaurant" is one way to begin the process. An effective approach is to make notes as you talk through the customer experience. What you want to document is:

◆ How the guest arrives, enters, and moves throughout the restaurant

◆ What activities take place

◆ Who interacts with the guest, and how

◆ The space, furniture, or accessories the guest needs for comfort or function

◆ Where these items are located and if they are to be design features

◆ How your staff interacts/communicates among themselves

◆ What support services/facilities/personnel are required

◆ What tools/space or equipment are needed for these functions

Often, the initial response is: "Well, you come in the front door. . . ." *Hold it! Not so fast.* Start at the parking lot or on the street in front of the restaurant. Take nothing for granted. Prior to preparing the operational plan, many restaurateurs believe that they have a good grasp of their concept and how they plan to operate. However, once they begin to discuss the inner workings of the restaurant, they realize that there are many unanswered questions.

Gary Thomas was going through this process for his newest restaurant venture, a 160-seat two-level Italian restaurant complete with wood-burning oven and display kitchen. He and his partners were thinking through the bar operation. "We will feature a large selection of boutique beers, bottle and draft," he said. "How much bottle storage do we need?" asked his manager, "how many taps?" As they got into the discussion, they discussed their need for a remote draft beer system and separate keg cooler, storage for backup cases of bottled beer, and bottle recycling. "Well, I've always kept reserve cases of beer in a section of my walk-in," he said. "Besides, we will have plenty of storage behind the bar." How much storage is "plenty"? Determine quantities—cases or bottles—that you think you need to store. Taking space allocated to other functions may not solve your overall storage needs. If you determine that you need an 8- by 10-foot walk-in cooler for your food storage and then take the back shelf unit for beer storage, you may compromise the kitchen operation. These are the kinds of issues that you will deal with as you develop your operational plan.

Leave blanks or put question marks in places where you are unsure of the answer. When Gary was asked, "What are your thoughts on the tabletop finish for the dining room? Do you want a finished wood or stone surface to set the plates on? Are you thinking of tablecloths, or base cloths with toppers?" He thought a minute, and said, "I don't know, I'm considering either a glass or paper topper over a cloth. Let's come back to that." He did not need to come up with an answer immediately. By noting that this was an unresolved issue, he could mull it over while he developed the other aspects of his service.

In fact, as the other procedures unfold, they may influence his decision of table surface material. His choice will also have an impact on many other decisions. If he decides to use tablecloths, there are storage requirements. Who changes the linen, and where is soiled linen collected? Bulk soiled linen control and storage must also be planned. So, while the answers to these questions are critical, it is not necessary that they be answered now. Just start putting your thoughts and ideas down on paper. This is not a neat and orderly process. Use the following outline to guide you through your restaurant. If areas do not apply, skip them. If your operation has a feature not covered here, add it. Get the essential elements down on paper so that you and your development team can get the feel of how the restaurant will function. Subsequent rewrites will fill in the details and may cause you to change your operating procedures or rethink earlier decisions.

Parking

Zoning regulations often dictate the minimum requirements for parking. But this may not be adequate to accommodate your clientele. If parking is not close or convenient for your customers, they may not patronize your establishment as frequently as you would like. When discussing parking, indicate if you need or want a covered dropoff, your assessment of overall parking needs, and other considerations that will influence or affect the design and layout of your parking area. In downtown areas, public parking garages and lots may be all that is available.

In commercial developments where communal parking lots are the norm, you may indicate a need for designated parking. Make notes about lighting, security, walkways, and covered entrances. If valet parking is planned, space will be required for the valet, key control, and cash control. If the valet is cued by the server so that the guests' car can be waiting, a phone or intercom may be required. If related issues come to mind, note them. Even if you are working with a preselected site, these comments will help in the planning and design process. Cover the following points in your notes and text:

♦ Spaces required for guest comfort

♦ Proximity to entrance

♦ Design considerations: covered; lighting; designated spaces; bicycle, bus, and truck parking; signage

♦ Security issues: valet, attendant, fenced

♦ Maintenance concerns: snowplowing, sweeping

Guests enter the building parking lot off the frontage road. Need directional signage. Review parking lot lighting, cleaning, and snow removal plan with landlord. Restaurant entrance to have awning or canopy. Back-light canopy. No parking in front of entrance. Indirect lighting at drive-up. Do we need late-night security for bar clientele? Locate designated handicapped parking. Designate area for employee parking.

or

On-street parking is limited. Off-street lots adjacent to restaurant are available. Note promotional programs with lot attendants. Primary traffic flow is east to west on Stanley Street. Consider valet parking. Check with local contract services.

or

Primary market will drive and want close-in parking. Need drop-off close to front door. Parking can be across street or adjacent, within one block. Lot should handle 80 percent of customers, two people per car.

It is perfectly acceptable to write notes to yourself to followup on related or unresolved issues. A valet service that provides bonded valet attendants and handles all aspects of the valet service will let you know what their requirements are for space and equipment. Flagging maintenance or marketing concerns may trigger other design-related issues for your development team.

Signage

Graphics, your logo, name, and tag lines are critical elements of your restaurant. Although it is not a room within your restaurant that must be planned for and designed, signage must still be planned for since it requires utilities and space, is an integral part of the building design, and must be consistent with your image and concept. Your signage helps create your identity. The size, location, and design may be affected by building or lease covenants and zoning regulations. These issues, if relevant, will be addressed by your design team when they review applicable codes and regulations. Indicate what you want and let your development team work out the details. Notes on signage should discuss:

♦ Placement

♦ Design and style

♦ Directional/informational signs

Illuminated sign at parking lot entrance. Large sign on building must be visible from highway and frontage road. Logo on awning. Also sign at parking entry. Illuminated. Neon.

or

Building sign to be understated, on building front only. Building design and colors to identify restaurant. Old-style lettering, indirect lighting. Parking lot to have small signs identifying our designated spaces and my private space.

Building/Restaurant Entry

When you say "the customer comes in the front door" you need to think about the entrance. The entry may be exclusive to your restaurant or a common building entrance with your restaurant entry as a secondary doorway farther inside the building. Do you need a vestibule or air lock? What else is there in the entryway: retail display, "specials" signage, newspapers? Even the size and type of doors may be significant for you. The entrance to your restaurant may be the "first impression" your guest has of your operation. The text on the entry will include comments on the building exterior as well, since this is all part of the entry experience of your customers. Consider the following:

♦ Exterior appearance and image: colors, windows, awnings or canopies, planters

♦ Entryway: style of door or doors, materials, hardware, floor finish, vestibule

♦ Lighting

♦ Signage or graphics

♦ Other functions/amenities: public phone, bench, news racks, displays or advertising, umbrella rack

I want guests to get an immediate sense of the restaurant when they walk in the front door. Large, single wood door with glass. Hardware selection very important. Door to open into vestibule that can accommodate 10+ people. Vestibule to have same rustic materials as bar. Mural or special artwork on walls. Snow/water a problem. Flooring material to be nonslip. Need wipe-off area outside door.

Waiting Area

When your guests enter the restaurant, what do you want them to see? Where do you want them to go? Guests don't necessarily have to approach a host when they first enter the restaurant. You may want them to have a choice of either direct access into the lounge or bar or to going to a host area. Perhaps the waiting area is more of a refuge where your guests can relax comfortably while waiting for their table without being hassled about a drink or food. Cover these points:

♦ Capacity: how many guests this area should accommodate, standing or sitting

♦ Type of seating: bench, chairs

◆ Design elements: displays, artifacts, artwork, views into dining room or bar

◆ Interaction with staff: host, greeter, manager, coat check

When entering the restaurant, customers must be able to by-pass host area and go directly into bar. A couple of large chairs or couch for people who don't want to go into lounge. Table with display of food/accessories to be very visible and dominant feature. Space to be small. Customers to feel more comfortable waiting in lounge.

or

Customers will enter a comfortable waiting room off the entry doors. This space will have a large saltwater aquarium that will establish our image of a seafood house. Nautical paraphernalia and wooden chairs will be available for waiting. Large groups are our specialty. Need to hold 20 to 30 people at a time.

Host

If they are greeted by the host, what is the host's function? You may think this is obvious. Well, is it? Sure, they welcome them to the establishment. But then what? Is there a greeter and a seater? Does the host take them to their table? What if there is a "wait?" Where do you keep track of the wait list? How do they find guests who are waiting? Where do they wait? How do you track tables and seating? Where do you list reservations? Are retail sales handled by the host? If you offer high chairs or booster seats, who gets them, and where are they stored? This is the level of detail that you need to delve into or a vital function may be left out.

◆ Functions performed

◆ Staff required

◆ Work space: counter and storage

◆ Equipment needed

◆ Design features

◆ Guest/staff interaction and flow

Host area to be informal. Provide "sideboard" rather than "podium" for host's stuff. Host to be approachable, not behind desk. Room for reservation book (verify size), phone, desk lamp, menus. Storage for backup T-shirts—2-foot-wide cabinet. Wall display shelving for retail items: breads and sauces. Sales handled by bartender.

or

Guest will approach host, who is standing and facing waiting area from behind desk. Host to confirm reservation in book or take name. If table not ready, direct guest to bar. Host and seater work as team. When table ready, seater will find guest and escort to table and present menu—need rack on side of host stand for food, wine list, special desert menu, and to-go menus.

Coat Room

Coat storage needs to be thought through. If you just think, "yea, let's have a coat closet," the resulting space may not be adequate. Is it a staffed "coat check" room or self-serve? Are wall hooks sufficient? Is security a problem? How many coats need to be stored? Are other, ancillary items required such as umbrellas or booster chairs?

♦ Self-serve or staffed

♦ Capacity: quantity and type of coats (full length or short)

♦ Location

♦ Other uses

Need coatroom. Practically all guests will have a coat in winter. Mostly waist or ¾-length ski jackets. Upper and lower coat bar OK. Some space for full length. Hat storage necessary. May have wall coat hooks in lounge. Coat check to be staffed. Host will direct guest to coat check adjacent to host stand. When slow, host will also handle coatroom.

Public Rest Rooms

While governing building codes require toilet facilities, many restaurants include amenities that are not required, such as providing more lavatories than necessary or larger compartments or seating areas. If your restaurant is multilevel, you may want additional facilities on other levels for the convenience of your guests. Product vending, electronic ticker tape or sports scores and advertising may also be featured. Do not overlook maintenance. Backup supplies storage and access to a mop sink are essential.

- ♦ Location: preference—near entry, bar, kitchen, or in far corner

- ♦ Quality standard: basic, flush valves, old style

- ♦ Amenities: larger vanities, extra fixtures, mirrors, product vending

- ♦ Maintenance issues: storage, ventilation, lighting

    Rest rooms to have same design materials as dining room. Bar guests to have access without going through primary dining area. Need mop sink closeby. Full-length mirror in ladies. Flush valves, no tanks! Heavy-duty fixtures but nothing fancy.

Retail Sales Specialty Displays

Many restaurants regard retail sales as a significant profit center. Logo clothing and trinkets, private-label sauces, and similar items may need to be displayed. Additionally, consider how sales are transacted. Is there a staffed retail counter? Is it a function of the host? Visual displays are very powerful sales incentives. Sales of deserts, house specialties, and bakery products may all benefit from visual presentations within your restaurant. If these elements are to be features in your restaurant, this is where you need to elaborate on them.

- ♦ Product line

- ♦ Quantity

- ♦ Display/space requirements: refrigerated, secured

- ♦ How transactions are handled

Retail sales to be handled by host. Host to have independent register to handle these transactions, primarily our breads and sauces. Need wall display and subtle graphics/signage to promote—6 feet of wall space, 2 feet deep. Bread rack? Secondary secured display case in vestibule, 4 feet long. No clutter.

Bar

To say you are going to have a bar does not address the space adequately. You need to determine how big a bar you want. Is it a feature or tucked in a corner? Do you want a bar that has low seats or standard bar stools? How many seats or stools? How many bartender stations? How does the bar function? When you follow the guest through the dining experience and he orders a drink, think through how the drink order flows. Who takes the order, where is it rung up, what does the server do, and what does the bartender do? Document the features/specialties or "gimmicks" that are specific to your bar operation: draft beer, boutique beers, wine, flavored vodkas, frozen/slush drinks. Some operators require the bartender to make espresso drinks. These are the details that will affect the design of your bar. Highlight these points.

♦ Size: number of stools or overall length

♦ Operational highlights: menu offerings, entertainment

♦ Stations: number of bartender workstations and server pickup points

♦ Server procedures and equipment requirements

♦ Bartender procedures and equipment requirements

♦ Design features/orientation

Bar to be very dominant and visible to guests as they enter lounge. Bartender to be able to see door. Traditional-looking bar: dark wood, tall back bar, mirrors, glass shelving. Red wine storage as well as liquor to be visible. 15 to 20 bar stools: padded seat with back. Customers can eat at bar. Separate area from dining room but can overlook or have low wall. Two bartender stations, carbonated beverage guns (get free from syrup supplier), draft beer (four faucets). Keg cooler to be in basement. Center faucet on front bar, accessible to both bartenders. Manual glass washing, no machine. Bartender to make all espresso drinks. Need two-group machine: grinder, trash, refrigeration. Specialty grappa display at back bar. Some feature at bar corners—light, sculpture—without interfering with customers. One POS behind bar. Remote printer for server drinks on back bar—inconspicuous. Wait station at each end of bar. Servers need POS, water, ice, coffee, iced tea, refrigerator, bus area: 4 to 5 feet. Not visible to customers but server needs to see tables from server station. Each bar station to have cocktail/ice unit (3 foot), blender station, at least 2 feet of multi-tier glass storage.

The discussion of service procedures will elaborate on the specifics of types of glassware, glass and bottle display and storage, types of bottle coolers (top load or doors), glass frosters, and the intimate details of mixology and service, down to the way in which garnishes and mixes are prepared and stored. The more detail you as the operator provide, the more efficient and less cluttered your bar will be.

Bar Storage

Your review of the bar operation will lead you to the issue of resupply. Ice, backup beer, liquor, and wine, dry goods and supplies need to be readily available. In large restaurants, separate storage areas or ice machines may be required at the bar, especially if the bar is on a separate level. Storage for bar supplies includes the carbonated beverage system, beer, liquor, wine, and paper products, fruit and bar snacks.

♦ Storage needs: list items

♦ Capacity: lineal feet of shelving, pounds of ice

♦ Location: immediate access to bartender or server, behind bar, adjacent room

♦ Design features: ventilation, temperature control, security, utilities

Need 4 lineal feet of liquor storage for backup liquor and miscellaneous supplies. Lockable room. Ice machine, 250-pound storage. Keep soda "bag-in-box" system in basement. Glass recycling containers at bar and large bin or room for bulk recycling of glass/cans in basement. Room to have drain for washing down.

Server Stations

Dedicated areas for your wait staff to get setups, condiments, coffee, and water or to access the POS system or perform other activities are necessary for your restaurant to function. In bars and lounges where food is served, the standard or more traditional bar pickup area may not be sufficient to accommodate all these activities.

♦ Functions performed

♦ Stations required or number of employees

♦ Equipment needed

♦ Design considerations: access, visibility

Two server stations needed on lounge: one adjacent to bar, one in seating area. Bar snacks need to be served warm: roll warmers, heated food well? Storage for backup. Water, ice, coffee, and coffee brewing: regular and decaf. Limited refrigeration for cream. Setups for food service. Cocktail trays—space to set down and work. Cup racks, glass racks: two each. Need quick access but cannot be visible to customers *at all*! Separate POS station, 1 unit, with related stuff (validator, printer). Area must be dry, protected from water or spills.

Lounge

When your guests are directed to the lounge, what do you want them to find? Who greets the guests? What kind of seating do they find? Your clientele and the food and drink you serve will affect these choices. Consider the other functions that may occur in the lounge, such as live entertainment, TV, or pool. If circulation and mingling are important, bar-height tables or drink rails may be more appropriate in some areas. Guest flow in a lounge has a significant effect on guest comfort. In lounges that cater to tourists or visitors, guests may feel uncomfortable walking into an unfamiliar lounge if they can't walk in easily, look around, and move through the lounge area.

♦ Capacity: area, number of seats

♦ Type of seating: indicate table and chair styles, sizes, and heights

♦ Service considerations: aisle space, server stations, table spacing

♦ Design features: image, visibility, access, circulation requirements, acoustical concerns

♦ Finishes and materials: flooring, colors

♦ Operational issues: guest/server flow, entertainment, dancing, smoking

Bar to have own identity. Entry to bar to be like entering parlor or living room. Bar clearly visible and welcoming. 40 to 50 seats plus bar stools. Some informal seating—couches, lounge chairs—need side tables for drinks and food. Table and chair seating to be deuces and four-tops. No booths, possible banquettes (straight booth benches). Need one six- to eight-top, round, for local regulars. Small chairs, padded seat, no arms. Tabletops to be of wood or other natural material. No cloths, mats, or topping. Some high-top tables to break up room if necessary. Divider between bar and seating area.

Dining Areas

Seats and tables are your primary source of revenue. Yet many operators do not think about the kind of seating they want, the mix of table sizes, flexibility, ability to accommodate private parties, or the "see and be seen" crowd. When you think about seating, discuss the type of chairs: arms or armless, size or shape. The nature of your clientele may influence this decision.

Cliff Grafton owned and operated a restaurant that catered to a high-end crowd that lingered over dinner. Comfort was a critical factor for Cliff. He needed a large, sturdy, well-cushioned chair. He also needed some with arms since he had customers who asked for them specifically. The large chairs and nature of his menu and service also demanded a large table—42-inch squares—with comfortable spacing.

By making this requirement known to his design team, they were able to plan the dining areas with realistic seating counts. The size of the tables also affects their spacing and your overall seating capacity. Although at this point you may not know the dimensions of the tables, if you indicate that "large pasta bowls and platters for family service must fit on tables" this is a "flag" that will be dealt with further in the design program.

As you go through the motions of your customer's dining experience, other factors will come into play. The use of serving carts or trays and tray stands require maneuvering room. The efficacy of multiple levels, whether to enhance views or break up a large expanse of tables, will be affected by your style of service. In your business plan, you may have based some of your sales revenue on group business, private functions, or special events. As you decide on types of seating and the requirements for your dining areas, be sure that the facility you plan can, in fact, accommodate the type of business you have projected in your financial calculations.

♦ Overall seating capacity

♦ Number and capacity of separate dining areas

♦ Seating styles: booths, banquettes, high tops, counters, traditional chair/table

♦ Table sizes and adaptability: flip-up panels, toppers

♦ Chair sizes and styles

♦ Table spacing, if critical

♦ Seating mix

♦ Specialty tables

♦ Service procedures

♦ Design features

Entry to dining area to focus on wood-burning bake oven and exhibition cooking line. Also want guest entrance to be a visual for seated customers. Dining area to be open but to have low dividers to prevent "ballroom" look. The guest is escorted to the table by the host. Host presents menus. Table is set with flatware roll-ups in cotton napkin (large), water glass, bread and butter plate (B&B), salt and pepper shakers (S&P), centerpiece–flower/plant/something. Busser serves water—large metal pitcher from sidestand. Server takes drink order and goes over menu and specials. Drinks/appetizers rung in on POS at wait station. Drinks picked up at bar. Runner brings apps from line. Server presents bread, served from large basket with tongs. Bread serving baskets kept at three locations: display table, space at exhibition kitchen front counter, and at wait station. Must be visible. Restocked from large bread display and cutting board near bake oven. Seating capacity of 120 to 140 seats. Four-tops (36-inch) with flip-ups to convert to rounds. Deuces along window (30 by 30 inches), four-place booths—6 feet± center to center. Need dining area for 20 to 30 people that can be isolated for private parties but still comfortable for regular dining. Two rounds for 6 to 8 people as feature tables. Larger chair than lounge seating—not bentwood. Padded seat, wood. Counter seating at wood-burning pizza oven for 6 to 8 people. Interaction between line and guests encouraged.

Patios

Patio areas, although seasonal, have requirements that must be considered during the planning and design of a restaurant. Access to bar and food service and the need for wait/bus stations plays an important role because patios are usually farther than the primary dining areas are from the kitchen and bar. Portable bars or workstations that do not require utility connections still need space. Seating requirements and flexibility are no less important here. Outside seating presents other concerns. How is outside furniture secured after business hours? Are awnings, umbrellas, or some other form of sun/weather protection required? Railings are often required by code to control alcoholic beverages. In addition to the points outlined for the dining areas, address the following.

♦ Seasonal or permanent equipment needs

♦ Security

♦ Maintenance

Patio seating for 40: 48-inch rounds, solid resin top, umbrellas. Chair to match, no arms. Need portable wait station and bar, power and plumbing for equipment. Floor drain for maintenance. Provide natural gas line for outdoor barbeque.

Wait Stations

If you cannot service your guests effectively, you may not achieve the level of financial success you have projected. You need adequate work spaces for your wait staff and bussers. Attempting to maximize seating at the expense of sufficient server stations will compromise your service. Be realistic about what must occur at these stations. As you "walk" your customer through the restaurant, think about where condiments, setups, POS systems, bussing areas, beverages, and backup supplies are kept. Some restaurants have carbonated beverage faucets at their wait stations. This requires utilities and routing of lines that will be noted in the design program. The issues to cover are the same as those for lounge server stations, although your response will probably be more extensive.

- ◆ Functions performed
- ◆ Stations required or number of employees
- ◆ Equipment needed
- ◆ Design considerations: access, visibility

Primary wait station to be adjacent to pickup line. Shield from customer view but servers need to be able to see their customers while at wait station. Utility sink with gooseneck faucet, ice bin, cup/glass racks—4 each, coffee brewing—check with vendor—iced tea, setups, napkins, condiments—12 to 15 feet overall. Isolate POS from wet area by 2-foot space. POS, printer, credit card validator, trash can. Separate section for bussing— bus tubs, 3 feet. Five servers may be using station at one time. Need adequate circulation.

Kitchen

The kitchen area is not the space left after the dining room and bar have been designed. On the other hand, you do not want your restaurant to be all kitchen with a few seats! It is an integral piece of your restaurant that has to be planned in conjunction with the rest of your restaurant. Your operational plan will discuss your kitchen from three vantage points.

The Service Staff. The food service staff interacts with the kitchen to pick up products, access self-serve products that are restocked by/from the kitchen, or to return products such as soiled dishes to the kitchen. Go through the motions of what they do and what they need to perform their tasks properly. If, for example, the server dishes up his own soup, how many different soups are offered? Where are bowls, utensils, and garnishes kept? Use these checkpoints as a guide:

♦ List the tasks performed by each position: host, cocktail and food server, busser, food runner, expediter.

♦ Indicate where these tasks take place.

♦ State what space, equipment, tools, or supplies are required, and how they are restocked.

♦ Include what tasks or equipment can be combined or placed adjacent to each other.

♦ List design features.

Server is responsible for taking orders, keying orders at the POS, self-serving bread and soup, taking drink and dessert orders, and serving coffee and beverages. Orders are taken at table onto pad and keyed in at primary wait station. Drink orders print remote at bar and are served by cocktail server. Food runners are stationed at line. Expediter assembles table and garnishes plates. Runner trays complete table, grabs tray jack, and proceeds to table. Room required near tables for jack stand. Runner is responsible for getting special utensils.

The Kitchen Staff. The functions that occur in the kitchen must be reviewed individually. Break down each task performed—receiving, storage, bulk preparation, finishing/line cooking, holding, plating, pickup, and related support functions—by your kitchen staff. Work through your menu and consider these points.

♦ Focus on each task, individually.

♦ Itemize the specific functions within each task: for example, where products are set on delivery for check-in, receiving procedures, breakdown, labeling, storage, and related administrative activities.

♦ Determine the space, tools, and equipment needed.

♦ Determine staffing and workstations.

♦ Consider small appliance needs.

♦ Decide the work space needed adjacent to primary equipment for supplies and complementery tasks.

♦ Plan for storage of backup supplies.

♦ List design features or concerns: visibility, noise, maintenance, exhibition cooking.

Breaking down the operation of your kitchen to this level of detail will allow you to develop workstations that enhance productivity and comfort. It will also force you to think through each function and reduce the chance of omitting a critical element. A chef was explaining his receiving procedures to his development team. "I like to transfer produce into clear food storage boxes immediately after I receive it. So be sure to have a place where I can stack these food boxes in the receiving area." This was a simple request. But had he not included this procedure in the operational plan, the design team may not have been aware of it and would not have planned for it. Perhaps he would have found a space for the food boxes, but why compromise your effectiveness because of faulty planning?

> All goods will come in through the service door. Need a 8- by 10-foot area for staging. Table, scale, phone. Walk-in cooker (7 by 12 feet), reach-in freezer (two- door), dry storage—16 lineal feet, 24 inches wide, five shelves high. Additional storage for nonfood supplies.

> Bulk prep area: double convection oven, six-burner with oven, steam-jacketed kettle—40-quart, worktables—10 foot, sinks. Lots of wall shelving. Table adjacent or across from line. Rack above convection oven for sheet pan cooling.

> Baking area: Bake oven, wood table—6-foot, bins underneath, 60-quart mixer. Pantry: 6-foot refrigerated salad table, worktable behind.

Wood-burning oven station: primary focal point at exhibition kitchen. Work area to include 6-foot refrigerated prep table, rolling area, cool area for dough storage. Dough made in bulk prep, transferred to line with low mobile rack—sheet pans. Customers seated at bar stools in front of this area—six to eight stools. Small pickup area 3 feet wide, with heat lamp. Need storage for "to-go" boxes.

Grill station–expediter station: between wood oven and pasta station. Remote printer, ticket rail. 3-foot charbroiler, six-burner, between grill and pasta—share. Work area on left, 2 feet wide, refrigeration, place for *bain marie.* Double pass-through shelf, 18 inches wide, heat lamps.

Warewashing and Handling. Warewashing requirements depend on how you operate and the type of utensils you use. Just planning to have a "pot sink, dish machine, and soiled and clean dish tables" shortchanges the needs of this area and may cause excessive breakage or wasted space. Some operators run most of their pots and pans through the dish machine and do not need a large potwashing area. Chefs and kitchen managers have different styles for handling the staging, washing, and resupply of sauté pans and utensils used by the line cooks. These items often need quick turnaround, and warewashing facilities must be located and designed to meet this need. Dish and pot storage varies as well. Some operators wash all bar glassware at the bar. Others wash at the bar and the main warewashing area, wherever the glasses land, and then "stage" the cleaned glasses for later transfer to the bar. Where and how these glasses are staged and how they are transported affects the space and equipment required. Consider the following:

♦ Overall customer counts: necessary to size equipment

♦ Variety of dishes, glassware and pots, pans, and utensils

♦ Anticipated quantities

♦ Where these items are used

♦ Where they are to be placed when in use

♦ How and where are they stored: glass and cup racks, hooks, shelving

♦ How do they get to/from work areas and warewashing

Bussers clear table by hand, take soiled dishes to bus tubs at bus station or directly to dish dropoff. Glasses racked by busser, flatware in "soak" by busser. Bus tubs rinsed and stacked by dishwasher for reuse. Clean dishes stocked on shelving at dish area. Par level maintained at line. Dishwasher maintains par level.

Delivery/Service Personnel. You need good access for deliveries and maintenance services. Stairs, ramps, and space for large hand trucks or carts may be necessary. Think about the kinds of deliveries you will receive, where they need to go, and where they will be used. Loading docks and space for delivery truck to park and unload without blocking customer traffic is of prime concern. A large-access hallway with a small door or a double door with a center jamb may create problems when you attempt to move equipment. Restaurants often minimize the requirements for deliveries and service because space is at such a premium. Small hallways, insufficient receiving areas, or poor access to storage areas causes wasted time and effort for both employees and delivery personnel.

Street-level loading area. No tractor trailer service. Back door—door bell, peep hole, self-closing. Big door—4 feet. Space for truck turnaround. No stairs, if possible. Ramps.

Trash areas have specific requirements that need to be documented. The size of the dumpster, a place to wash and store trash cans, bottle/can recycling, grease recycling, and wood storage for fireplaces or grills are items to consider. Security and visibility are also issues to discuss.

Dumpster is 5 by 7 feet. Grease recycling is 3 by 6 feet. Need can wash-mop sink, heavy-duty faucet/hose. Area to be enclosed/shielded. Lockable area for wood storage—one cord. Need space for recycle bins—3 at 2 by 2 feet.

Support Areas

Restaurants require auxiliary spaces for activities that support the restaurant operation. When these are overlooked, primary storage or work areas are compromised to accommodate these functions.

Receiving/Staging Area. When deliveries arrive, they need a landing space. They need to be counted, weighed, inspected, and possibly broken down and repacked. This requires space. Expecting this function to take place in your "prep" area or on the loading dock may be unrealistic. If the space in inadequate, proper receiving procedures may not occur.

Office. Office space can be as small as a step-in closet, a luxury space with casual seating, or a corner of the dry storage room. Listing the functions that occur in the office should be your first task, followed by the equipment (computers, files, safe, desk space) and personnel. There are operators who like their office adjacent to the "back door" so that they can see who comes in and out. Others prefer to be tucked in a remote area of the building.

Storage. Restaurants need storage for items that are not part of everyday service. Replacement china, glassware, and tabletop accessories are bulky items that need to be available but do not necessarily need to be immediately accessible. Basements, attics, or secured sheds behind the restaurant building may serve for this type of storage. Restaurants that have banquet or meeting space require storage for related items: tables, chairs, podiums, audiovisual equipment. Be realistic about your storage needs. Shortchanging your storage requirements will not reduce the space you really need. You need a place to keep firewood for your fireplace or wood-burning oven. To say, "I'll find a place after we are open." only delays the decisions and limits your options. Some items can be secured outside the restaurant. Patio furniture, yard maintenance tools, snow shovels, and seasonal displays can be kept in sheds or even off premises. List this requirement as a real storage need and let your design team figure out how to incorporate the space into your facility.

Employee Lockers/Rest Room. Unless you want your staff to use the public rest rooms in your restaurant and tuck their personal belongings on shelves and under tables in the kitchen, you need to provide a space for them. Lockers should be sized based on need. Cooks often bring their own knife sets. Security for street clothes and valuables should be provided. Restaurants often provide space for employees to lock bicycles. Restaurants in resort communities should consider space for employees to keep their before/after work toys—skis or golf clubs. How many employees will be on during a shift will help determine the number of lockers and related space required.

❖ PREPARING THE OPERATIONAL PLAN

At this point, you should have most of the information necessary to compile your operational plan. This is not a report that needs to be "presented," but it does need to be accurate and thorough. It is a working document. Incomplete sentences, pictures, and key words can all be used to make your point. Remember that the purpose of this document is to give the design team the essential information they need to prepare a usable and worthwhile design program.

You could collect all your notes, put them into a file folder, hand them to your development team, and say, "here it is—you should be able to prepare the design program from all this." But you shouldn't. Like all documents that you prepare, from menus to employee handbooks, there will be editing, rewriting, and most important, rethinking of your procedures. Although this is not the last time you will be able to change your approach to service or modify your operating style, it makes good sense to give your development team an operational plan that you are comfortable with.

Throughout your draft plan, many items may have been left undecided or you have posed questions that may not have been answered. As you fill in these blanks, you may alter your procedures. When management was planning George Wong's Restaurant, they knew they wanted an exhibition kitchen featuring wok cookery. Their initial operational plan stated,

> Feature three-chamber wok facing dining room with island hood. Need refrigeration, workspace, pickup area (3 feet). Raised platform? Closed-circuit TV of chef? Other specialty cooking?

When they reviewed their draft plan, these questions had to be answered.

> Chef to have view/eye contact with guests. Put exhibition cooking on pedestal. Cooking of specialty Asian food to be "demon-

strated." Use cooking platform for cooking classes. Have camera/TV monitors throughout dining room for guests to see how foods are prepared and presented. Add rotisserie at cooking pedestal: 20 or more birds. Add work space and sink at this area.

Some answers may alter your previously planned procedures dramatically. The operational plan for the Columbine Restaurant is a good example.

Servers will bring roll basket and whipped butter to table after taking entrée order. Rolls will be held at wait station in heated bin. Need decision on type of rolls: buy or bake on premises?

When they did their research on rolls, they decided that bread from a local bakery was the answer. And the bread was better if not heated, just sliced and served. With this new information, they altered their plans.

Servers will slice bread at bread station at line. Bread station to have wicker baskets of fresh loaves—design feature—maple cutting board and oversized bread knife. Stack of bread baskets for table service.

After you have filled in the blanks and answered the questions you included initially in your operational plan, meet with your management team (chef, general manager, bar manager, staff from your existing restaurant) to check the plan for consistency.

OPERATIONAL PLAN FOR REMODELING AN EXISTING RESTAURANT

Operational plans are not limited to new developments. They are often equally vital when remodeling or planning additions. Small renovations are deceiving. The Highland Bar located within a hotel underwent a renovation to create an entry directly off the street. The remodel necessitated the relocation of the bar wait station. Since the primary motivation for the remodel was to create the outside entrance and a separate identity for the bar, the design team simply took the space formerly allocated to the wait station and relocated it. Unfortunately, the existing space was inadequate and poorly configured. It was not until well into the construction process that the bar management noticed the size and placement of the wait station and lobbied hard to correct the problem. Had they developed an operational plan, even for this seemingly simple remodel, they would have saved time and money and had the servery they needed to support the staff effectively and care for their guests.

Remodeling, expanding, or renovating an existing restaurant requires the same thoroughness of planning that a new restaurant requires. Systems, procedures, and the style of service you offer changes over time. Wait stations, parts of the cooking line, or preparation areas that were once very effective may not meet your changed needs. First these areas are irritating to the line workers, then to management, and finally, these problems begin to show up on the financial statement as excessive labor, lower sales, or falling customer counts and gross revenue. At some point, management decides to make changes.

The advantage that existing restaurants have is that they can plan their renovations based on actual experiences. Bartenders can say that they need more glass storage because they know from working the bar that the space allocated doesn't give them enough stock. Servers can explain that with the expanded menu and appetizer selections, they need additional refrigeration at their work area.

The questions that operators of existing facilities face are:

♦ Who will coordinate/manage the remodel effort? Since many of these projects are small, the more structured development process is not often used.

♦ Who will participate? Management sees problems and inefficiencies differently from employees. While employees often focus on their specific task and how to make their job easier without regard for other, related activities, their input is critical. They see and experience operational flaws and difficulties that management may not recognize.

Once you are confident that the operational plan represents the image, style of service, and procedures that your will use in your restaurant, you can turn it over to your design team to use as the basis for the design program.

F i v e

Preparing the Design Program

The successful design of your restaurant is often based on the information you provide to your development team. How clear and comprehensive the information is will determine how effective your design team is in turning your concept and ideas into a restaurant facility that meets your needs and expectations. The best way to communicate your ideas and requirements is to prepare a written design program. This program addresses all the physical aspects of your restaurant. It presents them in a format that can be understood easily and followed by the various design professionals who will contribute to the design of the restaurant. It becomes a working document that will be revised and referred to by your design team. It also serves as a constant reminder to everyone involved of what your design intent is and the critical features that, when combined, create your concept and style.

Many architects and design professionals expect this information to come from you. And it should. You provide them with the operational plan, which describes in great detail how the restaurant works. It is from this document that your design team extracts the raw data that will become the building blocks of the design program. But the operational plan is not a substitute for the design program. And the design program is not just a rehash of the operational plan. They are two very different and essential documents. Where the operational plan *describes how your restaurant functions*, the design program extracts and elaborates on the spaces, tools, equipment, and related physical elements necessary to *enable you to perform as planned*.

Regardless of how well these design professionals understand the restaurant business or claim to know the concept you are creating or know the best tools and equipment to prepare and serve the menu you

143

are proposing, they do not know the details or the nuances of your particular operating style or cooking techniques like you do. The most effective way for them to develop this background so that they can prepare an effective and accurate design program is for you to insist that every member of your design team read and understand your:

♦ Business plan

♦ Capital expenditures budget and financing package

♦ Operational plan

Your operational plan may state: "The primary wait station will have the coffee brewer, ice and water station, an undercounter refrigerator, storage space for table setups, and a separate bussing area for two bus tubs." From this information the people developing the design program will ask questions to determine:

♦ The size and utility requirements for the equipment mentioned

♦ Work space required adjacent to this equipment

♦ Relationship of this equipment and work space at the wait station

♦ Requirements or preferences for materials or finishes

♦ Lighting or acoustical concerns

♦ Visibility and access out of or into the wait station

When discussing how the bar was to function in his operational plan, Tom Murphy wrote: "Draft beer, two faucets. 15 boutique beers, 12 to 24 bottles each. Two-station bar. Blended specialty drinks. Hand glasswashing, no machine. Check into back bar display of flavored vodkas." From Tom's perspective, he was very specific about how his bar was going to work. But, several questions needed to be answered to satisfy the design program.

♦ How many kegs of beer needed to be stored, and what size keg of cooler was required?

♦ Is the refrigeration for the cooler self-contained, remote, air- or water-cooled?

♦ Does he prefer top-load or front-load bottle coolers?

♦ Will the boutique beers be displayed?

♦ What accessory equipment is needed for the blended specialty drinks: ice cream cabinet, small refrigerator, fruit display/cutting area?

♦ What is needed for glass storage and space for washing?

♦ What are the results of research into the flavored vodka display options?

Once the people writing the design program understand these details, they can, with your help, prepare a functional document. The design program is dynamic. It will updated and refined as the restaurant progresses. Items that were desirable may become expendable. Features that were initially essential may become impractical. However this document evolves, it is still the guidebook that steers the design.

However they are prepared, design programs should be:

♦ Written and made available to every member of the design team

♦ Comprehensive and include, at minimum, the items listed on the worksheet

♦ Reviewed and edited by the owner and/or the owner's representative

♦ Edited and updated to reflect changes in the concept, operating style, or design elements

♦ Used and referred to continuously by your design team members

The worksheet shown in Figure 5.1 incorporates the necessary information.

DESIGN PROGRAM WORKSHEET

Room name: _____

Room number: _____

Function/use: _____

_____

Size/capacity: _____

Access/egress requirements: _____

_____

Adjacency: _____

Architectural/design features: _____

_____

Lighting: _____

_____

Specialty systems:

_____

Service requirements: _____

_____

Utilities: _____

_____

Finishes: _____

_____

Furnishings/fixtures:

_____

Equipment: _____

_____

Comments: _____

_____

_____

FIGURE 5.1

ELEMENTS OF THE
DESIGN PROGRAM

❖

Room Name and Number

Every room and space should be assigned a name and number. Where two spaces have the same or similar names (dining room, hallway, storage) the reference number will identify them clearly. Your design team will assign the numbers. These numbers will be used on various schedules and notes on the drawings and specifications.

Function/Use

This information describes in more detail how the space will be used. A room labeled "storage" doesn't tell the full story. This reference is used to elaborate on the name or describe the space in greater detail, such as "dry goods storage for nonfood items" or "private dining room/meeting room; also used for ballroom dance classes."

Size/Capacity

This is essential information. How many seats or tables do you want the room to accommodate? Seating capacity is always dependent on the style of seating, table sizes, and spacing. Rule-of-thumb square feet per seat formulas can work if you know the style of seating or seating arrangements planned. Informal dining seating may be calculated at 10 to 12 square feet per person. More spacious dining may be calculated at 15. Theater-style meetings or functions may be as tight as 10 square feet per person. This information will be elaborated on within this form. Coatrooms are sized by number of coats. How many coats must be hung? Full length or short? Some coatroom spaces are used for storage of booster seats, extra chairs, or tables. This should be noted here.

In the operational plan, you may have written, Small dining room to accommodate 25 to 30 people, banquet style. Service to this area to be self-contained so that doors can be closed and group left undisturbed." The design program will expand on this. "25 to 30 seats, 30-inch centers at 30-inch banquet tables. U-shaped or double-wide layouts. Chairs are 18-inch armless, stackable—three tiers. Need adjacent storage." The statement regarding the self-contained waitstation will be noted under "service requirements."

Access/Egress Requirements

Traffic patterns are very important for service and customer flow. Your requirements for access, direct or indirect, will be recorded here. Do you need direct access to the kitchen or bar? Is this access through a public corridor or a serviceway? Consider traffic to rest rooms. Is it acceptable for access to the rest rooms to be through another dining room? Should corridors or aisles be oversized to handle this traffic? Another issue discussed under this category is size and style of doors. Perhaps double doors are needed to move in large equipment, a piano, or portable bars? Patio dining and circulation to outside areas fall under this category as well. Note if rooms are to open onto patios, decks, or gardens.

Adjacency

This refers to how rooms are related or connected. Service requirements may dictate that the bar be adjacent to the kitchen entrance so that the wait staff can pick up drinks on their way out of the kitchen. Perhaps the bar must have a pass-through to a private dining room. With direct-draw beer systems, some operators need a large keg cooler sharing a common wall with the back bar. In your operational plan, you may have noted that "customers should be able to walk directly into the bar without having to wrestle through the crowd waiting for dining seats." This should be picked up by the person preparing your design program and noted here. Coatrooms are sometimes desirable near the host station so that the host can deal with coats without moving too far from his station. For other concepts, the coatroom may be desirable far from the host or waiting area to avoid congestion. If these issues are important to your concept or style of operation, they must be noted. The relationship of storage space to public and back-of-the-house areas is frequently critical. Your control procedures may be most effective when all the alcoholic beverages are stored adjacent to each other within view of the office. The employee lockers and rest room may need to be near the service door but away from receiving or storage rooms. If dining room 103 must have adjacent table storage accessed from within the dining room, or if the private dining room needs a door directly to the outside parking area, note it here. This information lets your design team know how the pieces fit together.

Architectural/Design Features

Your concept will include references to design styles or elements that depict your theme and image or are required for your restaurant to function. Large, arched windows, a stage, or level changes may be desirable. You may need a display table for homemade deserts or specialty foods; special ceiling heights or shapes, railings or displays, fireplaces or fountains. When the operational plan states: "Large fireplace—gas logs—will be focal point at the entry. The mantle will be stone with large design element mounted above. Accent lighting to highlight this feature," this requirement is recorded in this section. If necessary, include rough sketches of your ideas. Any additional information that you can provide will improve your restaurant.

Lighting

The design, selection, and placement of lighting and light fixtures is based on function as well as aesthetics. While your design team may feel very comfortable in implementing your design intent, there may be some operational lighting requirements that are frequently overlooked. Adequate lighting for maintenance, the ease of re-lamping, location of switches and dimming devices, and lighting zones are covered here. Workstation lighting must be sufficient without being too conspicuous to guests. The standard lighting in walk-in coolers may not be adequate for your needs. Many operators specify fluorescent lighting in their coolers for greater coverage. When the operational plan states: "Chandeliers in main dining room. Inconspicuous focal lighting on wall art. Booth lighting to be zoned separately from rest of room," these are flags to the design team and are noted here. Lighting may be required in millwork and cabinetry either to highlight decorative elements or for task lighting.

Specialty Systems

Sound systems, phone systems, TV and cable systems, theater lighting, alarms, and any items that are designed and built into your restaurant are defined here. Some systems may require their own schedule. Telephone systems are not usually provided through the general contractor, and the requirements for these systems vary greatly. The number of lines, type of equipment, where lines are routed, and other special needs must be defined or they will not be included in the design. The telephone schedule at the end of this section can be useful in defining these requirements.

Service Requirements

You know what you need to service your guests' needs properly. Server stations, bus stations, auxiliary coat storage, and the use of carts, portable, or mobile equipment should all be noted.

Utilities

The utilities required for listed equipment will be picked up in the design process. But often, convenience utilities may be needed that do not tie into any equipment schedules. Hose bibs for maintenance in trash areas or kitchens, additional electrical outlets for portable equipment, maintenance or future items, and gas connections for seasonal equipment are a few examples. Sophisticated POS systems require dedicated circuits and phone lines. Highlight these needs here. Some information regarding utilities will come from vendors who supply equipment. Coffee equipment is a prime example. By noting that some of the equipment will be provided by vendors and needs to be verified, you are flagging a potential oversight.

Finishes

Durability and maintenance are important factors in the selection of finishes. In some places, such as walls in warewashing areas, behind the cooking line, or in trash areas, excessive heat or moisture will dictate the choice of materials. Carpet may be used for noise control as well as aesthetics. The use of wheeled carts will affect the way the carpet is installed.

Furnishings/Fixtures

Chairs, tables, booths, banquettes, stand-up rails for eating or drinking, and specialty millwork are explained here. Special or unusual spacing for tables or seating plans should also be mentioned.

Equipment

The specifics of your equipment needs are listed here. Often, a chef or manager will do a rough sketch of how the "line" should be laid out or how a server station should flow. When listing equipment, note any accessories or features that you need, such as casters, shelving, controls, or finishes. Attach these and make them an integral part of the design program.

Comments

List concerns or notes that are afterthoughts or do not fit the foregoing categories, such as acoustics or signage.

❖ # DESIGN PROGRAM SUMMARY

The summary sheet (Figure 5.2) gives a quick listing of the required spaces and total area required. A factor should be added for circulation space to give a realistic overall space requirement. This number will be important when researching potential sites. A seemingly ideal location that is 3700 square feet when your design program indicates a need for 4300 square feet may need to be reevaluated.

Room Number	Room Name	Area (sq. ft.)
Total		
Circulation		
TOTAL		

Comments: _____

_____

_____

_____

FIGURE 5.2   Design program summary.

Telephone Schedules

The telephone schedules make it very clear to your design team and phone company what lines you need and where you want them. Additional lines may be needed for portable phones, restricted customer phone, or rollover for credit card validation. Make notes to accompany the schedule that describe additional required features, such as intercom, speaker, conferencing, or paging.

SCHEDULE OF REQUIRED TELEPHONE LINES

Line Number	Description	Remarks	Phone Number
1	Restaurant line	Published number	
2	Restaurant line	On rollover	
3	Kitchen	Separate	
4	Fax		
5	Modem (credit cards)		

TELEPHONE SCHEDULE

Area	Location Reference (See Drawing)	Line Numbers	Equipment
Host	A	1,2	Wall phone
Bar	B	1,2	Desk phone
Bar	C	5	Wall jack
Kitchen	D	3	Wall phone
Office	E	1,2,3	Desk phone
Office	F	4	Wall jack
Office	G	5	Wall jack

Room Checklist

It is surprisingly easy to overlook a space or room when planning your restaurant. You may not realize it until well into your design phase, and because it wasn't listed in your design program, the design team may have presumed that you did not want or need it. The following checklist will help reduce the chance of overlooking a space or may alert you to a space that would be beneficial in your restaurant. Additionally, you will want each of these rooms to be individually labeled and numbered.

- Outside entry
- Vestibule/air lock
- Coatroom
- Waiting area
- Host stand or cubicle
- Cashier
- Retail sales kiosk
- Bar
- Bar service area
- Bar storage
- Liquor storage
- Beer storage: nonrefrigerated
- Beer storage: refrigerated
- Keg cooler
- Carbonated beverage system
- Wine storage
- Red wine storage: temperature controlled
- White wine storage: refrigerated
- Return bottle storage
- Bar server station
- Lounge

- Game room
- Dining room
- Server areas
- Private dining room
- Banquet room
- Server pickup
- Broiler station
- Fry station
- Saute station
- Pantry station
- Desert station
- Pasta station
- Grill station
- Pizza station
- Specialty cooking station
- Preparation area
- Bakery area
- Pastry area
- Butcher shop
- Ice cream room
- Dishwashing area
- Potwashing area

- ♦ Dish storage
- ♦ Glass storage
- ♦ Pot/pan storage
- ♦ Utensil storage
- ♦ Smallwares storage
- ♦ Walk-in cooler/freezer
- ♦ Specialty coolers/freezers: meat, fish, dairy, ice cream
- ♦ Dry goods storage
- ♦ Clean linen storage
- ♦ Soiled linen storage
- ♦ Nonfood storage
- ♦ Secured/specialty storage
- ♦ Trash room
- ♦ Recycling room
- ♦ Janitor's closet
- ♦ Wood storage

- ♦ Paper storage
- ♦ Chemical/cleaning supplies storage
- ♦ Employee rest room
- ♦ Employee lockers
- ♦ Employee changing room
- ♦ Employee dining area
- ♦ Administrative office
- ♦ Administrative storage
- ♦ Receiving area
- ♦ Loading area
- ♦ Mechanical room
- ♦ Public rest rooms: men
- ♦ Public rest rooms: women
- ♦ Public rest rooms: ADA access
- ♦ Outside storage
- ♦ Remote/off-site storage

S i x

Planning and Design

To be a successful restaurateur, you must first develop your restaurant successfully. When playing golf, you don't rush to tee-up on the first hole with your putter because you are anxious to putt, do you? Similarly, you do not wake up one morning and decide to build a restaurant. You take the time to prepare properly. This preparation means that you have completed certain activities that have brought you to this phase of your development.

If you are ready to begin the planning and design process, you have already:

♦ Prepared a business plan

♦ Written your operational plan

♦ Completed your design program

♦ Secured financing

♦ Selected a project manager and the initial members of the design team

The overall objective of the planning and design process is to produce a well-conceived and comprehensive set of construction documents (drawings and specifications), based on your design program, that communicate clearly to the contractor and subcontractors how to build your restaurant.

If you compare the development of your restaurant to the preparation of a complex entrée, the construction documents should be regarded as the "master recipe." Like many complex recipes, there are subrecipes within them. Entrées are made of component pieces: sauces, fillings, starches, vegetables, and garnishes, each with its own

157

recipe and list of ingredients. They may even have subrecipes within them. Together, these component recipes make up the master recipe for the complete entrée. Construction documents are the master recipe that defines what goes into building your restaurant and how these "ingredients" are assembled and fit together. Like a recipe, the true test of its success is how well it works: looks and tastes in the case of a recipe and communicates your desired intent in the case of the drawings and specifications.

The more detailed the drawings and specifications are, the less room there is for misinterpretation or unwanted creative license being taken by a contractor or supplier. However, too much detail may also result in unnecessary expense or a missed opportunity to benefit from creative field decisions that may save you time and money. The degree of detail required depends on the complexity of your development and the skill of your contractors and suppliers. The recipe for an omelet may simply state, "3 eggs, ¼ cup grated cheese, ¼ cup diced ham, seasoning to taste." The professional cook knows how to combine them and cook them. But the recipe for galantine of duck may require significantly more direction.

The completeness of your construction documents will depend, in part, on your approach to construction:

♦ Formal bidding

♦ Negotiated contract

♦ Design/build

It will also depend on how demanding you are of your design team. Decisions regarding design details and construction methods are made:

♦ During the design phase, well coordinated and with input from all members of your design team

♦ On site, during construction by your contractor and some members of your design team

♦ As required, by the person building or finishing the work with no other input

Many contractors and subcontractors know how things are built and go together. It may not be necessary to give them detailed drawings of a standard door jamb or raised floor platform. But they may be less comfortable with building a server station from a quick sketch or ¼-inch scale drawing when dimensions are critical and a lot of equipment must fit in a confined space.

Planning and designing your restaurant is a component of the development process. The documents created during this phase, if prepared properly, make achieving your overall objective—operating a successful restaurant—more probable. It is now necessary to make every effort to ensure that the process is not compromised. Your primary concerns during this phase should be that:

♦ The documents reflect your concept and are true to the design program.

♦ The facility contains all the components, features, and design elements that you require.

♦ Your equipment, furnishings, and fixtures specifications meet your needs.

♦ The mechanical, plumbing, electrical, and specialty systems meet your requirements.

♦ The documents are complete, coordinated, and comprehensive.

♦ You have not been forced to make unnecessary changes or sacrifices.

♦ The design is within your budget.

ROADBLOCKS TO ACHIEVING YOUR OBJECTIVE

There are unseen forces that may compromise your design and concept and thwart your best efforts to prepare a comprehensive set of construction documents. Be aware of them, guard against them, and do not let them affect your planning and design adversely.

1. *Egos of your team members.* It is probable that some members of your design team will modify, change, or ignore some of the elements of your design program because they don't like them or disagree with

them. Since they consider themselves experts, they may make these alterations without your knowledge or consent. Although their input is important, they should not be permitted to alter your concept arbitrarily.

2. *Personal agendas.* Designers often have styles, ideas, or design elements that they believe will work well in a restaurant. Your restaurant may present an ideal opportunity for them to try out these ideas, whether or not they are suited to your concept.

3. *Conflicts within the team.* You will find that individual professionals often regard their scope of work as the most critical. The result is that they compete for space. If you need a coatroom to accommodate 125 coats plus booster chair storage and this room is adjacent to your dry storage area or prep area, the kitchen spaces may be unnecessarily squeezed to accommodate a too spacious coatroom. Front-of-the-house versus back-of-the-house battles over space occur frequently. Your kitchen designer may not even see the space that he has to work with until after the space plan is complete and your architect has allocated the overall space. This forces your kitchen consultant to fight for critical space. Such battles are always at your expense.

4. *Quick and easy.* There is always more than one right answer. But many designers and consultants take their first attempt and consider it an acceptable design solution. Do not accept design solutions with which you are not comfortable. Insist on seeing a few options or alternative solutions.

5. *Tried and true.* "This is the way it is done" or "Sidestands work best like this" should not be taken as gospel. Many excellent design solutions and approaches result from taking a fresh look at standard problems.

6. *Time constraints.* Your design team members are working on more than just your restaurant. You are not their only client. As a result, they may feel pressure to crank out your drawings and, in the process, gloss over details that need to be better defined and thought through.

7. *Poor or self-serving advice.* Consultants, suppliers, and contractors may make recommendations to you that are based on criteria other than your best interests. They may recommend higher-priced furnishings or equipment, materials or finishes that are in stock, systems that are purchased through a preferred manufacturer, or features and accessories that are not needed. These choices may not necessarily be the best solutions or products for your restaurant.

8. *Lack of knowledge.* Sometimes, members of your design team will make a recommendation or specify a product because they think it is the best available. Unfortunately, they may not be aware of improved materials or new products. While you should expect the people you hire to be the most knowledgeable in their fields (and through the interview process you have reason to believe this to be true), do not be shy in asking about products, materials, or equipment that you have seen or read about.

9. *Unwillingness to change or alter drawings.* As silly as this sounds, many designers and architects regard their drawings as important works unto themselves. Although many architectural drawings have been displayed in galleries as a form of artistic expression, the documents prepared for the construction of your restaurant probably don't qualify. Even if they did, you did not commission a work of art, you are building a restaurant! This is mentioned because many designers will fight against changes or will be reluctant to alter a drawing because they are proud of their work and don't want to mar it. It is also seen as "not moving the documents along." Changes to the drawings are not seen as progress. Economics may also play a role. Some changes to the drawings do not qualify as "additional services." In such instances, the time spent making these changes is not billable. You must recognize, therefore, that their motivation to keep your plan "as is" may not be based on what is best operationally or aesthetically, but on a selfish desire to avoid changing or altering a drawing.

❖ COORDINATION

Nothing is more important in the planning and design of your restaurant than the effective coordination of the members of your design team. The best designs and ideas can be totally undermined by poor coordination. Ideas do not become reality and designs that looked good on paper don't work if coordination is lacking. An item as simple as a water heater requires collaboration among the architect, mechanical engineer, electrical engineer, structural engineer, food-service consultant, and perhaps, the interior designer. Why all these people? Because:

♦ The size and rate of recovery are based, in part, on the demands of the food-service equipment.

- ◆ The architect must allocate a room or appropriate space for the unit and related ductwork.

- ◆ Electrical service required for the controls, fans, and heating element is designed by the electrical engineer.

- ◆ The floor or platform the unit sits on must be designed by the structural engineer to handle the weight.

- ◆ The door location, if viewed by the public, may require a design treatment by the interior designer.

Nelson's Bar was undergoing a major upgrade. The intent was primarily to relocate the entry so that the public perceived the bar as totally independent from the office building in which it was located. A side benefit to this remodel was that the server work areas and storage areas could be redesigned and improved based on changes made to the menu and operating procedures. Management assembled several members of the bar staff to work on designing the required changes. They made rough sketches of their ideas and reviewed them with management. Much time and energy was spent thinking through how these areas would work and what new equipment and spaces were needed. Management gave these sketches to the owner who reviewed and approved them. As the project proceeded and construction was well under way, the manager would stop in and visit with the construction superintendent. During one of these visits, he asked about the progress of the service areas. The superintendent looked through his drawings. There were no details of the service areas and, as far as he was concerned, "someone else" was handling those areas. In a panic, the manager went to the owner. Yes, they had reviewed and approved the sketches made by the staff, but it was clear that no one reviewed them with the architects or followed through on coordinating these revisions with the development team. At this point, the changes were hastily implemented. The resulting remodel suffered. The tight schedule prevented a thorough review of shop drawings and specifications, utilities were improperly located, cabinetry was not built to receive the new equipment, and no one was happy with the end result. Poor coordination compromised a carefully planned and thought-out conceptual design. It was an easily avoidable and all-too-frequent oversight.

The job of coordination belongs to each and every design team member. But the responsibility for making sure that all the pieces work together falls on your owner's representative or project manager. Although your architect will typically coordinate the consulting engineers—structural, mechanical, plumbing, and electrical—the management and coordination of some of the other specialists may fall through the cracks. This is why your project manager must play this critical role. Earlier chapters have addressed an effective approach to choosing and managing your development team. Your project manager, chosen by you, must have as his sole interest the successful execution of your design program into a working restaurant. He will mediate conflicts, resolve discrepancies, make decisions, and in general, keep the focus of the design team on your objective.

All members of your design team will attempt to help you create the restaurant you want. But their orientation and prejudices will move them to address the concerns of their particular discipline. Your architect, traditionally the project coordinator, may not fully understand the operational aspects of your restaurant. Kitchen designers know kitchens. Electrical engineers understand the restaurant power and circuitry. Mechanical engineers focus on the movement and treatment of the air in your restaurant. No one, outside your project manager, will fully consider the requirements of all these disciplines in the context of your functioning restaurant. Of course, many architects, interior designers, and foodservice consultants are well versed in restaurant operations and do look out for the functional implications of their designs. But they may weigh the benefit of design versus function differently from the operator. And the operator may not be comfortable enough with design to fully understand the decisions that he is being asked to make. This is where your project manager comes in. In the initial stages of the design process, it is the project manager who will ensure that special interests or stronger personalities do not compromise the design program. He will, as your representative, review and resolve the continuous conflicts between operational and aesthetic requirements. Often, both can be accommodated without compromise. But it takes a skilled and unbiased mediator to find the solution that works best for the restaurant.

❖ PROFESSIONAL DISCIPLINES AND THEIR RESPONSIBILITIES

The specific disciplines that may be involved in your restaurant development have been described earlier. The planning and design stage of your development requires that all of these people work together in a coordinated effort to design the facility that will become your restaurant. This point cannot be overstressed. Your restaurant building is a tool or machine. It is the vehicle that enables you to operate your particular style of restaurant. How this machine is planned and the features and functions it includes will determine how well you can operate.

The following list identifies the disciplines that will be contributing to your restaurant design and will be involved in the preparation of your contract documents. Understand that their scope of service may vary from those presented here. Some professionals may offer services that encompass more than one discipline. The essential purpose of this list is to impress on you the array of talents that will be working on your restaurant development and whose contribution must be managed and coordinated.

- Owners' representative/ project manager
- Architect
- Specification writer
- Structural engineer
- Mechanical engineer
- Electrical engineer
- Interior designer
- Food facilities designer
- Landscape architect
- Graphic artist
- Sound system consultant
- Acoustical engineer
- Lighting consultant
- Security system consultant
- Purchasing contractor
- Foodservice equipment supplier
- Exhaust hood manufacturer
- Hood fire protection supplier
- Fire sprinkler supplier
- Walk-in cooler manufacturer
- Refrigeration system consultant
- Water filtration system supplier
- Specialty floor manufacturer
- Hardware supplier
- Lighting supplier
- POS supplier
- Carbonated beverage supplier
- Wine supplier
- Coffee/tea/beverage supplier
- Phone company representative
- Satellite or cable company representative

❖ THE COST TO BUILD VERSUS THE COST TO OPERATE

Many of the decisions that you make during the design process will be budget related. While your design program has specified much of the design criteria for your restaurant, there will always be details that must be refined or choices that require decisions. The selection of materials will be determined, in part, based on their cost. In some cases you will reduce the coverage or square footage of expensive finish material to reduce the cost without compromising the most vulnerable areas. But some of these decisions may be made by your design team without their full understanding of the impact their cost savings will have on your day-to-day operation.

Wall, floor, and base finishes in the kitchen provide a typical example. Areas that are subjected to excessive moisture or water—dish- and potwashing areas, some preparation areas, janitor's sink and mop closets—need to be finished with materials that are truly waterproof. Fiber-reinforced plastic (FRP board) or ceramic tile is ideally suited for this purpose. The walls behind cooking equipment need to be finished with a material that can withstand excessive heat and can be subjected to heavy scrubbing and abrasive cleaners. Stainless steel or tile works well in these areas.

The juncture of the floor, base, and wall finishes must be watertight as well and finished with materials that can stand up to the anticipated or expected working and maintenance environment. Compromises or poor selections of materials for these areas may save initial cost but will require additional expenditures for maintenance and replacement prematurely.

Other decisions that adversely affect day-to-day operations are the quality of hardware, solid versus hollow-core doors, quality of light fixtures, number of floor drains, and the number of convenience electrical receptacles. It is advisable to plan your restaurant with all the features and amenities that you want. Then, during your budget review process, evaluate the specific areas where costs exceed your budget and make informed decisions. Do not compromise until you know what the true cost of the compromise is.

The cost of compromise can be evaluated based on its impact or effect on:

♦ Maintenance

♦ Expected life and replacement

♦ Future availability of parts

♦ Equipment performance

♦ Service

♦ Guest comfort

♦ Labor cost

♦ Operating costs

♦ Storage space

♦ Circulation, traffic flow, or work space

♦ Seating capacity or flexibility

You may not know what decisions your design team has made that will adversely compromise your day-to-day or long-term costs. How can you find out? There are 11 primary checkpoints that can prevent or identify unintentional or inappropriate decisions affecting your maintenance.

1. *Clearly state your expectations.* Specify low-maintenance, heavy-duty, commercial-grade, or energy-efficient materials. It is not necessary to identify brand names. What you are calling out is a standard of performance. Based on this standard, the person writing the specifications will write the appropriate text. There are many electronically controlled, computer-activated or computer-managed products on the market. Without knowing them specifically, you can establish the standard by indicating that you want "dining room lighting to have preset levels that can be set by management." This will alert the spec writers of your "standard of performance."

2. *Describe your requirements for flexibility or future expansion.* Unless you make it clear that you anticipate adding a counter-model steamer or want the space and utilities to add or use future appliances or equipment, your design team will plan and engineer your space for what is specified. Some additional capacity is required by code, but

never enough to allow for significant equipment additions. By indicating in your design program, during project meetings, or during the review process that additional electrical load, gas capacity, hot-water demands, or general expansion plans are required, you will be saving yourself significant expense down the road. Increasing primary utility feeds now is usually much less expensive and easier to accomplish that adding them in the future.

3. *Indicate specific materials where necessary.* Because of your research or from previous experience, you may be familiar with materials or finishes that appeal to you. Even if you dont know the name, describe the material so that it can be found by the specifier "that plastic wall material" is enough to identify Marlite or FRP board. Getting samples to ensure that the selection is correct is an easy solution. Epoxy paint, quarry tile floors, or stainless steel on certain wall surfaces may be listed in the design program. Repeating your requirements only reinforces them.

4. *Visit and learn* from well-maintained and well-operated restaurants. See what brands, equipment, and materials they use. The owner of the Mogul Restaurant believed in hosing down his kitchen every night. He was adamant about having faucets strategically placed throughout his kitchen so that he could attach a hose and wash down the floor and walls. This requirement led to others: watertight electrical boxes behind the range line, extra floor drains, waterproof wall finishes, and floors with integral coved bases and a good seal at the wall. When restaurateur Pam Johnson met with him to discuss her upcoming restaurant, he strongly recommended to her that she consider similar cleaning techniques and to plan for them in her design. These were not excessive demands. But had they not been brought up either in the design program or during a project meeting, these features may not have been included in the design.

5. *Ask to see samples of finishes specified.* If you are unfamiliar with materials proposed, get samples or find out who uses them locally. A highly touted sealer may not hold up to heat or scrubbing with heavy-duty cleaners or abrasives. Products may vary from manufacturer to manufacturer in terms of color, surface characteristics, thickness, or durability. By examining a sample, you will be able to make a more informed decision.

6. *Test products at your site*, if possible. Many coatings, sealers, and finishes can be applied in small quantities over small areas so that you can see how they look, feel, and perform. Many manufacturers and sup-

pliers will gladly offer to do this to demonstrate their product and earn a sale.

7. *Write for information* from ads in the trade press. Products designed for restaurant use are often promoted in trade or food magazines. Although many products promoted in the trade press are not uncommon, new products, equipment, and materials are marketed through these media as well.

8. *Ask your specialty consultants for ideas.* Your foodservice designer may know products and materials that are unfamiliar to your architect or interior designer. One of the many benefits of scheduled project meetings is the interaction that occurs among the members of your design team. When your interior designer is discussing materials being considered for the bar top or wait stations, your foodservice consultant may offer constructive comments or alternatives. Tile is often used on bar tops or serving counters. Aesthetically, it may offer many advantages. But maintenance, cracking or chipping, or the irregular surface may conflict with the intended use. Discussions among the design team members will address these issues and solutions, or acceptable compromises may be reached.

9. *Raise the subject again and again* during your design review meetings and make sure that the issue is addressed and resolved. Another benefit of scheduled project meetings is to address specific issues, assign responsibilities, and resolve questions. By making maintenance or special use an issue at these meetings, you make it a high priority with your design team.

10. *Review the plan of your restaurant from a maintenance viewpoint.* Throughout the design process, you will be reviewing the drawings. Go through the motions of filling a mop bucket, getting a hose, or other maintenance activities. The design program for Clarence's Grill called for a janitor's closet with a mop basin and rack for mops and brooms to be located near the receiving/storage areas. The conceptual plan incorporated this requirement. However, when Clarence looked at his plan from a maintenance viewpoint, he realized that while the mop sink was ideally suited for kitchen maintenance, it was difficult to transport a full mop bucket to the rest-room areas. Subsequently, he added a second mop closet near the public rest rooms to facilitate their cleaning and maintenance.

11. *Read the performance standards* of proposed equipment. Words like *high recovery, well insulated, heavy duty*, and so on, will let you

know the manufacturers expectations. Some materials are not recommended for certain uses. Heat, sunlight, temperature fluctuations, water, or alcohol may affect adhesives or material performance. Although it is reasonable to assume that your design team will not specify a product that is unfit for the intended use, they may not comprehend fully the uses intended.

❖ THE DESIGN PROCESS

The members of your development team have been given a considerable amount of information which they must read and understand before they put pencil to paper. What happens now? If you glance back at the restaurant development diagram, you will see that many design-related activities have been under way since your development started. These activities have been triggered by other activities. These will, in turn, initiate other tasks either when they are completed or have reached a certain milestone. The design process has, in fact, been progressing. You have:

- ♦ Prepared your business plan

- ♦ Developed your preliminary operational plan

- ♦ Drafted your design program

- ♦ Done a preliminary inspection and evaluation of the site

- ♦ Selected and assembled your design team

- ♦ Assigned responsibilities to your development team members involved in the design

- ♦ Established a preliminary schedule

There are two critical activities that occur at this time:

1. Verification of field conditions

2. Code review

These activities, if not performed properly or thoroughly, can jeopardize your design and may force you to redesign your entire restaurant.

Verification of Field Conditions

It is not uncommon for there to be existing drawings of your space. These drawings may be of the previous tenant's space or prints of the original building's construction documents. They may include architectural plans and details, mechanical and electrical drawings, or a partial set of these documents. Drawings provided by a landlord or broker may show space boundaries and some of the interior fixtures or features. And the document itself may be a photocopy or not "true to scale." As complete and accurate as these drawings may appear, do not forego field verification.

Just because there are existing drawings does not mean that they are correct or accurate. Often, changes made during construction are not reflected on the drawings. So walls located on the drawings may not actually be where they are shown. Inaccuracies on drawings may not have affected previous tenants but may have a significant impact on your design. Many aspects of drawings are schematic and do not accurately show actual sizes, routing, or location. Other factors that affect the accuracy of existing drawings are the following:

1. *Drawings do not reflect your total space.* The space allocated to you may have changed from the space leased by the preceding tenant. Adjacent tenants may have taken over a corner or moved a wall to increase their space. Additionally, common areas such as an elevator lobby, a vestibule, public rest rooms, or a coatroom may not be shown but may be subject to your design influence.

2. *Drawings are not updated to reflect design or construction changes.* Partitions may be relocated. Doors or windows may have been moved or closed off. Ceiling heights or floor levels may have been altered.

3. *Specification changes or model upgrades result in sizes different sizes from those drawn.* In addition to some equipment shown schematically (not to true scale), different models or manufacturers may result in sizes and utility requirements different from those shown.

4. *Construction methods used may alter dimensions shown.* If a wall thickness is changed in the field to accommodate plumbing piping or ductwork, it may not be shown on the existing drawings. The method used to connect walls or the finishes used may also alter the true dimensions.

5. *The condition of the structure, materials, finishes, equipment, and furnishings*—wear and tear, water or fire damage—is not indicated. Merely knowing that the water heater or electrical panel is adequately sized may not tell the entire story. If the equipment is in poor repair, replacement may be the most economical choice. When replacement is being considered, location, size, and features become important criteria. The condition of finishes may dictate how a surface is refinished. Patching and repairing may not be sufficient. A covering layer of drywall may be required to salvage a badly damaged wall surface. In such cases, the interior dimension of a room or area will change.

6. *Changes to or requirements of adjacent spaces may have altered the dimensions of your space.* Sound or noise attenuation or fire separations may have been added between your space and an adjacent space. Relocated doors or hallways or some negotiated compromises with adjacent tenants may also have altered your space.

When your design team talks of making a site visit to verify field conditions, they are referring to the physical characteristics of the existing space. These characteristics may be readily apparent or hidden and include:

Site Characteristics.   Surveys are used to determine property lines, utility line locations, easements, elevations, existing site features, and actual building placement on a site. It is usually not necessary to get an updated survey unless the site or building has be altered. If building expansion is being considered, soils testing may be required for calculating structural loads. It is important to verify that existing conditions are, in fact, existing. What is often not indicated on site plans, whether your location is a freestanding site, building, or space within a building are:

♦ Tenants, buildings, or spaces adjacent to, above, or below your space. This affects the barriers required between spaces for noise or fire. It also may affect routing of ductwork and other utilities. The activities generated by these tenants may also affect your development. Deliveries, trash, and pedestrian and automobile traffic may affect your design or circulation.

♦ The flow of traffic past or around the space. This information may determine the orientation of the signage, restaurant entry, location of the bar, or other access or visibility issues. Adjacent signage that may affect your sign placement in terms of visibility.

♦ Views and site lines from your building, proposed patios, or windows. What you learn here could affect the design of awnings, patio walls, landscaping, and other elements to either shield or enhance these views.

♦ The condition of parking lots, landscaping, exterior lighting, and outbuildings.

♦ Additions or remodeling that may not be noted on the site plan.

♦ New or relocated roof-mounted equipment.

Dimensions. The first requirement is to confirm what space is, in fact, allocated to your restaurant. Often, common areas such as elevator lobbies, rest rooms, or vestibules may be subject to your design control even though the space is not included in your leaseable space. Or access to necessary areas that are not within your leased premises, such as parking garage elevators, trash dumpsters, or public rest rooms, may affect the layout of your restaurant. It is better to show too much than not enough.

The true measurements of the space you have to work with must be field verified. All dimensions must be verified even if the area does not seem critical or if "all the other dimensions seem to be accurate." There are numerous stories of restaurant designs not fitting because they were based on drawings prepared for previous tenants or drawings that were checked, but not completely.

Giovanni's based their seating plan on an existing floor plan. The person assigned to verify the interior dimensions checked several dimensions and found them to be consistent with the drawings. Unfortunately, he did not check all dimensions and did not check the plan's written dimensions against the drawing. By using the existing drawing as the base plan, the design team prepared the seating plan. The chairs, tables, and booths were ordered off this plan and confirmed with the design team. When the furniture arrived and was being installed, it became very clear that the seating plan as drawn would not fit in the actual space. After minutes of trying to figure out if the booths were the right size or the tables were too big, someone measured the overall length of the dining area and then scaled it on the drawing. The plan was off by 4 feet! This painful lesson could have been avoided if the person assigned to field-verify the existing conditions did the job thoroughly and correctly.

Verifying dimensions entails checking the actual measurements of the space, features, and fixtures, including:

♦ Interior wall-to-wall dimensions

♦ Finishes, type of glazing, fire ratings of doors

♦ Thickness of partitions

♦ Ceiling heights

♦ Distance between a dropped ceiling and the structure above

♦ Size and location of door and window openings

♦ Changes in elevation of floors because of stairs, ramps, or curbs

♦ Location of utilities: floor drains, water supply, electrical panels, water heaters, mechanical systems, ductwork routing and enclosures, fire detection and protection systems, fire dampers, and access panels, and other existing conditions

♦ Identifying and dimensioning structural elements: columns, bearing walls, cross-bracing, stair and elevator towers, or other structural elements

♦ Exterior dimensions of the storefront, building facade, parapets, signage location, patio space, awnings, and other features.

Construction Materials and Finishes. Determine the construction of existing walls, floors, and ceilings. This is necessary because it will affect how you build or modify existing conditions, how new construction is detailed, and the type and application of new finishes. It may be necessary to punch holes in existing walls or ceilings to determine what is inside or how they are constructed. Such inspections will also help determine the routing of utilities. Does an electrical conduit come up from the floor, down from the ceiling, or run horizontally? Is there a need for blocking or insulation? What are the quality and condition of the materials?

Utilities. The location, size, capacity, and condition of all existing utilities must be shown. Although these may be abandoned or relocated, it is important to know what exists. It may be possible to reuse, add to, or maintain all or part of the existing utilities without compromising your design. Inspecting these items will also determine their condition and if they are worth saving and reusing or if they need to be replaced or upgraded to comply with current codes. These items include:

♦ Electrical panels, transformers, wiring, and receptacles

♦ Control panels, disconnects, and switches

♦ Gas meter, gas piping, and valves

♦ Water meter, piping, and valves

♦ Filtering systems

♦ Water heater

♦ Grease trap

♦ Floor sinks and drains

♦ Heating and air-conditioning units and ductwork

♦ Related routing of conduit, pipes, and ductwork

Existing Equipment, Furnishings, and Fixtures. Remodels or takeovers of existing restaurants may require taking an inventory of items that are to remain. It may be necessary to inventory all items that are existing and later verify which items will actually be left in place. This inventory will also help if the items left in the space are not included but are available for purchase. These items may be built-in or freestanding and include:

♦ Kitchen and bar equipment

♦ Light fixtures

♦ Chairs, tables, booths

♦ Furniture and artifacts

♦ Specialty systems: sound, phones, alarms

When inspecting and inventorying these items, it is necessary to note the:

♦ Manufacturer

♦ Model number

♦ Dimensions

♦ Features

♦ Utilities

♦ Condition

Several members of the design team may be involved in performing these site inspections since they each bring their own specialty and expertise to the investigation. This information will be used to prepare a reference plan and building sections of the existing space that will be used to inform the other members of your design team of existing conditions that affect their work. These documents will be used as the starting point for the schematic design of your restaurant.

Code Review

Most building or remodeling projects are required to have a permit. The permit or permits are issued by governmental agencies, usually building departments. These permits are issued after these agencies have reviewed your documents for compliance with governing codes. These "codes" are laws and regulations that govern what you must do, can do, and can't do when planning, designing, and building a restaurant. Since the codes that govern your particular location and building cover many specific areas, are prepared by many agencies, may overlap, and can be interpreted differently, it is necessary for your design team to determine what codes apply to your restaurant, to become familiar with them and to comply with them. The initial process they use to do this is often referred to as a *code review*.

Requirements vary greatly depending on your jurisdiction. It is necessary for your design team to understand what is required in terms of drawings, specifications, and documentation and what professional certification may be required of the individual members of your design team. There are certain elements of the design process that are not optional and must be addressed. Code compliance is one of them. Attempting to bypass or disregard these requirements may cost you time and money.

The codes that may apply to your restaurant include:

1. *Zoning regulations.* Your primary zoning issue is "approved use" of the space. This determination is part of your preliminary code review when you are researching a location. Your site selection process should eliminate any locations that are not "zoned" for restaurants, liquor li-

censes, cabaret licenses, retail sales, or other intended uses you propose. Zoning regulations will also affect signage, building heights and setbacks, patios and outdoor dining, railings and fences, awnings, parking requirements, and noise (music and entertainment). Zoning regulations are often set by municipalities and vary greatly.

2. *Building codes.* This is the overall regulation that deals with the construction of your restaurant. The primary function of building codes is to "protect the health and safety of the public." The building code sets the requirements for permits, building size, access and egress, construction materials, and the life, fire, and structural safety aspects of the building.

3. *Plumbing, mechanical and electrical codes.* These govern their specific discipline with the same primary objective as building codes.

4. *Health department regulations.* This code governs all aspects of your food and beverage receiving, storage, preparation, cooking, service, and related areas. It often specifies acceptable materials and finishes, equipment design and construction standards, exhaust and ventilation requirements, lighting, circulation space, sanitation requirements, and toilet facilities. These regulations vary greatly, and if not consulted in advance, can dramatically alter your design.

5. *Americans with Disabilities Act.* This regulation defines the access, egress, and circulation requirements necessary to accommodate people with disabilities. Many restaurants have been required to make significant modifications to their spaces to comply with these regulations.

6. *Local covenants or restrictions.* Aside from the applicable governmental regulations, you may have to comply with guidelines established by condominium associations, management companies, malls, neighborhood groups, or building owners. This is another critical area where project management and coordination play a key role. It is the responsibility of your design team to determine which codes apply to your space and to document how these codes affect the design of your restaurant. But some nongovernmental regulations as described above do not fall clearly under anyone's jurisdiction. Although these requirements may have become known during lease negotiations, the responsibility for following up on them may not have been clearly assigned. It is, therefore, necessary for your project manager to bring these requirements to the attention of your design team.

7. *Franchisee or licensee requirements.* In addition to the foregoing requirements, you may be subject to rules and regulations established by your parent organization, franchiser, or licensing agency. These groups often have specific requirements for furnishings and equipment, basic restaurant design, colors, and materials. Noncompliance may result in redesign or construction delays.

Phases of Design

The architectural profession has divided the design process into three phases:

1. Schematic design

2. Design development

3. Construction documents

This approach breaks the design process down into workable components that force and encourage review and approval before the next phase begins.

Schematic Design Phase. Based on your design program, field-verified drawings, and the information gained from the code review, your design team will prepare a plan of the restaurant that shows the required spaces and their interrelationships. This is a loose, broad-stroke plan of your restaurant. It is your design team's first pass at incorporating the requirements of your design program into a finite space.

Many decisions are made during the schematic design phase that establish the basic layout and organization of your restaurant. It is the basic building block of the construction documents and must be developed with input from every member of the design team. Too often, subordinate consultants—food service, interior design—and engineers are not included in this schematic design process. As a result, the plan that is presented to the owner may have fatal flaws in terms of space allocation or orientation that the owner does not see. If the plan is approved, the momentum is established to move forward rather than regroup and revise the "already approved" schematic design.

The schematic design should not be presented to the owner until all members of the design team have had an opportunity to review and critique it unimpeded by the owner's preview. They should review it from their specialized perspectives and push and shove the pieces around until all their concerns are heard and resolved. The presentation may be formal or informal. But the objective is the same: to show and explain the design team's interpretation of the design program. The design team members will explain their placement of rooms and spaces, guest and service flow, and seating. They will point out other features and amenities that your design program prescribed. When necessary, they will explain why they could not satisfy certain requirements or how they had to make modifications to your program based on physical constraints.

The schematic plan and elevations will be primarily architectural; structural, mechanical, plumbing, and electrical systems and equipment and kitchen and bar equipment are not presented at this time. However, because the schematic plan was reviewed by these disciplines, there can be a confident belief that the space required to accommodate these items is included in this plan. The schematic design phase is an ideal time for the design team to present perspective sketches or illustrations to help communicate the design ideas to the restaurant developer. A lack of familiarity with plans and elevations can be overcome with simple yet clear illustrations of key view or design elements.

The drawings presented may be freehand, but to scale. With computer drafting it is often easy to present these drawings in a more finished-looking form. However they are presented, they should include three principal elements:

1. *Site plan* (if applicable), showing:

♦ Building orientation on site

♦ Access and egress

♦ Parking

♦ Landscaping and outside seating areas

♦ Trash area and other outbuildings

2. *Floor plan*, showing all rooms and spaces as described in the design program, including:

♦ Room names

♦ Seating

♦ Floor elevation changes

♦ Rest rooms for men and women according to code requirements

♦ Kitchen work areas with equipment and exhaust hood areas defined

♦ Kitchen storage and support areas

♦ Traffic pattern for customers, servers, and staff

♦ Site lines to kitchen, service areas, rest rooms

♦ Location, size, and shape of bar

♦ Space allocated for mechanical and electrical systems

3. *Interior elevations* or sketches, which show:

♦ Key design elements

♦ Changes in floor elevations and ceiling heights

♦ Basic structure

Review. The purpose of the review is to determine if the plan proposed complies with the design program, operational plan, and your general design ideas. It is not a pass/fail test. Some parts of the plan may be acceptable and other rejected or modified.

Your focus should be on the following:

♦ Are all rooms and spaces shown?

♦ Are the sizes acceptable?

♦ Do the relationships work operationally?

♦ Are walkways and aisles adequate?

♦ Does the seating plan—seating mix, table and chair sizes, style of seating—comply with your requirements?

♦ Are work stations adequate and located properly?

♦ Is customer flow acceptable?

♦ Is server flow functional?

♦ Is circulation within the kitchen acceptable?

The schematic review may prompt program changes or refinements. You may want to move the office to gain a better view of the receiving area, or rethink the size of the employee locker room to gain additional dry storage space. The hallway at the receiving area may need to be widened to serve as a staging area so that the dry storage area size can be maintained. Seeing the spaces you defined in the design program on paper may give you a better idea of how the spaces interact. From this viewpoint, your programming priorities may change and relationships you thought were critical become insignificant.

Your program may have indicated that the pantry area be easily accessible to the convection oven at the prep area. But on seeing the plan, you realize that while this may work for the pantry worker, the flow within the prep area is disjointed and the oven should be at the other side. As you think about why the pantry needed access to the convection oven, you realize that the pantry person can use the adjacent range oven just as effectively. It is not uncommon for parts of the design to be approved while others are still being refined. Server station locations and seating layouts are often adjusted and relocated as the plan is refined. The organization of equipment under the hood or the details of the cooks table are shuffled as preparation methods and workstations evolve.

Review and refinement of the schematic plan may take several attempts. Remember that your approval of the schematic design does not preclude you from making changes as the design progresses. Your design team expects changes and refinements in the early stages of the design process. However, as you move into design development, the nature of the changes should be more refinement. Significant design changes will not be expected and may be met with strong opposition.

It is true that the further along in the design process you are, the greater the impact your changes have on all the design disciplines involved. However, do not let the design team pressure you into not making a change based on the cost in design time or dollars. One way of evaluating the cost/benefit of making a change is the "Saturday night rule": Consider the consequence on your service, customer comfort and your overall ability to perform on a busy Saturday night if you do not make the change. Is it worth the time and money to make the change now, or can you function well enough without it? This quick analysis can be used throughout the design and construction phases as one tool to assess the merits of a design change.

Budget Update. This is one of several budget reviews that will occur during the design process. Even at this stage, you can begin to get a handle on construction costs and the furniture, fixtures, and equipment budgets. Architects and engineers have reference books or software programs that provide budgeting formulas. They may have actual cost figures from similar projects they have completed recently. If you are working with a contractor on a "design/build" or "negotiated bid" basis, the contractor will review the schematics with the subcontractors and arrive at reasonable budget figures. Similarly, interior designers and foodservice equipment firms can work with you to generate reasonable budgets based on your schematic design. Although these budgets are preliminary, they will be more refined than the budgets presented in your business plan and they will be updated and refined regularly.

Use a detailed line-item budget form to track your costs. The form used for the capital expenditures budget in your business plan is a good working document. But many of the categories will require breakdowns to categorize your budgeted costs further. Where necessary, develop subschedules so that you have a clear understanding of where your money is being spent.

1. *Contract services.* You should have written, signed contracts for all the professional services you have retained, explaining clearly the fees being charged. Where expenses are additional, request estimates for budget purposes. Hourly contracts should have estimates and weekly updates or "not to exceed" amounts.

2. *Construction.* Construction budgets are frequently divided by areas, known as "divisions." Since this amount will account for a significant part of your total development budget, it is important to refine it as quickly as possible. Your contractor should use the standard categories described below.

♦ Division 1—General conditions: permits, supervision, temporary facilities, activities related to project management, and establishing and maintaining the work environment and administrative activities necessary to complete the construction process.

♦ Division 2—Site work and demolition: subsurface work, clearing, earthmoving, foundation work, site utilities, drainage, landscaping, and related work.

♦ **Division 3—Concrete:** formwork, reinforcement, cast-in-place, special finishes, precast units, and decks.

♦ **Division 4—Masonry:** stone, brick, block, and related components.

♦ **Division 5—Metals:** Structural steel framing, joists, decking, general framing, ornamental metal, and fabricated items.

♦ **Division 6—Wood and plastics:** rough carpentry, heavy timber construction, structural wood members, finish carpentry, architectural woodwork, and prefabricated plastics.

♦ **Division 7—Thermal and moisture protection:** water- and dampproofing, insulation, roofing and siding, traffic toppings, and sealants.

♦ **Division 8—Doors and windows:** wood, metal, and specialty doors and windows, storefronts, hardware, and glazing.

♦ **Division 9—Finishes:** stud and metal framing, plaster, gypsum wallboard, tile, terrazzo, acoustical treatments, suspended ceilings, resilient flooring, carpet, specialty flooring, coatings, paint, and wallcovering.

♦ **Division 10—Specialties:** chalkboards, lockers, grills and screens, corner guards, access panels, fireplaces, signage, rest-room accessories.

♦ **Division 11—Equipment:** kitchen, bar and service area, and laundry equipment falls under this category and is often treated as a separate package "by owner" or "by others." Any work related to this activity, such as staging or installation, should be listed.

♦ **Division 12—Furnishings:** chairs, tables, booths, specialty cabinetry, artwork, and accessories are often supplied "by owner" or "by others." Any work related to this activity, such as staging or installation, should be listed.

♦ **Division 13—Special construction:** sound booths, disco booths, special ceilings, and sound and vibration control.

♦ **Division 14—Conveying systems:** elevators, dumbwaiters, and escalators.

♦ **Division 15—Mechanical:** plumbing (water and gas), heating, ventilation and air conditioning, fire protection, refrigeration, and related controls. Refrigeration is often treated as a separate item with a separate subcontractor; it is also frequently considered part of the foodservice equipment package. Verify that it is included in one or the other. Final connection of the foodservice equipment falls under this division.

♦ **Division 16—Electrical:** primary service, distribution, power, lighting, controls, communication systems, wiring, and electrical controls for specialty systems provided by others. Final connection of the foodservice equipment falls under this division.

These divisions cover all aspects of construction. By breaking the budget down into this detail, you are less likely to overlook something. As the budget is refined, even these divisions will have subschedules or further line-item detail.

3. *Specialty Items.* Many items fall outside the general construction budget and must be accounted for separately. These items are typically provided "by owner" or "by others." These specialty items are listed in the capital expenditures budget form. When budgeting these items, you should get proposals from potential suppliers rather than develop "guesstimates." Phone calls to potential vendors will provide at least a realistic budget figure.

4. *Furniture, fixtures, and equipment.* The single line items presented in your initial budget will now need to be refined. Unit cost times the yardage or square footage based on the plans will provide a more accurate figure for carpeting, specialty flooring, and wall finishes. Kitchen and bar equipment can be tied to a more specific listing and line-item schedule. Seating can be costed-out based on a schedule prepared from your preliminary plan.

5. *Freight, taxes, delivery, and installation.* These items can amount to a considerable sum and are frequently overlooked. Freight can be as much as 10 or 12 percent of the actual cost of the furniture, fixtures, and equipment (FF&E). Delivery and installation are separate from freight. Freight gets your FF&E from the manufacturer to a local warehouse or staging area. Delivery gets these items from the staging area to the site. Installation involves uncrating, assembling, setting in place, and securing or sealing to walls or floors as required. Final connections of utilities are handled by the general contractor through the subcontractors. These budget items can account for thousands of dollars and should be based on realistic estimates.

Design Development Phase. This phase refines the schematic design, establishing critical dimensions, structural elements, and systems: steel versus concrete, placing equipment, coordinating mechanical and electrical systems, selecting finish materials, and expanding on the interior design of your restaurant. Throughout the schematic design and design development phases, the design team should be interacting and communicating. The project manager should be intimately involved in these meetings or receive copies of all correspondence.

As design development progresses, you and your operational staff will still be refining and modifying your operational plan. Product research may force you to alter plans. You may find a some great bread basket that changes your approach to service. As these ideas are refined, they need to be coordinated with your project manager, who will, in turn, incorporate them into the design program. These changes will work their way through the design team.

Review. Once again, it is necessary for you to review the drawings and budgets. An important role of the project manager is to walk you through the drawings and make sure that you understand them. Changes made to the design program should be reflected in these drawings. If these changes have been omitted or altered, you need to know why and the reasoning behind the design team's decisions. You may have expanded the work area at the main wait station to 15 feet of counter space, basing this number on a rough layout you did of this area. If the drawings show only 12 feet of work space, you need to know why. Perhaps the added length eliminated a table or encroached on an aisle or service corridor. Operationally, the 3-foot loss may be critical. You need to weigh the cost of the table against your service procedures or modify the work area.

The updated budgets should also be reviewed. While parts may still be based on assumptions, allowances, or square-foot costs, these budgets are getting progressively more detailed. Your focus during this review should be on the following:

1. *Have your changes been implemented?* The refinements to your operational plan may require changes to the design program. Keeping these changes current is necessary if you expect your restaurant to function properly.

2. *Are you comfortable with any compromises you are asked to make?* Yes, there will be compromises. Limitations of space or constraints imposed by materials or shapes of spaces will require some rethinking

or adjustments in the design of your restaurant. Budget compromises may also play a role now or later in the development process.

3. *Are the critical dimensions correct?* You need to know or figure out what the critical dimensions are for your restaurant and be certain that they are not violated to make a plan work on paper. These may include:

♦ Accurate dimensions of kitchen and bar equipment

♦ Spacing of equipment away from walls for utility connections and ventilation

♦ Kitchen aisle and circulation space

♦ Serving aisles and public trafficways

♦ Server station sizes and related circulation space

♦ Door openings

4. *Does the equipment lay out as planned?* As the plan is refined, changes in the operational plan may affect the size or model of equipment. The new, larger models may not be shown, requiring work surfaces or sinks to be reduced in size. You may have shifted equipment to better organize work areas. These changes should be reflected in the plans.

5. *Is the revised seating plan acceptable?* Your seating plan will be massaged and adjusted constantly. Restaurateurs know that seats and seating units are the revenue generators for their business and they are always refining the seating layout.

6. *Do the server stations work?* As the equipment requirements for these areas becomes more refined and the tasks performed at these stations are more clearly defined, the size of these workstations becomes more exact. Trying to squeeze 10 feet of necessary counter space into 8 or 9 feet may adversely affect service and negate the benefit of any increased seating.

7. *Are changes required based on recent revisions to the design program or operational plan?* You should realize that improvements, refinements and changes to your operational plan and design program are a natural part of the development process. Any modifications to the drawings required because of these improvements should not be regarded as poor planning. It is, in fact, smart planning to have the foresight to improve your operation before you create built-in deficiencies.

Throughout the design and review process, you have been refining the plans based on your design program and your operational plan. The design team has been at these meetings raising questions that will help them refine their drawings and specifications. Before the design team gets too involved in the construction documents phase, there are critical operational issues that need to be addressed that may not have been covered in earlier document review sessions. These are details that affect operations and need to be addressed from an operational viewpoint.

1. *Location of light switches and thermostats.* These should be located based on who controls these functions.

2. *Zones for lighting control.* It is the operator who knows how the dining areas will be sectioned and if certain types of seating require different light levels. A wall of booths may need to be controlled separately from the overhead lights to create a different look or mood.

3. *Location of miscellaneous electrical receptacles.* Convenience outlets and special receptacles for hand-held or counter appliances are not always scheduled with the equipment or planned for on the electrical drawings. Placement and requirements for vacuums, flashlights, holiday lighting, promotional signage, or similar items need to be identified and located on the drawings so that overall loads and panel sizes can be designed properly.

4. *Placement and utilities requirements for owner- or supplier-provided equipment.* Although such items as coffee brewers, POS systems, computers, a sound system, and a security system are often noted or scheduled, they are often marked "verify." This means that no definite provisions have been made for these items, although the various trades involved are aware that more information will follow. Problems arise when this information is provided at the last minute and it is different from what was expected. This is a good time to get the answers to these questions and fill in these critical blanks.

5. *Placement of floor drains and floor sinks for general maintenance.* In addition to the required drains for walk-ins, ice machines, bain maries, and beverage equipment, floor drains are necessary for general maintenance and where liquid spills are anticipated. Adding a few floor drains in the design phase is inexpensive insurance and will improve maintenance activities.

6. *Door hardware.* How you plan to operate your restaurant will affect the type of hardware you will require. If your dry storage room is always open because your staff needs ready access to it and the expensive products are stored elsewhere, you may not even need a door, let alone any hardware! Some rooms require closers so that the door will always be in the closed position. Others, like liquor rooms, may need a lockset that is always in the locked position and requires a key to open. Back-door entrances to some kitchens have no exterior handle and must be opened from the inside. This minimizes unauthorized access. By preparing a draft schedule of your required hardware needs—closers, hold-open devices, type of locksets, push/pull/kick plates, vision panels, panic bars, bells, and alarms—you will be making decisions that are consistent with your operational plan.

It is best to go over these items just before your design team begins the construction documents phase. The plan and seating layout have been established and you have developed a good sense of how the restaurant will function.

Construction Documents Phase. This is the phase where all the details come together. The details of architectural, structural, mechanical, plumbing, electrical, foodservice, interior design, and specialty systems must be coordinated. Written specifications for each of these areas must be prepared and coordinated with the drawings. There will be a lot of interaction between the various disciplines involved in your restaurant development. Your project manager will continue to hold project meetings and review progress. The drawings and specifications that each discipline of the design team prepares will come together to form a cohesive set of construction documents for your restaurant. You are building one restaurant facility that has many parts. All the parts are related and a well-prepared set of documents will reflect that.

Earlier, these drawings and specifications were referred to as a "recipe." As in a recipe, it is critical that the ingredients are listed and the instructions written so that they can easily be understood and followed. Where information appears on a set of construction documents can determine if it is seen and whether the work will be performed in a proper sequence or by the proper trade or at all! Although you may argue successfully that the information was there and the contractor is, in fact, responsible for performing the work, you will still have lost time and disrupted the construction process.

Clearly, there is more than one right way to approach the preparation of construction documents for a restaurant. But too often they are drawn and written without the focus on their purpose that is to enable a general contractor and his many subcontractors, working together, to build your restaurant facility as designed, on schedule, within the approved budget and without compromising your concept or design intent. If information is contradictory, vague, in the wrong section, or missing, your restaurant development may suffer. The following guidelines will make your job of monitoring this process easier and may help to avoid unnecessary costs, delays, or reduced quality.

The contract documents are identified by discipline or trade so that those responsible for performing the work can quickly and easily reference the documents that apply to their work.

C	Civil	P	Plumbing
L	Landscape	E	Electrical
A	Architectural	K or FS	Foodservice equipment
S	Structural	F	Furnishings
M	Mechanical	ID	Interior design

An important function within the job of coordinating these documents is to determine where information that affects multiple trades should be located and how best to reference this information so that it is seen and used. Electricians focus on the "E" drawings, plumbers on the "P" drawings. If there is important information in other sections that affects their work, it needs to be flagged on the drawings that they use.

Civil Engineering Drawings. The drawings prepared by the civil engineer relate to the site and survey work. Property lines, reference elevations, utilities, and the location of buildings, roads, walks, and driveways are indicated on these documents.

Landscape Drawings. These documents are prepared by a landscape architect or landcaping contractor. They show the design and placement of all trees, plantings, irrigation systems, site grading and related schedules, and specifications for their purchase and installation.

Architectural Drawings. These drawings consist of plans, elevations, sections, details, and schedules. They are linked together by reference numbers and various symbols that direct the reader from the plan and elevations to the more specific sections, details, and related schedules.

They may also key to drawings in other sections that provide more detail or require careful coordination.

Several plans are necessary. These plans, described below, require coordination within the design team.

1. *Demolition plan.* When remodeling an existing facility, it may be necessary to remove existing partitions, mechanical systems, electrical or plumbing fixtures, or other features. The demolition plan defines the scope of this work.

2. *Site plan.* This plan shows all site conditions, dimensions, building location, utilities, easements, paving, landscaping, signage, reference elevations, legal descriptions, and reference information. Trash areas, wood storage, bike racks, patio seating, railings, and planters are shown on this plan.

3. *Architectural floor plan* (each level). These plans show all walls and partitions, dimensions, room names and reference numbers, floor elevations, door swings and reference numbers, all finishes and reference numbers, built-in casework, toilet rooms and plumbing fixtures, stairs and handrails. Reference numbers key to schedules.

4. *Reflected ceiling plan.* This is a plan of what occurs at the ceiling. Design elements, lighting, sprinklers, access panels, grills and registers for heating, ventilation, and air conditioning, exhaust hoods, ceiling finish/tile patterns, and anything else that occurs at the ceiling is shown on this plan. Although some of this information may also appear on drawings prepared by other disciplines, the architectural-reflected ceiling plan shows all these elements together and ensures that there are no conflicts.

5. *Roof plan.* HVAC units, exhaust ductwork, vent piping, gas lines, remote refrigeration packages, roof drains, skylights, parapets, crickets and slopes, access hatches and ladders, and screens to shield these items from view and rooftop signage are indicated on this plan.

6. *Foodservice equipment plan.* The kitchen, bar, service areas, host stand, and many back-of-the-house areas are packed with equipment from several different sources. Most equipment is designed, located, and specified by the foodservice consultant. Some items are provided by specialty vendors and other items are selected and provided by the owner. Regardless of the source, all of these items must be shown on the equipment plan and referenced to an equipment schedule.

7. *Furnishing plan.* Seating (chairs, tables, booths, banquettes), display tables, decor items, planters, plants, and artifacts are shown on this plan and keyed to a schedule.

Schedules. Schedules make it very easy for those bidding or costing your restaurant and those building it to understand what you want. Keyed to reference numbers on the drawings, they provide the specifics of quantity, size, sources, models, finish materials, and colors, accessories, and other features. The information is located in one place so that if you decide to change the tile size or color, changing the reference information on the schedule will be reflected wherever the reference symbol is indicated. If descriptive text rather than reference numbers are noted on several different drawings, changes may be overlooked in one place and you will not get the finish you expected or you may be charged extra because it was not shown properly.

Where detailed specifications expand on scheduled equipment items, the schedules may be very generic, listing only a description such as "worktable" or "convection oven." The detailed specifications will expand on this item, giving all the pertinent information regarding manufacturer, models, accessories and features, utilities, and finishes.

All disciplines should use the same reference numbers where applicable. The foodservice equipment schedule is the primary schedule for listing and identifying all the kitchen, bar, and foodservice-related equipment. Mechanical and electrical schedules that key to this equipment should, ideally, use the same reference numbers, so that item 23 refers to a convection oven on all schedules. Typically, there will be schedules for:

- Room finishes
- Doors and hardware
- Windows
- Foodservice equipment
- Furnishings
- Lighting fixtures
- Mechanical and electrical equipment

Reference Notes. Notes are added to the drawings to provide additional instructions or clarification. Often, they relate to coordination among the various trades. Most notes have reference symbols so that the note can be written once and keyed to all areas where it applies.

Legends. Symbols, shading, numbers, and letters within various shapes are used by all disciplines to convey information. While many of these symbols are standard within each discipline, variations are commonplace. Legends are provided to explain the symbols used.

Building Exterior Elevations. These drawings show how the exterior of the building will look. Materials and reference numbers, windows and doors with reference numbers, vertical dimensions, grade elevations and reference elevations, signage, light fixtures, section lines, and references to details and schedules are indicated on these drawings.

Building Sections. These drawings show a cross section of the entire building or space, indicating vertical dimensions, floors, soffits, roof, parapets, concrete slabs, and wood framing. Construction methods, conditions, and details are referenced.

Wall Sections. These drawings show, in larger scale than the building sections, the construction and dimensions of walls, including thickness and materials. One critical element in restaurant construction is the location of wall blocking for supporting wall shelving or wall-mounted equipment. The location of wall blocking is typically shown on the architectural floor plan, since it is usually done as part of the wall framing. The detail that describes how it is constructed will be shown as one of several "typical" wall sections.

Interior Elevations. These drawings, usually at ¼-inch scale, show what occurs at the walls of each room, from the finished floor to the finished ceiling. Although many designers limit the interior elevations to primary areas, it is highly recommended that every wall of every room and space be drawn in elevation. Interior elevations show doors, windows, wall openings and pass-throughs, equipment, furniture, wall mounted shelving, electrical panels, wall-mounted switches and controls, and wall and base finishes. During the construction document phase, these drawings can highlight conflicts with equipment and mechanical or electrical components. For example, electrical disconnect boxes appear schematically on the electrical drawings. This means that they are shown as a symbol on the electrical plan. Unless they are shown on the interior elevations, you may inadvertently cover them with shelving or other equipment. It is also necessary to show all items whether provided and installed by the general contractor, equipment supplier, specialty supplier, or owner. These items may include chalkboards, mirrors, lockers, or time clocks. Often, when these items are not shown, the space is assumed to be vacant and may be utilized by another discipline for other equipment.

Construction Details. These are large-scale details and drawings of how the many components of a building are assembled. Floor, wall, and ceiling construction, connection details, how casework and millwork look and are constructed, paneling and trim details, stairs and railings, and in general, how all the pieces fit together. This is another area where careful coordination is critical. Often, building components, millwork, cabinetry, and partitions include equipment that is provided by others. This equipment either sits on, is adjacent to, or is built into these items. The construction details must be drawn showing these items and referencing them to their appropriate schedule. All trades involved must be made aware that this equipment is an integral part of the millwork and provisions must be made for structural support, trim at openings, utility connections, drains, maintenance access, and air circulation.

A beautifully designed server station that does not show the drop-in ice/water station or coffee brewer and the related space needed for water and drain lines will either not be built as drawn or, if built as drawn, may not accommodate the necessary equipment. Bar details often don't show back-bar refrigeration or the supports necessary to hold the back-bar top in place when equipment must be moved for service or replacement. Similarly, front-bar details need to show the under-bar equipment and need to be coordinated with the placement of beverage guns and the routing of syrup lines, beer systems, electrical receptacles, and plumbing lines.

Engineering Drawings. The drawings, details, and schedules prepared by consulting structural, mechanical, plumbing, and electrical engineers are very specific to their discipline and are often shown schematically. They do not traditionally show related architectural features or how their work is coordinated with other disciplines. The routing of ductwork or electrical conduit may not be shown to scale, and it may not be clear how it gets from point A to point B. That aspect is usually shown on the architectural drawings or coordinated but not illustrated.

An electrical panel may require a 6-inch-deep recess into a wall. If the wall drawn on the architectural plan is only 5 inches thick, this presents a problem. Electrical conduit cannot be shown to drop down from the ceiling to a server station if there is no partition or chase within which it can be routed. Similarly, plumbing and other utilities may be shown schematically to go from point A to point B. But if they cannot get there within walls, ceilings, or underground, problems will occur and compromises may have to be made during construction. Supply registers for heating and air conditioning cannot be located behind booths or server stations without details showing how the air will circulate or how the millwork will be constructed to accommodate this.

Consulting mechanical, plumbing, and electrical engineers are responsible for coordinating the utility requirements for all furnishings, fixtures, and equipment. They receive schedules and specifications from the architect, interior designer, foodservice consultant, specialty consultants, as well as from each other to ensure that the necessary utilities are provided and properly located. The schedules that accompany their drawings include:

♦ Mechanical and plumbing equipment and requirements

♦ Refrigeration equipment and requirements

♦ Foodservice equipment and requirements

♦ Electrical equipment and requirements

These schedules are keyed to their drawings, the drawings provided by specialty consultants, and the architectural drawings.

Drawings of Specialty Consultants. Restaurant development often requires the services of specialists to design and coordinate specific areas of the restaurant. These include:

♦ Foodservice consultants

♦ Interior designers

♦ Sound system consultants

♦ Cable/video specialists

♦ Lighting designers

♦ Acoustical consultants

♦ Telephone systems designers

♦ Security systems specialists

♦ Beer/beverage systems suppliers/installers

These consultants and specialists provide a very valuable service. They know their industry and products. They have access to the latest technology, materials, and equipment to meet your needs. The timing of when these consultants get involved in your restaurant development, how they present their information, and how their information is coordinated within the construction documents will have a significant impact on how these items fit, are installed, and ultimately, function.

Each of these disciplines has his own priorities and concerns with regard to his equipment and how it is specified, where it is located, and how it is installed. The drawings and specifications they prepare should and often do provide this information clearly. The dilemma that faces the architect and the project manager is how to incorporate this information into the construction documents. Information supplied by consultants and specialty suppliers can be handled in one of two ways:

1.   Integrated within the construction documents

2.   Treated as a shop drawing

If the information is to be an integral part of the construction documents, it must be:

1. *Clearly identified.* Labeling of drawings is the simplest identification. If a wiring diagram of the sound system is part of the electrical drawings, it will be found easily by its title or label.

2. *Coordinated with the total package.* Using the same example, the wiring diagram of the sound system cannot be added to the electrical drawings and considered "coordinated." The speaker locations may need "blocking" or wall recesses, which requires coordination with the architectural drawings. If the CD player and amplifier are located within millwork, the interior design details must show this and indicate how the wiring is to be routed or concealed.

3. *Not contradictory with other documents.* PVC conduit for routing beverage lines, if shown on the foodservice drawings and plumbing or electrical drawings, must be shown in the same place and routed the same way. Since the plumbing/electrical drawings will show this rout-

ing in the context of other work by the same trade, these are the drawings that will usually govern. However, contradictory information may result in longer routes or more difficult access. This in turn may affect the installation of this equipment during construction.

4. *Located within the drawings where the appropriate trade will find it.* All specialty consultants include numerous notes on their drawings that inform and direct other trades that may have some involvement with their work. But if the information is not located in the appropriate place on the primary drawings used by that particular trade, it may be overlooked. The issue here is not "well, the note was on the drawings, you should have seen it." Rather, it should be placed where it will most likely be seen to avoid misunderstandings or delays.

Shop drawings show in very specific detail how a particular item is going to be fabricated or constructed. They are amplified drawings and specifications, usually prepared by the person or company that will actually make the product or perform the work. These drawings clearly indicate all components, connections, fabrication methods, materials, finishes, installation methods, or directions and descriptive text as required to describe their work. If the information is treated as a shop drawing, it must be:

1. *Referenced in the construction documents.* The trades responsible for installing or coordinating some aspect of the referenced work must be made aware that more comprehensive and extensive information is being provided. A note on the drawings is a flag that alerts them to this.

2. *Reviewed by all disciplines.* Every discipline should have an opportunity to review any shop drawing that affects their work even remotely.

3. *Coordinated with the construction documents.* The information contained in shop drawings is usually far more detailed and exact than the information normally provided on the construction documents. This expanded information may alter details shown on the construction documents. If necessary, clarification drawings must be issued.

The concern that you, as the developer, should have is that whatever information is presented in the construction documents be accurate. Showing sound-system speakers and wiring on a plan is fine if that is, in fact, where they will be located. If the plan shows one location and the shop drawing comes in with them located differently, decisions made based on the plan will be nullified. Access panels or blocking provided for speakers or TV monitors may be in the wrong place and you will bear the cost and time to relocate them.

Foodservice Consultants.   The planning and design of kitchen, bar, and related service and support facilities is often turned over to specialty consultants. As an integral member of the design team, they help plan the overall space so that the functional and space requirements for these are adequate. Once the spaces for these areas are defined, they prepare complete drawings and specifications. These documents usually include:

♦   Equipment plans and schedules

♦   Elevations and/or large-scale details/isometric drawings of equipment

♦   Equipment plumbing plan and schedule

♦   Equipment electrical plan and schedule

♦   Equipment ventilation plan and schedule

♦   Building conditions plan and related notes

♦   Detailed line-item specifications

All of these items are often included in the construction documents set of drawings. They are treated as a comprehensive document relating to the food and beverage facilities. These foodservice drawings contain vital information that needs to be coordinated with the architectural, structural, mechanical, plumbing, electrical, and interior design drawings. The critical aspect of this coordination is that the necessary information be on the primary drawings used by the trades in the field.

Unfortunately, these foodservice documents, when included in their entirety in the set of construction documents, are often redundant with other documents prepared by other disciplines. Some of this information should be used within the design team as reference documents and not included in the comprehensive set of drawings for construction. But often architects are reluctant to get too involved in the foodservice documents because they are very technical and detailed. They prefer to use the documents in their comprehensive state. There are, however, key issues that you, as the developer, need to ensure are well coordinated and included in the appropriate section before the construction documents are released. These issues are:

1. *Floor depressions and recesses.* Walk-in coolers and freezers are often specified with integral floors. These floors are frequently recessed below the finished floor grade so that there is no step or ramp required to enter the unit and the finished floor surface and base material can run continuously into the cooler/freezer. There are also details prepared by the foodservice consultant which show an isolated, insulated concrete slab that serves as the floor in these walk-ins. These recesses need to be coordinated with the architectural and structural drawings.

2. *Wall blocking.* The foodservice drawings show the location of wall-mounted equipment and indicate where blocking is required. The details relating to this blocking, where the blocking is located (horizontally and vertically), construction details, and area to be covered need to be indicated on the architectural drawings since the framing crew will probably be responsible for this work.

3. *Special architectural features.* Floor troughs, specialty wall and ceiling finishes, concrete curbs, or nonstandard equipment loads may be noted on the food-service drawings. Verify that these items are picked up on the architectural and structural drawings.

4. *PVC lines and related access panels.* These conduits are used as sleeves through which beverage syrup lines, beer lines, or refrigeration lines are pulled. Unless this information appears on the electrical drawings (if electrical PVC is used) or the plumbing drawings (if plumbing PVC is used), the contractor responsible for the work will not get the proper information. The access panels that allow for the installation trades to work the lines through these conduits may be provided by the general contractor. Therefore, it is necessary for this information to be noted on the architectural documents and possibly the reflected ceiling plan.

5. *Floor drains and sinks.* Verify that these are adequate and floors are sloped properly. Drain symbols show up on architectural, foodservice, and plumbing drawings. However, you want to be sure that they are shown where you want them on the plumbing drawings since it is the plumbing contractor who will be providing and installing them. Plan revisions and updates often result in drains being added or relocated. Coordination with the plumbing drawings is especially critical to en-

sure that these changes are picked up. The sloping of floors to these drains should appear on the architectural drawings.

6. *Sleeves for refrigeration and utilities.* Floor penetrations and sleeves for utility lines that go through floors or roofs are normally noted on the architectural drawings. Utility routing is usually not a problem since the trades responsible for the work figure out how to get from point A to point B. The coordination effort becomes more involved if a refrigeration subcontractor arrives on the site toward the end of construction and the routes for his lines are covered up with drywall. Although it may be true that he should have planned better, unless the routing of these lines is clearly delineated on the drawings, it can be overlooked and cause you delays and cost overruns.

7. *Exhaust hoods, ducts, and ductwork.* These systems fall under the jurisdiction of the mechanical engineer. Even if the hoods are provided by the foodservice equipment contractor, the mechanical engineer is still responsible for the air-handling systems for the entire restaurant and will probably be coordinating the exhaust, makeup air, and overall balancing of the systems. Be sure that dishwasher hoods, precipitators for specialized grease extraction, and hoods over isolated cooking equipment are shown in addition to the primary hoods. These hoods, since they affect the ceiling, will also appear on the architectural-reflected ceiling plan.

8. *Plumbing and electrical connections for equipment.* These requirements are called out in detail on the foodservice drawings and schedules. They are also noted on the plumbing and electrical drawings and schedules. It is essential that the information on the plumbing and electrical drawings be reviewed for accuracy since these are the documents that the trades will use and reference in the field. The concerns with utility connections are that:

♦ They are located close to where you need them.

♦ The connections are oriented so that equipment can fit tight to walls.

♦ Receptacles are located so that the cords do not drape across counters.

♦ The conduit and piping are concealed in walls wherever possible.

♦ The connections are accessible.

♦ Plumbing and gas connections have individual shutoffs.

♦ Drain piping does not interfere with cabinet storage space or protrude out into aisles.

♦ They are installed to facilitate cleaning.

♦ Quick disconnects, if required, are indicated in either the food-service equipment specifications or plumbing specifications.

9. *Convenience outlets and utilities not listed for specific equipment.* The foodservice drawings will sometimes specify utility requirements for general-purpose use. But it is important to verify that any necessary utilities that are not assigned to specific equipment or may be useful in the future be indicated on the appropriate plumbing or electrical documents.

Interior Design. The drawings and specifications covering the interior design of your restaurant affect all disciplines of the design team. Interior design includes all finish materials and colors, architectural details for railings, stairways, walls, doors, windows, soffits, millwork and cabinetry, design or selection of furniture, lighting and light fixtures, and the overall shape and form of your restaurant. Some of these areas are designed by the architect and others coordinated by the interior designer.

The interior designer will play a key role in the planning of the space, helping to creating the drama and feel that you described in your business plan and operation plan. The documents they prepare include:

♦ Furniture and fixtures plan

♦ Lighting plan

♦ Details of custom-fabricated millwork and cabinetry

♦ Detailed specifications

These documents usually do not overlap or conflict with other drawings in the construction documents. But there are still areas that need careful coordination with the other sections.

1. *Specialty lighting and switching.* Lighting that is designed and specified by the interior designer may be supplemental to the standard

lighting planned by the electrical engineer. The switching of these fixtures must be planned along with the switching of the general lighting.

2. *Clear references to foodservice equipment item numbers.* The millwork and cabinet details prepared by your interior designer will include the front and back bar, server stations, and the host area. These will include specialized equipment that must be considered in the design of these items. It is important that the equipment being located on or in this millwork be clearly identified so that the fabricator can easily reference these pieces and refer to the critical dimensions, access ports, and other features that will affect their design and construction.

3. *Acceptable finishes in foodservice areas.* Water, alcohol, heat, cold, and abuse are ever-present in restaurants. Materials that are not designed for these conditions, however appropriate they may appear, will age poorly and not provide the image you are expecting. Review the finishes proposed and verify that they will survive in a restaurant environment.

4. *Coordination of seating plan.* The seating plan that you developed and approved is based on certain sizes and shapes of chairs, tables, and other styles of seating. As the selection and specification of these items is refined, confirm that the sizes shown on the plans are consistent with the sizes specified.

5. *Coordination of server stations and design elements.* When millwork and cabinetry are detailed, conditions become apparent that may require the shape or size to vary. Drop-in pieces may require more space than originally thought. Utility chases or space may need to be enlarged. Whatever the reason, if these items grow or change shape, they may affect the seating layout or aisles.

Specialty System Consultants/Suppliers. The drawing and specifications prepared by these consultants/suppliers—sound, cable/TV, telephone, security/fire, beverage, point of sale (POS)—are very specific and are traditionally provided either as shop drawings or incorporated into the drawings prepared by the consulting engineers. Some components of these systems may be provided by the general contractor, such as support blocking, access panels, chases, or conduit for routing lines or wiring. The installation of the equipment is usually provided by the specialty consultant/supplier.

Telephone systems, in particular, are becoming more complex. Where restaurants used to have one or two lines, they now have lines for voice, fax machines, modems, credit card validation, and message centers. In the design program there is a schedule dedicated to defining the phone requirements for your restaurant. This schedule will clearly communicate your needs to the consulting electrical engineers and the telephone system supplier.

These specialty systems have exacting requirements for them to function properly. To ensure that this information gets to the proper party, it is necessary that the following items are coordinated within the construction documents.

1. *Special electrical wiring.* POS systems usually require isolated, grounded, dedicated circuits. Alarm systems may need to be on the same circuit as emergency lighting or have battery-backup units. Power for primary units—phone system, alarm panel, main sound system units—must also be planned and located.

2. *Conduit runs.* Master/slave relationships between POS terminals may require links between units. Some jurisdictions require phone and speaker cable to be routed within electrical conduit. If so, these conduit runs need to be shown on the electrical drawings.

3. *Access for routing wires and cable.* It is an indication of incomplete planning when you see exposed wiring, phone lines, and specialty cables at server stations or along walls and ceilings. This occurs because special systems are often installed toward the end of construction after surface finishes are complete and access to walls and ceilings is limited. Planning for these systems and providing conduit or pre-planned routes for this wiring will eliminate these unsightly tangles of wires.

4. *Blocking requirements for mounting equipment.* Wall-mounted TV monitors, speakers, special-effects lighting, or other heavy items usually require more than expansion anchors in gypsum wallboard. Wood blocking in walls or special connectors are typically specified. Since these need to be installed during construction, they need to be noted on the drawings.

5. *Phone jack locations.* The phone schedule identifies these requirements. Verify their location on the construction documents and coordinate them with millwork shop drawings.

6. *Adequate space and ventilation for primary equipment.* Electrical equipment and motors generate heat. When this equipment is located within closets or enclosed areas, proper ventilation is required for their proper function. Venting, exhaust, or supply air registers need to be designed in to handle this heat load.

Specifications. The written documents that accompany the drawings, referred to as *specifications*, describe the acceptable standards of performance, methods of construction, and quality standards for products and materials. Some specifications identify by manufacturer, model number, and features exactly what products are to be used. It is important, when evaluating bids, prices, or proposals to verify that the products or materials proposed meet these specifications.

The specifications for your furniture and fixtures and the specification for your foodservice equipment require careful scrutiny. Many products that appear comparable or claim to be "equal" may not be manufactured of the same-quality materials or have the same features or warranties.

Furniture Specifications. The selection and specification of your furniture—chairs, bar stools, tables, table bases, booths, and banquettes—is based initially on the look or appearance you described in your design program. There are other factors that must now be determined to ensure that you get the quality and performance you expect. In some cases it is advisable to get a sample and try it or go to a showroom and try several.

1. *Chairs*

♦ Style: design, appearance, arm or side chair, upholstered seat and/or back

♦ Size: based on design program and seating plan

♦ Frame material: wood, metal, plastic

♦ Finish: paint, stain, lacquer

♦ Frame color

♦ Upholstery: fabric, vinyl, leather

♦ Features: casters, stackable, swivel

♦ Manufacturer/model: many chair options are available as standard products

2. *Bar stools*

♦ Style: with or without back, swivel, upholstered or solid seat

♦ Base: fixed or movable

♦ Other features same as chairs

3. *Tables*

♦ Size and shape: Tables can be made in any size or shape to meet your needs. While there are standard sizes listed by many table manufacturers, custom sizes are not uncommon.

♦ Style: Thickness, type of edge, shape.

♦ Material: Your tabletop design will affect the material selected. If you always use a cloth or topper, padded plywood or particleboard may be adequate. If the table will be bare, design will play a key role in the material selection. Tables are made of all types of materials from wood to concrete.

♦ Finish: Tabletops are subjected to the same heavy abuse as bar tops and server stations: heat, cold, water, and alcohol. Whatever finish is selected must withstand these conditions.

♦ Features: Tabletops can have flip-up panels for expansion, built-in warmers and revolving servers, built-in lighting, or other custom accessories.

4. *Bases*

♦ Size: The size of the base is usually determined by the size and shape of the tabletop.

♦ Style and type of base: Round, spider, wall bracket with pin legs, cantilever, tilting for   storage, self-leveling or adjustable.

♦ Design: Bases can be very plain or serve as design elements.

♦ Finish and color: Bases can have any type of finish and color. Most bases are wood or metal and have finishes that can withstand the abuse of shoes and maintenance equipment.

5. *Booths and banquettes*

♦ Size: Length, seat depth, and spacing. Spacing is a factor of table width and booth seat depth. The length is a factor of desired seating capacity. Where spacing is tight, the depth of a table can be reduced and the length of a booth can be increased so that tabletop items can be spread out widthwise.

♦ Height: Privacy and design requirements affect this decision. Divider panels of wood, glass, or fabric can be added to booth backs to increase the height and add privacy or create a design element.

♦ Shape: Booths can be straight, oval, round, or any shape that works.

♦ Material: Upholstery, wood, plastic, metal, or other surfaces can be used for the seat and back.

♦ Design and style: Booth fabricators and designer offer many styles of upholstering, seat and back styles, bases, and trim.

♦ Colors or fabric: Choose materials that are made withstand the wear and tear booth seats and backs will suffer.

♦ Features: Added divider panels, coat trees, canopies, or lighting.

6. *Custom millwork and cabinetry specifications must consider*

♦ Wear and tear of restaurant use

♦ Health department requirements for cleaning and sanitation

♦ Effect of water, alcohol, heat, and cold on finishes and adhesives

Foodservice Specifications. The selection and specification of equipment for your restaurant involves more than just determining the type of appliance: six-burner range with oven, fryer, stainless work-table. There are many features and options that only the operator can choose and should not be left to others to decide.

1. *Purpose.* What do you need the equipment to do? Is it for a specific menu item or must it serve a variety of needs?

2. *Size/capacity.* Most equipment comes in a variety of sizes and capacities. Determine what batch sizes you are preparing, how long it takes to prepare, and when you will be using the equipment. These answers will help determine the size or capacity you need.

3. *Style.* Some equipment is offered in different styles. Countertop or floor models, wall mounted, matching bases with other equipment.

Equipment that is viewed by the public may require a different style from that which is hidden from view.

4. *Construction standards.* There are generally two standards of durability and performance: light duty and heavy duty. Large-volume operations use heavy-duty equipment, while smaller restaurants can operate very effectively with the lighter-weight series. The differences are in cooking performance (Btu/hr.), size, and construction materials.

5. *Utilities.* Several choices are available. Utility cost or availability, personal preference, or opinions as to performance affect this decision. Altitude affects the performance of some equipment and may be a factor in your decision. Many factories will adjust or calibrate their equipment to perform better at higher elevations. This requirement must be specified.

6. *Finish.* Stainless steel, painted metal, custom color. This decision may be affected by whether or not the public can view this equipment, and by budget or maintenance concerns.

7. *Options and accessories.* Understanding what optional features are available may help you make a decision. Casters versus legs, extra shelves, specialty shelves or slides, electronic ignitors for gas appliances, convection oven bases, drawers versus doors, remote refrigeration, door hinging, and many other options are available.

8. *Related equipment.* In addition to listed accessories or options, some equipment may require other components from the same or other manufacturers to complement its use. Flexible utility disconnects for gas or electric appliances that are on casters, dipperwells for ice cream cabinets, specialty faucets, and drains for sinks are a few examples.

Allocation of Responsibility for N.I.C., By Others, and By Owner. Do not assume that because something is shown on the contract documents, it is included in a budget or within the scope of a contractor's work. Throughout the construction documents there will be references on the drawings and on schedules such as "N.I.C" (not in contract), "by others," and "by owner." These notations are made because the items cited are necessary or are required by the design program but do not fall within the scope of work defined for the general contractor and subcontractors. In some cases, the owner or developer has elected to handle some items himself and has deleted them from the general contractor's scope of work.

The responsibility for providing, installing, connecting, and coordinating these items with the construction documents must be assigned. If the office furniture or safe is "N.I.C.," who is going to get it and install it? If the host stand is "by owner," the tasks of finding it, purchasing it, or building it and getting it to the restaurant so that it can be set in place must be assigned to someone. Furthermore, any ancillary work that must be performed on these items, such as installing a phone or light on the host stand, connecting utilities or building these items into millwork or cabinetry must be spelled out in the construction documents. Some items noted as "by owner" are provided by the owner but installed by the general contractor. These items must be noted clearly so that the contractor can schedule and budget for the necessary work. Items that are typically designated in this manner are:

1. *Specialty finishes.* Industrial flooring, carpet, designer tile, wallpaper, and paneling are often shown, although not included in the general construction contract. These items are frequently specified and purchased through designers or specialty contractors outside the scope of the general contractor. These finishes, however, may affect other details. The thickness of flooring must be considered when floor transitions are involved or floors will be uneven and tripping can result. The thickness of tile or paneling on walls may affect utility locations and require extensions on electrical boxes. Special finishes on counters may alter the height and affect guest comfort or function.

2. *Purveyor-supplied equipment.* Coffee brewers, beverage equipment, ice machines, and dishwashers are often supplied or leased by vendors in exchange for using their brand of product. Decisions regarding which purveyor to use are sometimes not finalized until well into the construction phase of the restaurant. Unfortunately, utility requirements, sizes, cutouts, or support requirements in millwork must be established in the very early stages of construction to avoid costly retrofitting. By assigning responsibility early for these items and setting deadlines for decisions that coincide with construction requirements, delays, incorrect fabrication, and cost overruns can be avoided.

3. *Plumbing fixtures and accessories.* Hand sinks, mop sinks (janitor's sinks), and paper towel and soap dispensers are frequently listed on the foodservice drawings with the note, "N.I.C." or "by plumbing contractor." The mechanical engineer, however, may have seen the items on the foodservice drawings and made similar notes on his drawings with reference to "by others." Verify that the reference notes on the drawings

prepared by one design discipline are consistent with the notes of the others. Some items, such as the paper towel and soap dispensers, are provided by purveyors when you use their product. But they are often shown as being provided by the general contractor since they are a standard hardware supply item. Determining who will provide these items will avoid duplication and unnecessary expense.

4. *Miscellaneous millwork and cabinetry.* The big pieces such as server stations and display cases are rarely unassigned since they are prominent design elements. The menu holders and accessory shelving are more frequently overlooked.

5. *Signage and menu boards.* These items are most frequently provided "by owner." Here too, the primary sign and menu board may be correctly assigned, budgeted and coordinated. But the smaller signage, such as the parking lot signs, directional signage, and restroom signs, are often overlooked.

6. *Outside furniture.* Seasonal furniture may be listed as "future" in addition to being "by owner." As the restaurant opening approaches, the patio may be functional and the furniture needs to be on site.

7. *Landscaping and fencing.* These items are sometimes left undecided and assigned to "by owner" since architects do not commonly include this work in their scope of services. Landscaping may require water connections for sprinkler systems, drainage considerations, and lighting that must be coordinated with the construction documents. Developers often work with local plant nurseries to provide design/ build services.

8. *Operational items.* Time clocks, bulletin boards, and lockers and similar items are shown on the plans and elevations but are usually provided "by owner." The size, mounting, or installation requirements and utility requirements need to be verified and coordinated.

Owner Review Process. The completed construction documents should be reviewed in their entirety. This is a standard procedure within the design team. Additionally, the project manager should "walk" the developer/owner through the documents to confirm that the latest version of the design program has been followed and that the operational plan still works. This review can occur at intervals throughout the preparation of the construction documents. It is helpful to go through the documents with a marker to highlight all references to "by owner," "by others," and "N.I.C." This makes assigning responsibility for these items easier. The specifications, particularly the furniture and fixtures and the foodservice equipment specifications, should be reviewed to verify that the models and features are correct.

Budget Update. Throughout the construction document phase, the budget will be updated and refined to minimize cost overruns or unexpected "budget creep." Subschedules will now apply to most of your initial one-line budget items. Landscaping, previously not included in your budget, may now be an integral part of your design and must be accounted for. Percentage fees, taxes, freight charges, and similar expenses must be updated and accounted for and reflected in your current budget. It is to your advantage to maintain current budget figures so that you can make informed decisions as to deletions or changes in the scope of your restaurant and to keep your development within your funding limits. Unless you are working under a design/build agreement, the test of the budget will come when the documents are bid or priced out. However, conscientious budget monitoring should keep the development on track.

Allowances.   Until your contract documents are complete, your design will continue to use "allowances' or reasonable estimates for groups of items. The cost of bathroom plumbing fixtures, for example, may be based on a standard, commercial grade. However, as the design develops, you may decide that you want colored fixtures or wall-hung or low-profile fixtures, all of which cost more than standard commercial-grade fixtures. The allowance budgeted by your contractor is now outdated.

   Hardware is another category that is frequently covered with an allowance. Until all the door hardware—locks, closers, knobsets, push and pull plates—have been determined, this allowance cannot be fine tuned. If the allowance was based on brushed aluminum and you decide to use polished brass, the budget figures will change.

   Often, permit fees are based on fixture counts, seating capacity, or other units of measure that may not have been finalized. Your design team will use their best guess as to what these figures will be. But until these decisions are made, the allowance remains in the budget. As your budget is refined, you need to eliminate all allowances and feel comfortable with the categories, subschedules, and prices presented. Here is a checklist of items that typically are budgeted based on allowances and are often overlooked as budgets get refined. You best defense against budget creep or budget shock is to review line-item costs at your weekly project meeting and demand updates.

- ♦ Permit and tap fees
- ♦ Percentage-based consulting fees
- ♦ Hardware
- ♦ Plumbing fixtures
- ♦ Landscaping
- ♦ Millwork
- ♦ Carpet and specialty finishes
- ♦ Signage
- ♦ Owner-provided items

Without a current, realistic budget, you may be required to cut back on essential expenditures that occur at the end of construction but are critical to your operational success. Areas that suffer are usually:

- ♦ Working capital
- ♦ Advertising and marketing funds
- ♦ Preopening payroll
- ♦ Kitchen smallwares

The best defense against compromising your development and the future success of your restaurant is to update and refine your budget continuously based on realistic sources and schedules. With the construction documents complete and thoroughly reviewed and the budget updated to eliminate allowances and account for all changes and revisions, you are ready to begin the construction phase of your development.

Seven

The Construction Phase: Building Your Restaurant

The complete and comprehensive set of construction documents that you and your design team have completed will now be used to build your restaurant. Unfortunately, a good set of construction documents does not guarantee that your restaurant will be built satisfactorily. There is a long road between the completion of the construction documents and the finished product. Your objective is to:

1. *Contract with qualified contractors, trades, and suppliers.* Finding, interviewing, and evaluating contractors who are interested in building your restaurant is an important responsibility that should not be delegated to someone unfamiliar with construction or unable to represent your best interests.

2. *Confirm your line-item budget.* Your previous budgets may include reasonable estimates and pricing based on incomplete drawings and specifications. Once a contractor and subcontractors are selected, these costs can be firmly established.

3. *Establish a realistic schedule.* Previous schedules and timetables may have been based on historical information or comparable developments. Here, too, your selected contractor and subcontractors can prepare detailed schedules based on their crews, other work they have committed to, and delivery schedules for materials and equipment.

4. *Manage the construction process effectively.* Within the overall schedule for your construction, there will be unexpected issues that need to be resolved, immediate answers needed to critical questions,

211

field decisions required, and coordination of "owner-provided" furnishings, fixtures, and equipment. These items, if not managed correctly, can cause serious delays and disrupt the overall construction schedule.

The construction phase is a component of the development process. Success during this phase means that:

♦ The restaurant is constructed as designed.

♦ Changes in the operational plan or design program are incorporated into the construction documents.

♦ Approved changes are coordinated with all trades.

♦ The restaurant is built on time.

♦ Your agreed-upon budget is maintained.

Many people think they are familiar with construction and how buildings go together. They think this because they have built additions to their home, been involved in some aspect of construction, such as working summers as a carpenter, drywaller, or painter, or have worked for other companies that have developed restaurants. But restaurant construction is not unlike learning a foreign language. You study in school, take a few night classes, even have a private tutor for a while. Then you go to the foreign country, stay in a resort hotel, chat with the waiter, ask directions to shops and restaurants, and have a discussion with the bartender. You are now, according to you, "fluent and able to get along fine." Well, you probably would not feel comfortable negotiating a lease or discussing a business venture in your new "fluent" language.

Understanding construction in a general way does not make you a bona fide contractor or project manager. Those restaurateurs and developers who say, "well, I know enough to be dangerous" probably don't realize how right they are. The process of building a restaurant is complex and requires a well-coordinated effort by people who know what they are doing. The construction process consists of three parts:

1. Preconstruction activities

2. Construction

3. Project administration

❖   PRECONSTRUCTION ACTIVITIES

There are several activities that occur before a contractor begins the actual work of building or remodeling a restaurant. If these activities are not properly performed or if they are omitted or abbreviated, your development may be jeopardized.

Selection of a Project Manager

This is the person who represents your interests during the construction phase. This may be the same person who represented you during the planning and design phase. Since many critical decisions will be made during construction or even as a result of the plan review process, this position must be filled before the construction phase begins. Typically, your architect represents your interests during this phase. However, you may also have your project manager continue to participate and act as your representative to coordinate and interpret many of the job-site decisions that may affect your concept or operating procedures.

Selection of a General Contractor

Contractors are usually required to be licensed by the state or local government. This licensing requirement, often a written exam, is to ensure that the contractor has an understanding of the codes, rules, and regulations covering his work. It is, however, no guarantee that he can build your restaurant. Your selection of a general contractor should be done according to the guidelines presented earlier. The selection process—competitive bid, negotiated bid, or design/build—will affect the timing of this selection as well as your participation in the selection of subcontractors and suppliers. The general contractor submits the construction documents to the appropriate agencies for review and permits.

Permits

The construction documents submitted for review are required by most jurisdictions to have been prepared by design professionals licensed to practice in the state. This includes architects and structural, mechanical, plumbing, and electrical engineers. Interior designers and food-service consultants have professional societies that offer certification, but this accreditation is not usually required for permits. The construction documents will usually not be accepted for review without the proper "stamps." Code compliance was discussed during the planning and design phase. Preliminary meetings and review sessions are often held with plan review officials during the design phase to get a "reading" on how they will interpret the codes. But these informal meetings do not replace their formal review of the construction documents. These reviews frequently result in comments or conditions being marked on the documents by these officials requiring compliance with certain provisions of the code, clarification that the design meets certain criteria, or requiring changes to comply with the code. Permits may be issued with the understanding that these requirements will be met or the corrections may be required before the permits are issued. In the latter case, the design team will make the necessary corrections, coordinate them throughout the documents, and reissue them.

It is essential that construction not begin until the necessary permits are secured. Many developers, anxious to get started, will get a demolition permit or sitework permit before the review process is complete on the other documents. This is fairly typical and usually not a problem. What may be a problem is the review and approval of nongovernmental agencies that have authority over the development. Landlords, shopping center management, franchise headquarters, or other groups whose approval is required must review and "sign off" on the documents. Failure to get their necessary approval may cause delays or changes to work already complete.

Selection of Subcontractors and Suppliers

The choice of the general contractor often dictates the subordinate trades that will be involved in your restaurant development. This does not mean that you have no control over their selection or that you cannot review their credentials and references. These are the contractors who will be implementing your design. If they are not qualified or experienced in restaurant construction, your project may suffer. During the selection process for a general contractor, you can require that all subordinate contractors be approved by you. It is then your responsibility to verify that they are familiar with restaurant construction, have the ability to perform, and that their references meet your requirements. Although the specifications may require certain brands or models, the source of supply for these items may alter your budget. Reviewing these supplier sources and recommending alternates may result in savings of time and money.

Selection of the Foodservice Equipment Supplier

The equipment package for your restaurant is a major purchase. The number of items, special features specified, related components, delivery time, and the complexity of coordination and installation make the selection of a source for these items very important. The drawings and specifications in the construction documents clearly define the products required and the scope of work involved. The foodservice equipment supplier is usually responsible for:

♦ Reviewing all construction documents for conflicts, omissions, or potential problems related to the foodservice equipment package

♦ Verifying utility requirements of specified items against construction documents

♦ Attending construction meetings, making field inspections, and taking field dimensions related to his scope of work

♦ Purchasing all items specified

♦ Receiving, inspecting, and staging all items prior to installation

♦ Coordinating the delivery of all items to the job site

♦ Assembling and setting all items in place

♦ Leveling and sealing all equipment

♦ Coordinating the startup and calibration of all equipment

Since many other construction activities are dependent on the installation of this equipment, coordination is crucial. If items are not delivered on time or if products are not as specified, major delays and construction modifications may be required. Therefore, the inspection and staging function becomes critical. If items arrive damaged, if component parts are missing, if door swings are wrong, or if model numbers or styles are incorrect, it is the responsibility of the vendor to resolve these issues without delaying the project. The contract for the foodservice equipment can be bid competitively or negotiated. It can be included as part of the general construction contract under the control and supervision of the general contractor, or it can be handled as an owner provided package with the coordination responsibility on your project manager. In either case, you want to select this supplier with the same scrutiny as you do the other members of your development team.

It is not uncommon for the foodservice equipment supplier to propose alternatives to the equipment specified. There are many manufacturers of comparable equipment on the market, and there are several reasons why they may recommend other brands.

♦ The alternative is a higher quality for the same price.

♦ The specified manufacturer cannot meet the delivery schedule.

♦ Local warranty or maintenance service may be better on the alternative proposed.

♦ They do not have access to the product specified.

♦ They have special freight, pricing, and rebate programs with the alternative manufacturer.

The decision to accept alternatives should be weighed using the criteria discussed in the section "Substitutions" later in the chapter.

Selection of the Furniture Supplier

Similar to the foodservice supplier, and often the same company or vendor, the furniture supplier will provide and install the chairs, tables, table bases, booths, banquettes, and other furniture items. Based on the specifications included in the construction documents, this vendor will be responsible for:

♦ Reviewing all construction documents for conflicts, omissions, or potential problems related to the placement and quantity of the furniture

- ♦ Purchasing all items specified

- ♦ Receiving, inspecting, and staging all items prior to installation

- ♦ Coordinating the delivery of all items to the job site

- ♦ Uncrating, assembling, and setting all items in place

- ♦ Leveling and adjusting all furniture

- ♦ Installing artwork or other accessories as required

Alternatives and substitutions may also be proposed for these items. Here, too, it is necessary to evaluate these products based on the criteria presented below.

Freight Management

Freight and shipping are line items on budgets that many developers accept as a cost of doing business. Suppliers add freight charges to invoices and they are rarely challenged. Freight can amount to as much as 15 to 20 percent of the cost of furniture, fixtures, and equipment. It is a line item in your budget that must be negotiated and scrutinized as much as any other. Many companies specialize in freight management. Equipment and furniture suppliers often use freight management companies to consolidate shipping, track and expedite shipments, and with negotiated contracts, save significantly on shipping charges. Some vendors offer free shipping with large-dollar-volume orders. This incentive may be enough for you to accept an alternative manufacturer.

Selection of Suppliers for Specialty Systems and Special Products

The general contractor will provide and coordinate most of the components of your restaurant construction. But there are systems and products that are provided by specialty vendors that you may want to deal with directly. These include sound systems, security systems, telephone, TV sets, VCRs, and cable/satellite systems. The products may be decor items, custom light fixtures, aquariums, plants, and interior gardens. Ideally, the requirements for these systems and products have been coordinated within the construction documents. But in reality, these items are often not finalized before the construction documents are completed and the specific requirements for these products are not indicated. These loose ends should be picked up when the shop drawings are reviewed. Each of these vendors should coordinate their requirements with the design team who will document these needs and, if necessary, coordinate these requirements with the design team and the general contractor.

Budgeting

With the selection of the general contractor, subcontractors, and primary suppliers, it is necessary to review the earlier line-item budgets and confirm or adjust the numbers and make necessary adjustments. The permit review process may have required changes that affect the budget. For example, altering the size of a water heater or grease trap will change their cost and your budget. Establish a firm budget that has no allowances or estimates. Where allowances or estimates remain, determine why these costs are not confirmed and make the necessary decisions to finalize them. If estimates must remain, monitor them closely so that they do not get out of hand.

Scheduling

A written schedule of construction activities indicating their sequence and timing is a standard document that is prepared by the general contractor. This chart is often posted on the jobsite and is reviewed and adjusted as necessary at the scheduled project meetings. Since many of these activities are interrelated, delays or adjustments in the work performed by one trade often affect the timing of one or several others. Maintaining this schedule and coordinating the work of the various trades on the job is the responsibility of the general contractor.

Project Management

The management of the restaurant development is different from construction management. While the general contractor will oversee, coordinate, and handle the administrative activities associated with building the restaurant, there are several activities that are either outside the usual scope of the general contractor's work or must be reviewed and monitored by the project manager on behalf of the restaurateur. These activities include:

♦ Scheduling, attending, and keeping notes on the periodic (weekly) job-site meetings. These meetings should be attended by members of the design team, all trades, and when necessary, suppliers.

♦ Participating in field decisions that affect the budget, design, or operational integrity of the restaurant.

♦ Reviewing and updating the budget periodically.

♦ Acting as the owner's agent to followup on "owner-provided" items and respond to questions or unresolved issues.

♦ Coordinating and participating in periodic field inspections.

♦ Initiating owner-required changes or revisions.

♦ Establishing and maintaining chain of communication between developer/restaurateur and general contractor.

Preconstruction Meeting

The general contractor and his subcontractors and suppliers have reviewed and understand the construction documents. They have prepared line-item budgets based on the drawings and specifications and understand the scope of their work. A preconstruction meeting with the trades and the design team brings these parties together to discuss coordination, schedules, timing, and concerns. It also gives everyone a chance to meet with the other people involved in the construction process with whom they will be dealing. Restaurant construction can take many months or longer to complete. These people will be working together during this time, and need to establish solid working relationships.

Adversarial relationships, however, do develop. In an ideal work environment, all participants in your restaurant development will work together to achieve your objective. In reality, there are personal agendas, personality differences, and scheduling conflicts within the design team, between the designers and the contractors, within the construction crew, among the owners, and any combination of the above. Being aware of these situations and dealing with them quickly and decisively will minimize their destructive effect on the development of your restaurant.

Formalization of a Chain of Communication

Establishing who has authority to be on the construction site and who can interact with the general contractor may seem insignificant or "something than can be dealt with if it becomes a problem." Restaurant developments create a lot of interest on the part of investors, partners, employees, potential vendors, and the general public. For safety reasons, unauthorized personnel should not be permitted on the job site. Those who are permitted should comply with the posted rules. But even those people who are permitted to stop by should understand the chain of communication. When the Desperado Roadhouse was under construction, a waiter from a sister establishment stopped by the check out the progress. He commented to the plumber that the wait station seemed small and the sink should probably go on the other side. The plumber, not wanting to do something wrong or have to redo his work, stopped what he was doing, called the job superintendent who called the project manager and spent the next 45 minutes trying to resolve this potential problem. An innocent question halted work on the restaurant for close to an hour. Had the chain of communication been clearly established, the plumber could easily have responded, "talk with Tony, the project manager" and continued on with his work, knowing that any changes would come through the proper channels.

❖   CONSTRUCTION

The construction of the restaurant is coordinated and managed by the general contractor. The schedule developed in conjunction with the subcontractors, suppliers, and the project manager clearly presents the projected activities and the timetable of events that will occur through the construction period.

Construction schedules are usually bar charts. They show start and end dates and the relationship of the activities to each other. The tasks listed below are representative of those listed on typical construction schedules.

- ♦ Permits received
- ♦ Excavation
- ♦ Site work
- ♦ Concrete footings
- ♦ Concrete walls
- ♦ Underground primary utilities
- ♦ Foundation waterproofing
- ♦ Underground plumbing
- ♦ Underground electricity
- ♦ Interior gravel
- ♦ Perimeter drains
- ♦ Slab-on-grade
- ♦ Backfill
- ♦ Wall framing
- ♦ Roof framing
- ♦ Specialty blocking
- ♦ Fascia
- ♦ Roofing
- ♦ Doors and windows
- ♦ Exterior trim
- ♦ Exterior paint

- ♦ Plumbing rough-in
- ♦ Electrical rough-in
- ♦ Fire sprinkler
- ♦ Mechanical rough-in
- ♦ Gypsum wallboard
- ♦ Insulation
- ♦ Tape and finish
- ♦ Interior trim
- ♦ Tile
- ♦ Paint
- ♦ Specialty finishes
- ♦ Kitchen/bar equipment installed
- ♦ Toilet accessories
- ♦ Door hardware
- ♦ Bathroom hardware
- ♦ Final connect plumbing
- ♦ Final connect electrical
- ♦ Floor coverings
- ♦ Final painting
- ♦ Punch list

Construction schedules vary in format and task listing. The important element of any schedule is that it clearly itemizes the activities required. As construction progresses, there are many critical conditions, review points, and activities that require action, decisions or clarification. While some of these may be performed by the general contractor or members of the design team, it is essential that your project manager be actively involved. Your project manager represents you and is responsible for protecting the overall integrity of the concept and design. That is why he must participate actively in these review and decision-making activities.

Field Inspections and Project Meetings

Throughout the construction process, it is necessary for the design team and the project manager to attend the scheduled job-site meetings and visit the site to inspect the progress and quality of the work. These inspections should be thorough and documented so that corrections required or work to be performed can be monitored. These meetings and inspections benefit the contractor as well as the owner. They provide another check on the construction process and help minimize errors, conflicts, or omissions.

The following areas should be addressed during the periodic field inspections and project meetings.

Field Use of Drawings and Specifications. The construction documents are prepared so that the trade traditionally responsible for performing a task knows where to find the necessary information. Typically, the information is on the drawings designated for that particular trade. The preconstruction meeting held with all trades and members of the design team will spend time reviewing the documents and identifying special conditions or design elements that require special attention or coordination. But when information affects multiple trades, there are instances when the information may not be presented where it will be found easily. Most often, the drawings prepared by specialty consultants contain notes and requirements that affect multiple trades. This information—conduit runs, blocking, floor recesses and similar conditions—is not always shown on the appropriate corresponding drawings. If these drawings are finalized after the construction documents are complete, the information will only be found on the specialty consultants' documents. It is important, therefore, that those trades involved in any aspect of the work be made aware of their task and its timing within the overall project schedule.

Schematic Versus Actual. Schematic diagrams within the construction documents usually show how elements of the electrical, plumbing, or mechanical system fit together. Symbols are often used to show valves, panels, pumps, or other components or equipment. These symbols represent the component, but they do not show the true picture or scale of the item. When the construction documents are prepared, coordination among the design team members should verify that the actual component fits where it is shown. This, however, is an area where the drawings do not necessarily guarantee that the finished product will be as drawn. A fast-food kiosk planned for a shopping center had to be, essentially, self-contained. This meant that the hand sink and small potwashing sink needed a water heater that had to be located within the kiosk. Height and visibility were critical issues since the unit was visible from all sides and there was no ceiling or roof area to hide the water heater. The foodservice consultant recommended an under-sink unit that would have enough capacity for both sinks and would be hidden from public view. The mechanical engineer agreed and specified one. The schematic drawing of the plumbing showed the sink and the water heater positioned under the drainboard. In reality, however, the water heater was too tall to fit under the drainboard when mounted on legs, as required by the health department. This problem, which was not identified during the design phase, became a construction issue. It was an awareness of the potential conflicts posed by schematic drawings that caught this problem before the water heater was ordered. This allowed time to resolve the problem, avoid delays, and made returns and restocking charges unnecessary. The placement of access panels, control devices, or switches is often indicated schematically. If the actual size and placement of these items are not shown on the construction documents, their actual size and location must be coordinated in the field and reviewed by the design team and project manager to avoid operational conflicts.

Field Conditions and Field Measurements. On the construction documents, all walls are plumb, floors level, corners square, and dimensions clearly noted. On the construction site, these conditions vary. When drawings are prepared for existing spaces that are being remodeled, the documents may reflect the significant variances but will not indicate all. Or they may note that these conditions exist and design corrections into the construction documents. Most construction documents clearly note that the drawings are representative of the design intent and that field conditions may vary or conflicts may occur. It is expected that the general contractor and the subcontractors will work together to minimize these variances and conflicts and notify the design team when they occur. These discrepancies may often be minimal, but there are times when critical dimensions or conditions have a significant impact on the design or function of the restaurant. These variances become important when ductwork, equipment, or millwork must fit or where dimensions must be exact. In restaurant construction, dimensions are often critical. Seating layouts can become uncomfortable if a few inches are lost. Fractional inches may affect the fit of equipment. The complexity of restaurant construction necessitates that all trades and suppliers work closely and coordinate their work. Field verification of conditions and dimensions is standard practice. The construction drawings will usually note critical dimensions that must be maintained for equipment to fit, traffic areas, or seating. Where field conditions require adjustments, they are made in the dimensions that are flexible. If conditions warrant, design changes or modification of construction details may be required to compensate for lost space.

Changes/Revisions. There will be changes and revisions during the construction phase, whether as a result of field conditions, because modifications to the operational plan require them, or because you realize there is a better way to build something or a better place to locate it. Changes and revisions do not necessarily result in increased costs or construction delays. But if they are not handled properly, they can cause unwarranted conflicts and result in extra costs and extended construction schedules.

Whatever the source or reason, changes and revisions must be:

1. *Initiated through proper channels.* Telling the plumber on the job to add a connection or move a faucet may or may not get the job done, may or may not get it done correctly, and may or may not cost you time and money. If the general contractor has proper control over his subcontractors and the subs have instructed their crews in the correct procedures for changes or revisions, your comment to the plumber would be redirected. Procedures often depend on the size and scope of the construction project and the relationship you have with the contractor. For your protection, however, all changes and revisions should be routed through your project manager and the design team. They will review your objective and may suggest alternative solutions. Once an approach is finalized, they will coordinate it with related construction documents and present it to the general contractor. He will determine how the change will be incorporated into the construction schedule, the related costs (if any), and coordinate it with his subcontractors and suppliers.

2. *Properly documented.* All communications related to your restaurant development should be documented in writing. They should be dated, signed, and routed through proper channels. Design changes often require drawings or sketches and dimensional information.

3. *Coordinated with other trades and suppliers.* Changes are not self-contained. They most always affect another trade or supplier or construction detail. Altering the size or shape of a server station will affect utility connections, equipment placement, millwork details, layout of floor and base finishes, and adjacent construction details. It may even alter seating arrangements. If these trades and suppliers are not included in the distribution of documents related to this change, they will not be aware of the changes and not alter their work accordingly.

Although many changes or revisions may be warranted or necessary, it is important to evaluate the cost/benefit of the proposed changes. Ask yourself, "What impact will the proposed change have on service, customer satisfaction, check averages, or customer counts?" If there is no significant impact, you must decide why you are making the change. Some design changes are aesthetic and may not be clearly measurable. But if the change enhances the concept or theme and that, in turn, builds your market, it may be justifiable. Cost, or the impact on your budget, is the other half of the equation. Before you make any change, you must consider the effect on your budgets. Realistic costs include not only the cost of the change, but the costs of related changes that result. These may be structural, plumbing, electrical, finishes, or architectural details.

Substitutions. Product specifications are continuously being improved and changed. Suppliers may have access to comparable products by different manufacturers. Delivery schedules may require the contractor to substitute products. Price may convince you to alter specifications and use another brand. There are many reasons why the product called for on the construction documents will be changed. While the reason for the change may be very valid, substitutions require meticulous coordination, specifically with regard to:

♦ **Utility loads and connections.** Similar equipment or components do not necessarily have the same utility requirements. The specific requirements of the substitute must be reviewed and coordinated with the construction documents.

♦ **Size.** Dimensions and clearances may vary.

♦ **Access for service or attachments.** Some brands have service access on the side, others at the rear or front. This may be an issue and should be verified.

♦ **Installation requirements.** Wall-mounting hardware, cutout dimensions, depth of recesses, or other installation specifications may change when products are substituted.

♦ **Compatibility with adjacent equipment or components.** Changing one item of equipment in a line-up or substituting parts may affect how the entire line's functions or looks. Incompatible components may affect performance or warranties.

♦ **Color, finishes, and design.** Aesthetic considerations are often critical in restaurant design. Alternative suppliers or brands may not have acceptable appearances or work with other design elements.

♦ **Code considerations.** Changing manufacturers may require resubmittal to health or building department.

Special Conditions and Construction. The construction documents identify special conditions and construction details that are required. Field inspections should verify that these items do not conflict with or interfere with access to or use of other equipment.

♦ **Blocking and special anchors.** Wall-mounted equipment requires support within the walls for proper anchoring. This equipment is often very heavy and cannot be held securely without solid blocking or specialty anchors. Blocking is not limited to foodservice equipment. Many decor items—mirrors, display shelving—are heavy or will carry heavy loads and need proper blocking for this support. Inspection of this work will prevent it from being installed improperly or mislocated.

♦ **Insulation.** Sound attenuation is a consideration between dining rooms, between the dining areas and the kitchen, or in restroom walls.

♦ **Access panels.** Proper maintenance and service of systems and equipment requires access to spaces above ceilings or in walls. The location of these panels is often shown schematically on the drawings. Exactly where they are installed is usually determined in the field by the contractor doing the work. The placement of these access panels is often dictated by the equipment or system that must be accessed.

Shop Drawing Review. There is a very distinct difference between the drawings and details of millwork, cabinetry, stainless steel fixtures, and custom equipment provided in the construction documents and the fabrication drawings submitted by the companies actually building the item. Shop drawings show in very specific detail how these items will be built. They often include large-scale drawings for clarity, exact dimensions, wiring and plumbing diagrams and schedules, specifications of "buy-out" items included, listing of items that are to be built-in or installed by them but provided "by others" hardware, material and finish specifications or samples, notes on installation requirements and requests for missing information or clarification of dimensions. Shop drawings are submitted for review and approval by these fabricators and suppliers to the general contractor, subcontractor, or purchaser of the item. It is the responsibility of these parties to review and approve these documents and to distribute the drawings for review to other parties whose work is or may be affected.

Deciding who should review shop drawings is always an important decision. If the general contractor or a particular trade is not providing the item, they are reluctant to review the drawings because of the implied liability or responsibility. Although this is understandable, these trades need to be aware of how these items are going to be fabricated and to determine if the fabrication affects their work in any way. This review can be accomplished during the job-site meetings. It is not uncommon for shop drawings to be reviewed and returned for corrections or revisions. Once shop drawings are approved and fabrication begins, alterations or changes can be costly and time consuming.

Shop drawings are usually provided for the following items and should be reviewed as noted:

Custom Structural Elements. Steel and wood structural elements and their connections are often submitted as shop drawings for review by the structural engineer and the design team. Structural elements are frequently overlooked by other design team members, leaving the architect and structural engineer to review them. However, the depth of these items may vary from original design and may have an impact on the exhaust hood mounting height or ceiling details in public areas.

Booths and Seating. The booths, banquettes, and tables are often supplied by a common fabricator. They will prepare a drawing of the seating plan to confirm the layout, booth styles, and dimensions. These drawings will note finishes required on the ends and back, table sizes and design, bases, and specialty hardware. This drawing will only show what they are providing. If chairs or bases, are being provided by another source, the count, style, and models must be confirmed against this drawing. Construction details for these items will also be provided, along with finish and fabric samples. The quantities noted on this drawing must be checked against the line-item furniture budget. Dimensions and spacing should be confirmed with field dimensions to verify that the plan will work as drawn. Blocking for table wall brackets must be confirmed. Installation requirements such as building access and door openings should be confirmed and delivery/installation dates verified.

Cabinetry and Millwork. This includes host stations, retail displays, specialty paneling, booth dividers, and custom trim. Verify dimensions, routing of utilities, drop-in equipment specifications, finishes, and hardware.

Bar and Back Bar. Bars are built with the combined efforts of several trades and suppliers. The "bar die" or vertical wall that the bar top rests on is often constructed by the general contractor or framing crew. They may also be responsible for applying the finish to the inside face of the bar die. The top and finish on the front may be supplied and installed by a millwork shop. The back bar may include lower cabinets, and top and upper back bar. Underbar equipment—sinks, cocktail units, drainboards, bottle coolers—must fit under the front and back bars. Review of these shop drawings must include:

♦ Confirmation that all specified equipment will fit as designed. Support brackets or legs added by fabricators to support the back bar may interfere with equipment placement.

♦ Verification of all dimensions and of combined dimensions of work provided by all trades. Finished bar tops are 42 inches above the finished floor. When one source builds the bar die and another fabricates the bar top, this overall dimension may vary. A variance of as little of ½ inch is noticeable to customers.

♦ Coordination of utilities, including receptacles, floor drains, and sinks.

♦ Verification of hardware, foot rail, service rail, access door, and gate.

♦ Coordination of carbonated beverage and beer line penetrations.

♦ Review of finishes.

Server Stations. Sidestands are designed to accommodate a lot of equipment and supplies in limited space. When reviewing these shop drawings, it is important to confirm, in addition to the standard items, that shelves and drawers are sized properly to handle utensil inserts or other containers, heavy-duty hardware and proper handles are provided, drop-in items are delivered to the mill shop or on site for field cutting of required openings, grommets for cords are provided, and chases or space for utilities are provided.

Railings. Handrails, drink rails, and other custom wood or metal railings will be reviewed by the design team for proper dimensions and mounting/anchoring devices. Your concern will be that they have the appearance you want, do not pose any unnecessary maintenance headaches, and do not have details that can catch clothing.

Exhaust Hoods. The design and engineering of exhaust hoods and makeup air systems is usually a function of the mechanical engineer. When hood systems are included in the foodservice equipment contract, they must still be reviewed and approved by the mechanical engineer. Fire protection systems are sometimes integral with hoods, and their design is included with the hood shop drawings. The placement of nozzles is based on the layout of the equipment below. If this layout has been altered, it must be noted on this plan. Dimensions for hoods are usually critical since they are often planned to fit between walls or fit the full length of a wall. Finish trim pieces to seal off the hood at the ceiling or side panels should be accounted for when reviewing scope of work.

Mechanical, Plumbing, and Electrical Systems, Components, and Fixtures. Shop drawings and specification sheets that provide the technical information on standard specialty products are often submitted for review and approval. These include toilet partitions, bathroom fixtures, bathroom accessories, electrical panel boxes, light fixtures, and control devices. Review these items for compliance with the specifications, proper size, material, finish and color. Some of these items are built-in to walls, ceilings, or floors. It is necessary to confirm that the depth of these items fits into the space allocated.

Specialty Light Fixtures. Custom or specialty light fixtures can be provided by the owner or by a specialty fixture supplier different from the vendor providing the more standard fixtures. Prior to fabrication of these items, shop drawings must be provided and reviewed. Custom, one-of-a-kind fixtures may not bear the required Underwriters' Laboratories (UL) label required by code and may need to be submitted to the local building department for their review. Additionally, it is useful for the electrical contractor to review these drawings since he will be installing them and may need to provide special adapters or hanging mechanisms.

Custom Remote Refrigeration Packages. Remote refrigeration packages are either part of the mechanical contract or included in the foodservice equipment package. When reviewing the shop drawing, confirm that all refrigeration units are accounted for, that the compressor sizes are compatible with the coils, that the utilities are correct, and that the space allocated to the unit is adequate. Remote compressor systems are either provided with or require a rack and structural support. It is important to verify that the space allocated and ventilation provided are consistent with the manufacturer's recommendations.

Walk-In Coolers and Freezers. Panelized walk-in coolers are traditionally included in the foodservice equipment package. Dimensions of these units usually vary from those shown on the construction documents because the actual dimensions are different from the nominal dimensions. Most units are referenced by whole-foot dimensions: 6 by 8 feet, 10 by 12 feet. In actuality, these units are slightly smaller. Additionally, since many walk-ins are comparable, price shopping is not uncommon and the brand specified is not always the one ultimately purchased. Shop drawings are reviewed for dimensions, door swings, interior and exterior finishes, floor and base details, lights, utility loads and connections, coordination with floor recesses or isolated slabs, and verification with shelving specification.

Custom-Designed Stainless Steel Equipment and Components. Foodservice equipment is fabricated out of stainless steel because of its durability, ease of cleaning and sanitary qualities. Fabrication standards are usually described clearly in the foodservice specifications. The review of these fabrication shop drawings must include:

♦ Verification of design and all dimensions

♦ Coordination of built-in equipment and equipment items that are incorporated into the fabricated items

♦ Verification of all utilities, connections, chases, internal wiring and plumbing, and coordination with building rough-ins

♦ Coordination with adjacent equipment and details

Specialty Systems. There are many specialty systems that are incorporated into restaurant design that require shop drawings. These systems may include POS, telephone, security, sound, and TV/cable. The drawings and specifications provided as shop drawings for these systems are usually one-line wiring diagrams, hardware, and component specifications and installation requirements. These drawings may be included in the construction documents but must still be reviewed and coordinated with field conditions. Materials, finish textures, and color samples are also submitted for review and approval. Not technically shop drawings, they are included in the review and approval process. These include custom carpets, stone surfaces, wallcoverings, fabrics, paints, stains, laminates, and specialty finishes. Small samples may not show the dramatic effect expected. In these instances, large samples or mock-ups are provided. These may be brought out to the site to judge how they will look and how the scale fits with the other design elements already in place. The intent of reviewing samples is to eliminate surprises and confirm that you are getting what was specified.

The review of these shop drawings must include a review of how the various pieces fit together. Where does the work of one trade end and another begin? Although this should be clearly noted in the construction documents, it is important to confirm that all suppliers and trades understand their scope of work so that the sequence of activities in the field is not disrupted. The exhaust hoods, for example, may be delivered and hung in place by the fabricator or equipment installer, and the welded connection from the ductwork to the hood may be the responsibility of the mechanical contractor. Millwork may be set in place by the cabinet shop, but the finish may be applied by the painting contractor under the direction of the general contractor. The coordination of these activities should be reviewed and confirmed during the shop drawing review process.

Utility Rough-Ins. One of the most critical inspections made during the construction process is verifying that the utilities—water supply, drains, gas piping, electrical outlets and junction boxes, ventilation ductwork, and service for specialty systems—are located properly. The construction documents will clearly indicate these requirements and there should not be any great discrepancies. But that is why field inspections are conducted. Although you do not expect to find problems or omissions, now is the time to verify that utilities are installed properly and make corrections before the walls are closed up. When verifying the size and placement of utilities, it is wise to have the construction documents and the documentation of any changes or revisions for reference. This inspection will verify both horizontal and vertical dimensions and the size of service. It is important to confirm that the work in the field conforms to the construction documents and to note any required changes or revisions.

Installation of Foodservice Equipment

The delivery and installation of the foodservice equipment is a major event in the construction of your restaurant. It is a time when the restaurant is coming together very quickly with many trades on site. Careful coordination will keep the development on schedule. The installer, often a subcontractor to the equipment supplier, should attend the project meetings that affect his work. During these meetings, the issues of installation dates and times, truck access and parking, delivery routes into and through the building, and areas of priority will be resolved. The foodservice equipment is not all installed at the same time. The construction schedule may require that exhaust hoods, walk-in coolers and freezers, sinks and dishwashing areas, and large, built-in items such as ovens or display refrigerators be brought on site and set in place before the site is ready for the other equipment.

Equipment installation includes:

1. *Uncrating.* Equipment is shipped on pallets, in crates, or in boxes. Parts and accessories are packed separately. Packing material and wires holding pieces in place must be removed. Uncrating generates a lot of debris that must be disposed of.

2. *Assembly.* When equipment is shipped, components such as legs, casters, doors, shelves, and attachments are wrapped separately. These parts must be put together properly. There are also components provided by the foodservice supplier that must be installed by other trades, such as gas valves and faucets. These are small items that are easily misplaced and need to be stored securely until delivered to the general contractor or appropriate subcontractor for installation. On large projects, the foodservice equipment installer will often require a receipt for these components. Assembly also includes piecing together the fabricated items.

3. *Setting in place.* Setting equipment in place may involve locating it under the hood in the correct order, installing it in millwork or cabinetry, hanging items from ceiling structures and walls, or securing items to the floor. This work on these equipment items is often done concurrently with plumbing and electrical work.

4. *Leveling, sealing, and trim work.* Foodservice equipment must be installed level and plumb for proper operation. This often requires simple adjustment of legs or more creative shimming. Health departments usually require equipment that is not mobile or portable to be sealed to walls and floors, usually with silicone caulk. Where spaces between walls and equipment is too great to be sealed effectively with caulking compounds, trim pieces are required. These trim pieces can be stainless steel, aluminum, or galvanized metal. Trim may also be accomplished with drywall, ceiling tiles, or painted wood. Installation of equipment and sealing and trimming of this equipment must be done correctly or the restaurant will have cleaning and maintenance headaches.

Final Connection of Equipment. When the foodservice installer sets equipment in place, this does not include mechanical, plumbing, or electrical connections. These connections are made by the general contractor through his mechanical, plumbing, and electrical subcontractors. Components such as cord sets, faucets, gas valves, and quick disconnects may be provided as part of the equipment package but are supplied for installation by the other trades. In the construction documents, the schedules on the mechanical and electrical drawings will clearly indicate what connections and components are required for final connection.

The details of exactly how these connections are to be made are usually left to the tradespeople on the job. When mobile equipment is specified with quick disconnecting or flexible connections so that it can be moved for cleaning with disconnection of the utilities, the connection should be made so that the equipment fits close to the wall. The use of connection elbows or the orientation of valves can affect this placement significantly. Field inspection of this work should focus on:

♦ Verification that all equipment is accounted for

♦ Proper placement of all equipment

♦ Verification that all components are on site and distributed to proper trades and installed properly

♦ Wall-, ceiling- and floor-mounted equipment is located correctly, secure, and sealed

♦ Equipment is level and properly sealed and trimmed

♦ Allied trades understand their work involved in final connection

♦ Coordination of start-up and calibration services.

Installation of Furniture and Fixtures

The delivery, assembly, and installation of the booths, tables, chairs, and other furniture is one of the last activities to occur. These items are easily scratched and damaged and should not be installed until absolutely necessary. Booths and banquettes may require coordination with the general contractor if end walls, divider panels, or trim pieces are to be installed. In some instances, furniture is fixed in place. Bar stools, tables, and patio tables, for example, may be specified as anchored to the floor. In these cases, the furniture supplier will be required to coordinate the anchoring mechanism with the general contractor and, perhaps, install the bases prior to the installation of the other furniture. Cantilevered table bases require the same coordination to ensure that blocking is provided and the walls are properly anchored.

Installation of Owner-Provided Items

Although owners take responsibility to provide equipment, products, or systems, general contractors and their subcontractors rightly assume that unless documented to the contrary, the owner will coordinate all aspects of those items. Therefore, if you are going to take responsibility for providing these items, any support or coordination required of the general contractor must be clearly noted in the construction documents. This includes:

♦ **Allocating space.** If you are providing the safe, a space needs to be designated for it and proper structural support or anchoring devices must be planned.

♦ **Blocking.** Proper support for wall-mounted equipment is always an issue in restaurants. Speakers, TV sets or heavy artwork or accessories need solid backing for mounting to walls or from ceilings.

♦ **Wiring, receptacles, and conduits.** The special systems listed above may require electrical service, special receptacles, or conduit runs for supplier-provided cables or wiring.

♦ **Coordination.** Even though the foregoing items may be provided by the owner, code requirements may require components that are not normally furnished by the supplier. Additionally, by noting the requirements on the construction documents or providing shop drawings for job-site review and coordination, these items will be expected and the construction schedule can accommodate them.

Inspections by Building Officials

Building officials make periodic inspections of the construction to ensure that the work is being performed according to the approved construction documents and that the applicable codes are being followed. Their inspection and signature on the permit indicates that they have inspected and approved the work noted. Each department—building, plumbing, mechanical, electrical, health, and fire—make several inspections at specified stages of completion. It is traditionally the responsibility of the general contractor to call the building department to request inspections, since work cannot progress until the inspection and "sign-off" occur.

Timing of inspections affect the construction schedule. Contractors are usually required to request inspections 24 to 48 hours in advance. They anticipate when work will be completed and call ahead so that the inspection will take place as soon as the work is complete. This timing, especially for final inspections, is often dependent on "owner-provided" suppliers meeting deadlines and providing necessary components. It is the project manager, therefore, who must coordinate and monitor these requests and coordinate the performance of these suppliers.

Inspectors can and often do require changes or revisions that may not have been noted on the construction documents during their plan review and permit process. Field conditions may dictate the addition of an exit light or sign, additional fireproofing or space between ductwork and combustible materials, relocation of wall-mounted shelving in exitways, or any number of other changes. Some of these issues may be negotiable and others not. Your design team and contractors may be able to propose alternative solutions. This is the nature of construction. If initial code reviews are thorough and the construction documents are submitted and reviewed according to proper procedures, these changes are usually minimal.

❖   ADMINISTRATION

The management and administrative activities that support your restaurant construction are as important as the construction process itself. Inaccurate, incomplete, or poorly organized documentation and follow-through can cause delays, cost overruns, and lawsuits. Depending on how responsibilities are allocated, these tasks may be assigned to the general contractor or to the project manager.

Contracts

Written agreements that clearly describe the scope of services being provided, areas of responsibility, and terms of compensation and that are signed by the authorized parties should be executed. These documents, which should be reviewed by legal counsel, make it clear what is expected of all parties.

Construction Documents

All companies and individuals involved in any aspect of the restaurant construction should have a complete and current set of construction documents and should receive all updates and changes. Too often, specialty suppliers and vendors are given only those sections of the documents that pertain to their scope of work. Unfortunately, this denies them the opportunity to review the documents for conflicts that may affect their work either directly or indirectly and the development loses this potentially valuable insight.

Project Directory

It is necessary to provide everyone involved in the restaurant construction with a complete directory of all the participants: owner, developer, operator, landlord/tenant coordinator, contractors, suppliers/vendors, and any other companies or agencies that are connected with the development. This directory should include company names, contacts, involvement with project, address, phone, and fax. Updates and changes should be distributed as they occur.

Bonds

Some projects require that contractors and suppliers be bonded. Bonding is an assurance by a bonding company that the job will be completed. If the contractor fails to perform, the bonding company is responsible for having the work completed. If this is a requirement, copies of these bonds should be on file.

Permit Fees

Fees required with document submittals to the building department must be arranged for. Some contractors advance these fees while others require that the payment be made directly by the developer. Submitting documents without the necessary fees will delay the plan review process.

Project Scheduling

The preparation and management of the overall project schedule is the "map" that keeps all the contractors, suppliers, and the restaurant management aware of when activities will occur.

Permit and Approval Procedures

The procedures for submitting documents for review and approval vary widely. It is the responsibility of the general contractor and the project manager to understand these procedures and follow them. The project manager is involved in this because some approvals may have to come from nongovernmental sources such as landlords, neighborhood groups, condominium associations, or similar groups.

Schedule of Shop Drawings

The construction documents indicate where shop drawings are required for approval. A schedule listing these drawings and tracking the approval process will help monitor the flow of these documents and ensure that no shop drawings are overlooked.

Samples and Colors

Similar to the shop drawing schedule, approvals are usually required for colors, materials, and finishes.

Applications for Utilities

General contractors arrange for temporary utilities to be supplied to the site during construction. Applications for permanent service of gas, water, sewer, power, telephone, and cable must be arranged for separately. These may require written applications and deposits.

Insurance

Insurance policies for professional liability, worker's compensation, vehicle use, general liability, fire, property, special hazardous, or other coverage may be required by the developer, owner, or leasor. These should be documented and filed.

Pay Procedures

Applications for pay and the procedures for administering pay requests for all contractors, suppliers, and vendors should be clearly defined in the contracts or other written agreements. The proper forms and procedures should be followed and copies of all documents properly signed and filed.

Test Reports

The construction documents and building authorities may require independent testing of structural elements: soils, concrete, existing structural members. These tests need to be conducted properly and the results presented to the required agency. Some owners require samples of materials to test for scratching or durability. These tests may be unsophisticated and are used to establish a comfort level. A document should be prepared so that those requesting the test can sign-off on the results.

Change Orders

Changes or revisions made during construction must be documented so that the owner or an authorized agent can approve the change and any related costs or changes to the construction schedule. Many small construction projects or remodels do not use the formal paperwork recommended by architects. However these changes are recorded, they must provide solid backup for the change and involve all members of the design team and the general contractor. These change orders should be signed to authorize the change, distributed as necessary, and filed.

Construction Meeting Notes

Periodic scheduled project meetings are held at the job site to review progress, plan schedules, coordinate work, and resolve problems or conflicts. These meetings are attended by all contractors, suppliers (when relevant), the project manager, and others involved in the development. Minutes taken during these meetings indicate when and where the meeting was held, who was in attendance, what actions are required or decisions made, persons responsible, and due dates. These minutes are distributed to all parties involved in the development and a master file maintained with the general contractor.

Daily Field Reports

General contractors keep journals of what takes place on the job site on a daily basis. This may include weather conditions, work performed, trades on the job, deliveries, inspections, accidents, and any other notable activity.

Startup and Calibration

The foodservice equipment and mechanical equipment may require special startup procedures. Some equipment must be initiated by a factory-authorized agent or the warranty will be voided. Refrigeration and ice-making equipment frequently needs calibration and adjustment. Gas appliances and thermostats may also need adjustments and calibration. Heating and air-conditioning units and exhaust hoods need to be balanced. This work is usually called for in the construction documents but may not be arranged for by the supplier or contractor if it is not reiterated or brought up at a project meeting.

Manuals and Warranties

New equipment is packed with an operating manual, warranty and service information, cleaning instructions, and other instructions and information. These booklets should be collected by the equipment installer and put into a notebook or binder for the operator. The general contractor may request several copies of these documents so that they can have one in their files and provide one to the owner or landlord.

Directory of Service Agencies

The manuals provided with the equipment usually contains a listing of regional service agencies or a national number to call for local service. The general contractor will prepare a listing of all contractors responsible for performing warranty work on the building and the plumbing, mechanical, and electrical systems. Each supplier should also provide a listing of service agencies for the products they provide. This composite list should be provided to the owner and operator and be kept on file with the general contractor.

Punch List

Near the completion of the construction, the general contractor, owner, project manager, and members of the design team will make a detailed inspection of the restaurant. This inspection will focus on all the construction details and finishes, equipment and systems, and any requirements imposed by the inspection authorities. They will list all deficiencies or items that need correction. This list, known as the punch list, will be consolidated and given to the general contractor. It is his responsibility to oversee the satisfactory completion of these items. The project manager may also be involved if items on the list are to be corrected by suppliers or vendors under contract to the owner.

❖ # PREOPENING STARTUP

The administrative details involved with opening the restaurant have been in process since the operational plan was drafted. Throughout the design and construction phases, the preopening activities were being formulated, executed, and implemented. With careful scheduling and planning, these activities were ready and waiting to be introduced into the restaurant facility. Toward the conclusion of construction, and with the approval of the inspecting authorities, management begins to take over the restaurant. This transitional period—before final inspections and the certificate of occupancy but when the facility is essentially complete—can be stressful for all parties.

Until the building is turned over to the owner by the general contractor, the general contractor is responsible for the facility. His objective is to complete his work, get the certificate of occupancy, complete his punch list, finalize his paperwork, and move on. Management, on the other hand, is anxious to take over the space, set up the restaurant, schedule staff training, and prepare to open the restaurant to the public. To avoid unnecessary conflicts, inspection delays, or unfinished work, management should:

♦ Schedule initial preopening activities with the general contractor— by being on the construction schedule, preopening activities become "legitimized" and expected.

♦ Involve only those employees who are necessary—too many people in the restaurant during the final days or weeks of construction can disrupt a tight schedule.

♦ Give priority to the trades—the sooner the construction trades finish, the sooner the restaurant facility will be turned over to management. Moving supplies into rooms where they are still working or blocking server stations with cartons and preventing final connection of coffeemakers slows down the work.

♦ Maintain the chain of communication—if problems or errors are discovered, work through the project manager to resolve them. Attempting to fix something yourself or directing workers to make a change is not in the best interest of the restaurant.

The culmination of the development process occurs when:

♦ The restaurant facility has passed all final inspections.

♦ You receive your certificate of occupancy.

♦ The punch list has been completed.

♦ All contractual and adminstrative activities are complete.

♦ Your preopening activities are complete.

♦ The restaurant is ready to be opened to the public.

This is a very satisfying moment. If your restaurant development has been successful, you will have planned, designed, and built a facility that will enable you to execute your concept and operating style smoothly. Like putting together a complex puzzle, the pieces must not only fit together properly, but you must have all the pieces. From this point on, your success will be measured by your operational performance.

Index